SCOOP

VOL. 1: BREAKING NEWS

WRITTEN BY
RICHARD HAMILTON

ART BY
JOSEPH COOPER

COLORS BY
PETER PANTAZIS AND ALBA CARDONA

INSIGHT COMICS

San Rafael, California

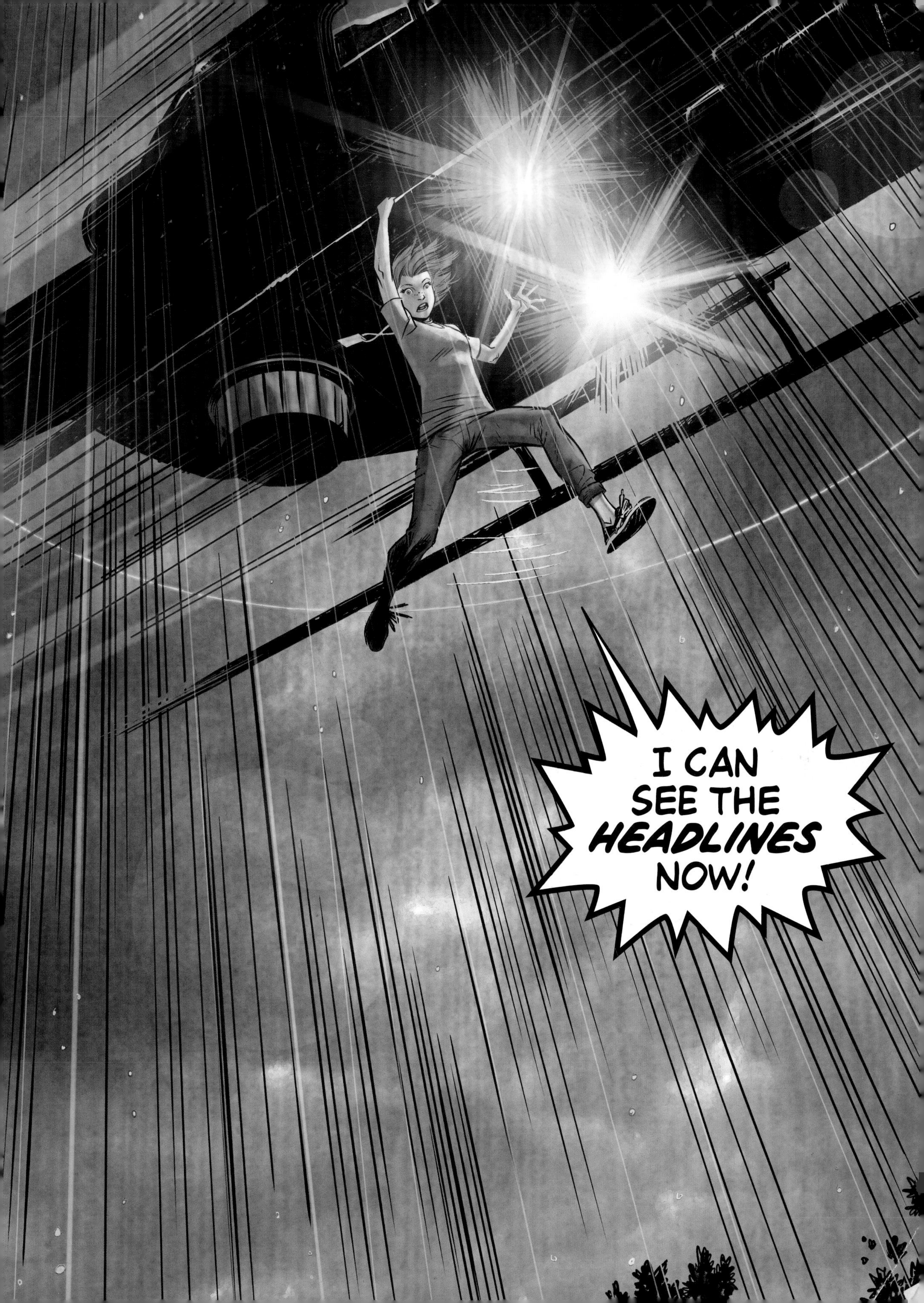
I CAN SEE THE HEADLINES NOW!

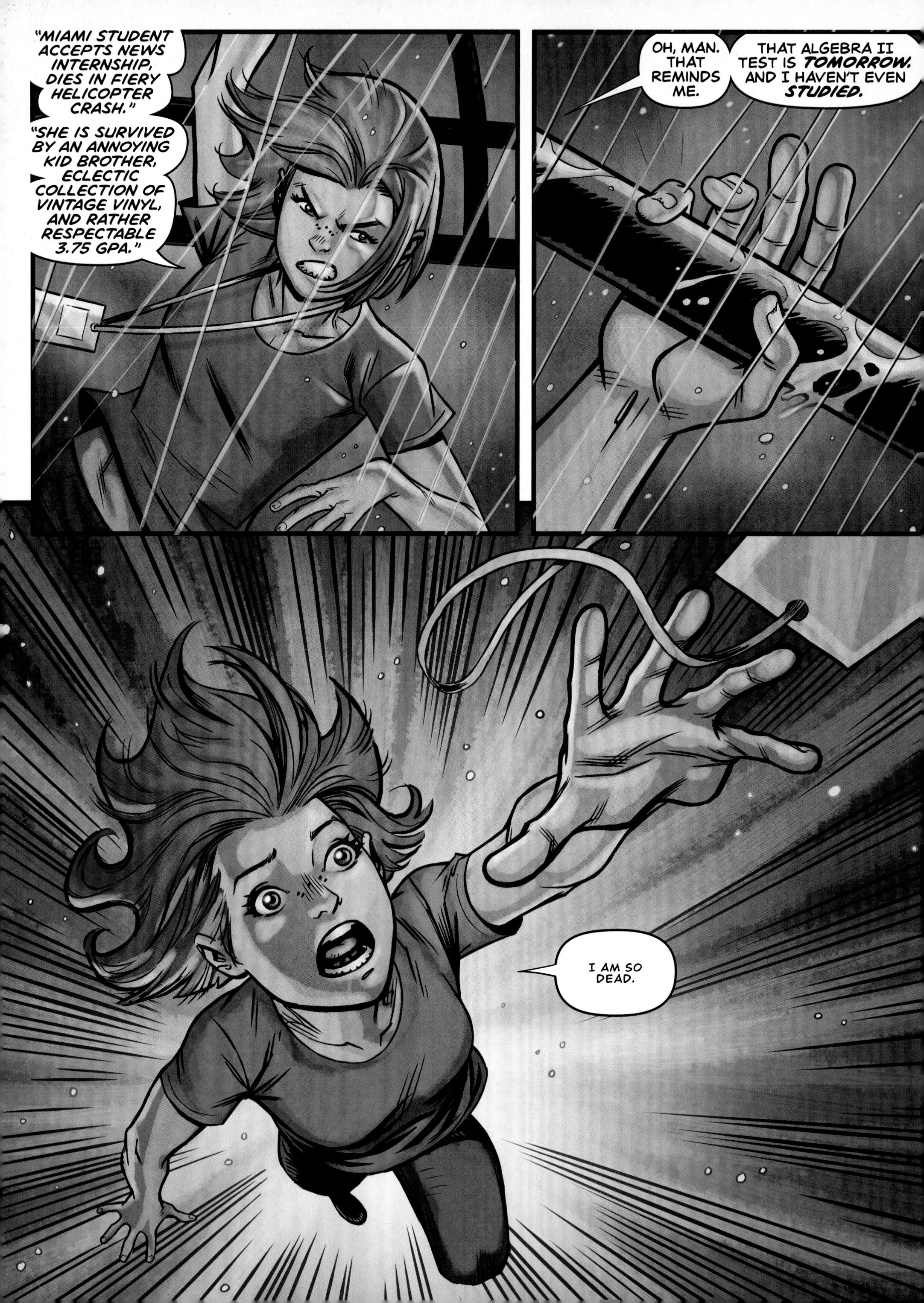
"MIAMI STUDENT ACCEPTS NEWS INTERNSHIP, DIES IN FIERY HELICOPTER CRASH."
"SHE IS SURVIVED BY AN ANNOYING KID BROTHER, ECLECTIC COLLECTION OF VINTAGE VINYL, AND RATHER RESPECTABLE 3.75 GPA."
OH, MAN. THAT REMINDS ME.
THAT ALGEBRA II TEST IS TOMORROW. AND I HAVEN'T EVEN STUDIED.
I AM SO DEAD.

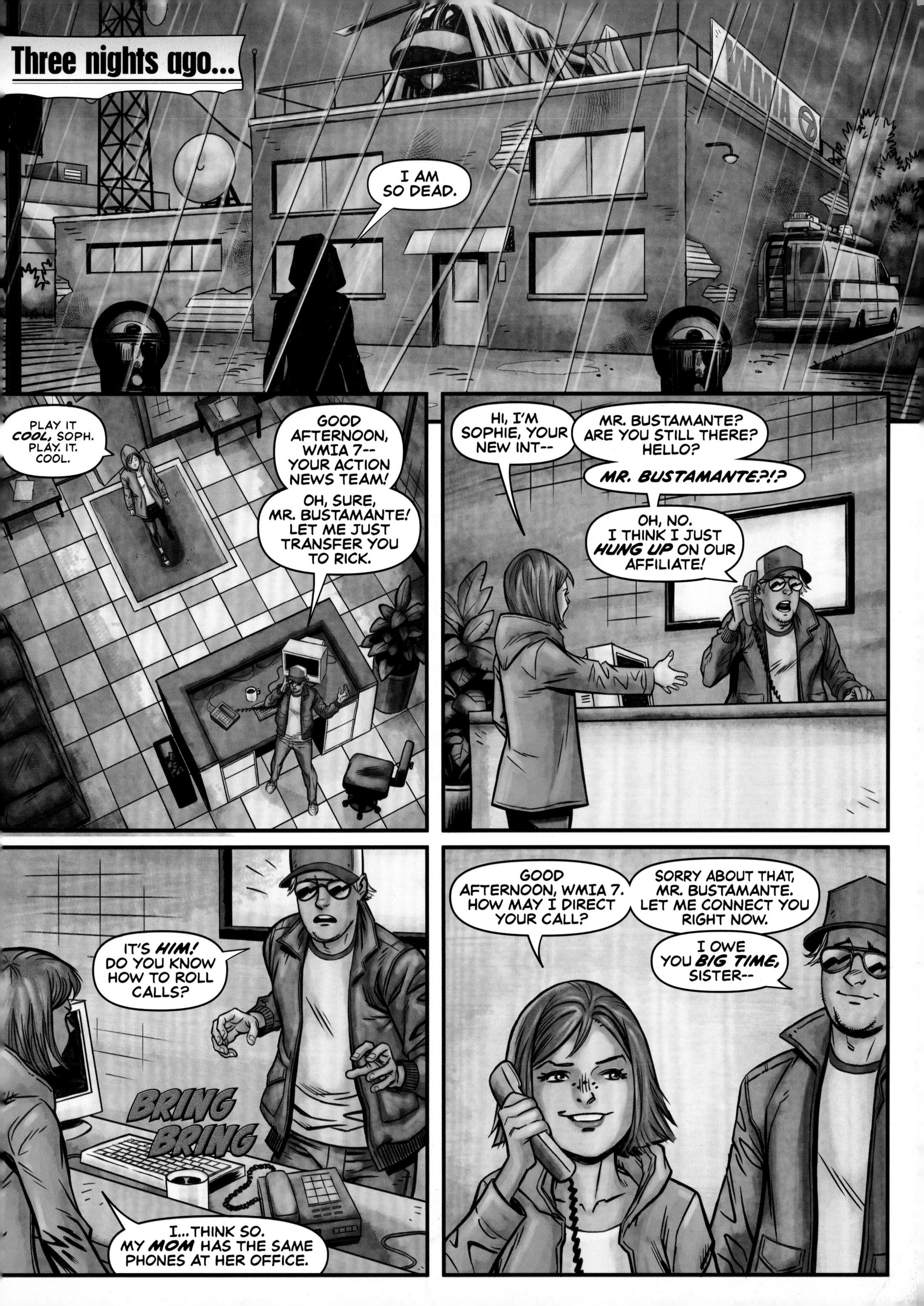
Three nights ago...
WMIA 7
I AM SO DEAD.
PLAY IT *COOL,* SOPH. PLAY. IT. COOL.
GOOD AFTERNOON, WMIA 7-- YOUR ACTION NEWS TEAM!
OH, SURE, MR. BUSTAMANTE! LET ME JUST TRANSFER YOU TO RICK.
HI, I'M SOPHIE, YOUR NEW INT--
MR. BUSTAMANTE? ARE YOU STILL THERE? HELLO?
MR. BUSTAMANTE?!?
OH, NO. I THINK I JUST *HUNG UP* ON OUR AFFILIATE!
IT'S *HIM!* DO YOU KNOW HOW TO ROLL CALLS?
BRING BRING
I...THINK SO. MY *MOM* HAS THE SAME PHONES AT HER OFFICE.
GOOD AFTERNOON, WMIA 7. HOW MAY I DIRECT YOUR CALL?
SORRY ABOUT THAT, MR. BUSTAMANTE. LET ME CONNECT YOU RIGHT NOW.
I OWE YOU *BIG TIME,* SISTER--

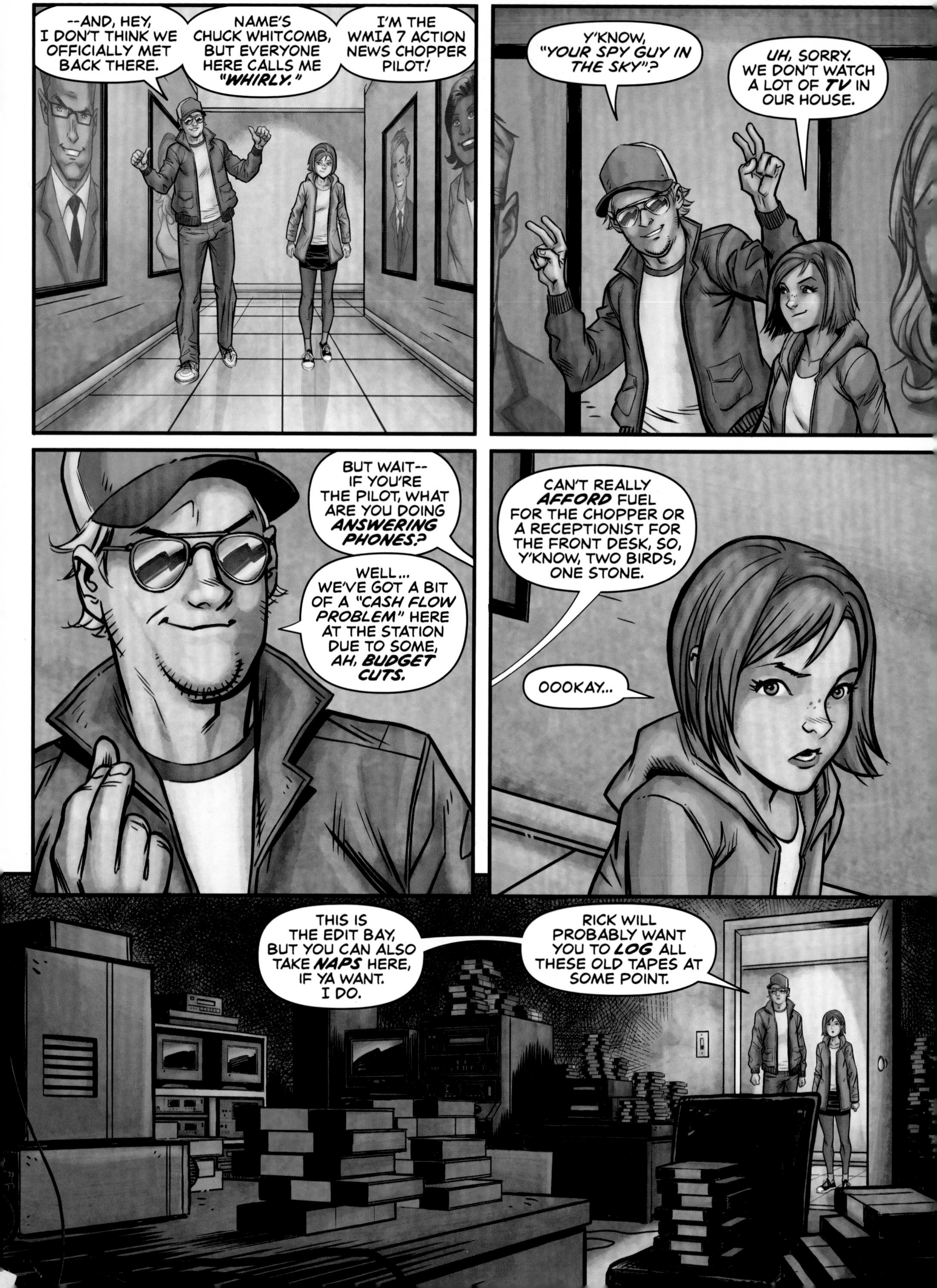
--AND, HEY, I DON'T THINK WE OFFICIALLY MET BACK THERE.
NAME'S CHUCK WHITCOMB, BUT EVERYONE HERE CALLS ME "WHIRLY."
I'M THE WMIA 7 ACTION NEWS CHOPPER PILOT!
Y'KNOW, "YOUR SPY GUY IN THE SKY"?
UH, SORRY. WE DON'T WATCH A LOT OF TV IN OUR HOUSE.
BUT WAIT-- IF YOU'RE THE PILOT, WHAT ARE YOU DOING ANSWERING PHONES?
WELL... WE'VE GOT A BIT OF A "CASH FLOW PROBLEM" HERE AT THE STATION DUE TO SOME, AH, BUDGET CUTS.
CAN'T REALLY AFFORD FUEL FOR THE CHOPPER OR A RECEPTIONIST FOR THE FRONT DESK, SO, Y'KNOW, TWO BIRDS, ONE STONE.
OOOKAY...
THIS IS THE EDIT BAY, BUT YOU CAN ALSO TAKE NAPS HERE, IF YA WANT. I DO.
RICK WILL PROBABLY WANT YOU TO LOG ALL THESE OLD TAPES AT SOME POINT.

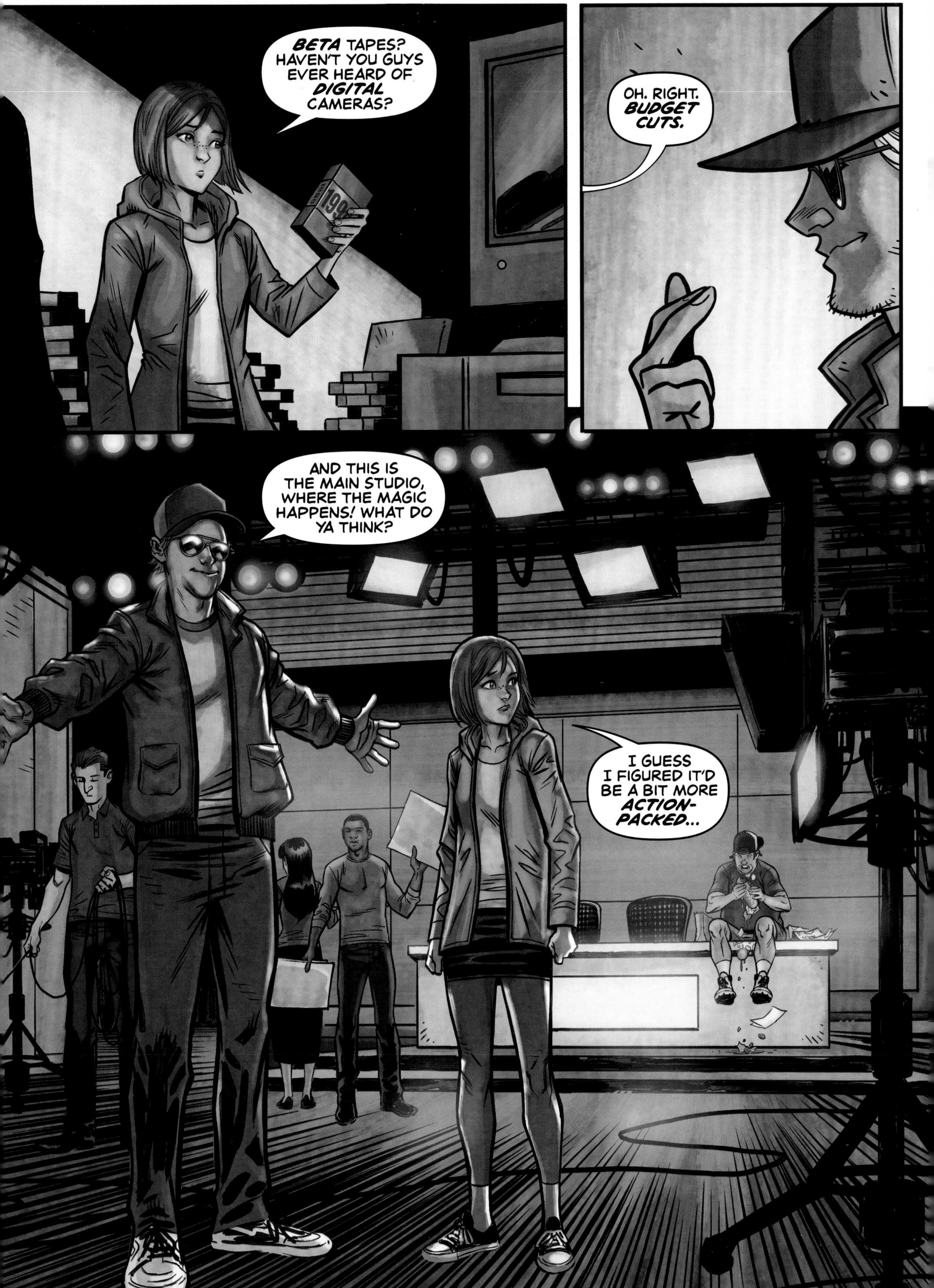
BETA TAPES? HAVEN'T YOU GUYS EVER HEARD OF DIGITAL CAMERAS?
OH. RIGHT. BUDGET CUTS.
AND THIS IS THE MAIN STUDIO, WHERE THE MAGIC HAPPENS! WHAT DO YA THINK?
I GUESS I FIGURED IT'D BE A BIT MORE ACTION-PACKED...

LOOK--THERE'S OUR WEATHER REPORTER, CANDY CARMICHAEL!

VELCRO! HAS ANYONE SEEN MY VELCRO?

THESE SUNS AND CLOUDS DON'T STICK TO THE MAP BY THEMSELVES, PEOPLE!

YEP. THEY REPOSSESSED THE DOPPLER LAST MARCH.

YES, SIR, MR. BUSTAMANTE, RIGHT AWAY! I'M SENDING OUR TEAM ASAP!

THERE WAS A HIGH-PROFILE MURDER IN SOUTH BEACH. EVERY OTHER NEWS OUTLET GOT THERE THIRTY-FIVE MINUTES AGO.

EVEN FIESTA DE NOTICIAS GIGANTES BEAT US. AGAIN.

WHY? WHY DOES THIS KEEP HAPPENING TO ME? WHY IS LIFE SO UNFAIR?

OKAY, GUYS. LET'S GET DOWN THERE. NOT THAT IT MATTERS...

AND CAN SOMEONE PLEASE FIND HAL?

START AT THE GOLF COURSE AND EXPAND YOUR SEARCH FROM THERE...

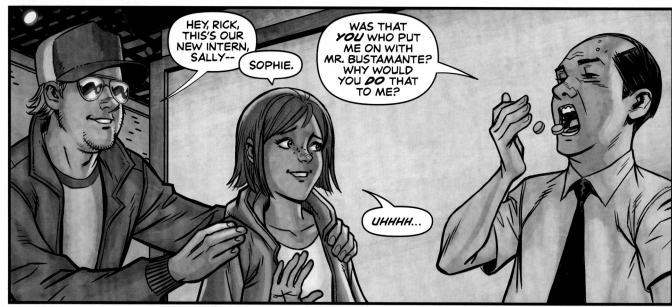

HEY, RICK, THIS'S OUR NEW INTERN, SALLY--

SOPHIE.

WAS THAT YOU WHO PUT ME ON WITH MR. BUSTAMANTE? WHY WOULD YOU DO THAT TO ME?

UHHHH...

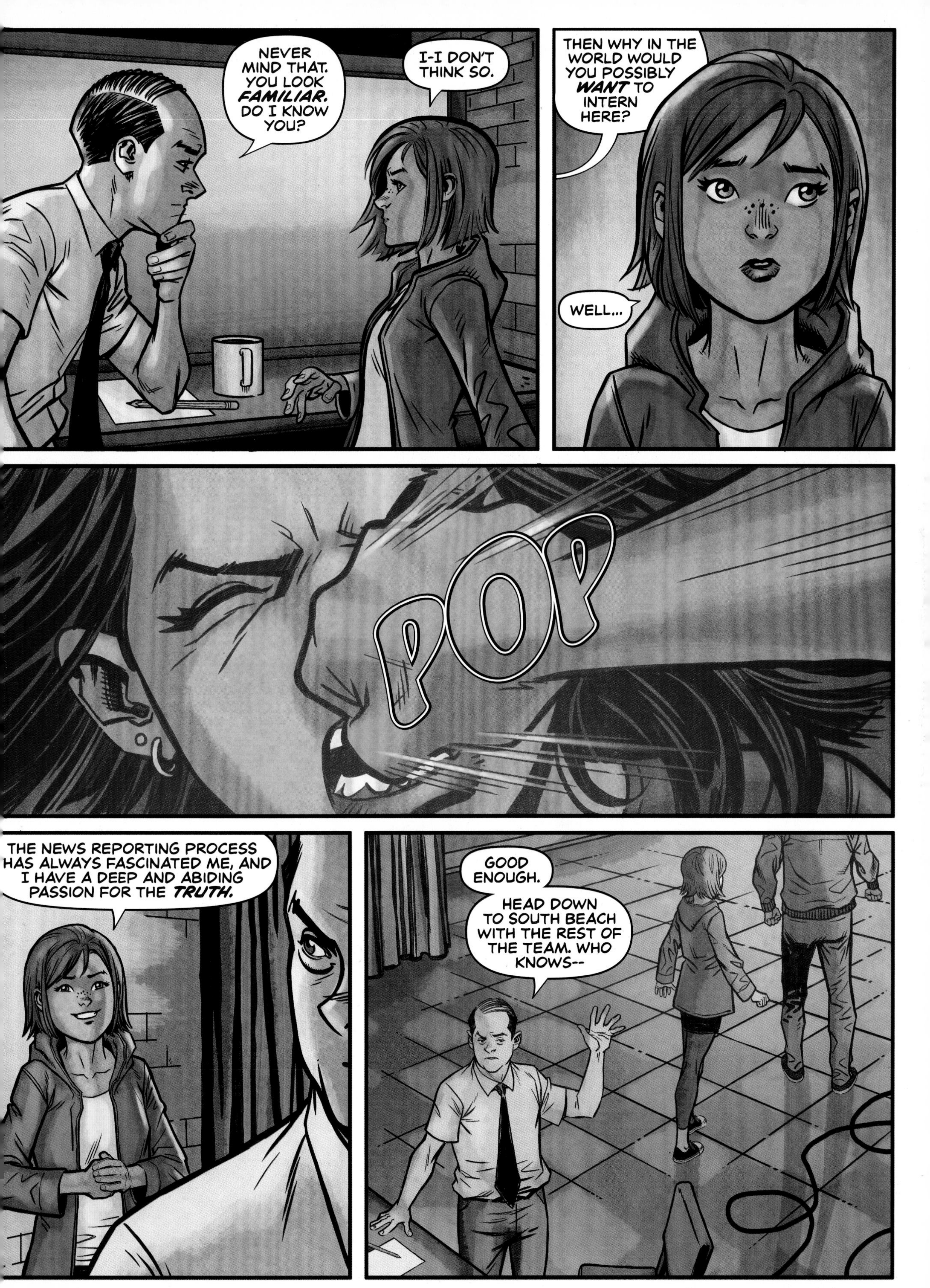

NEVER MIND THAT. YOU LOOK FAMILIAR. DO I KNOW YOU?
I-I DON'T THINK SO.
THEN WHY IN THE WORLD WOULD YOU POSSIBLY WANT TO INTERN HERE?
WELL...
POP
THE NEWS REPORTING PROCESS HAS ALWAYS FASCINATED ME, AND I HAVE A DEEP AND ABIDING PASSION FOR THE TRUTH.
GOOD ENOUGH.
HEAD DOWN TO SOUTH BEACH WITH THE REST OF THE TEAM. WHO KNOWS--

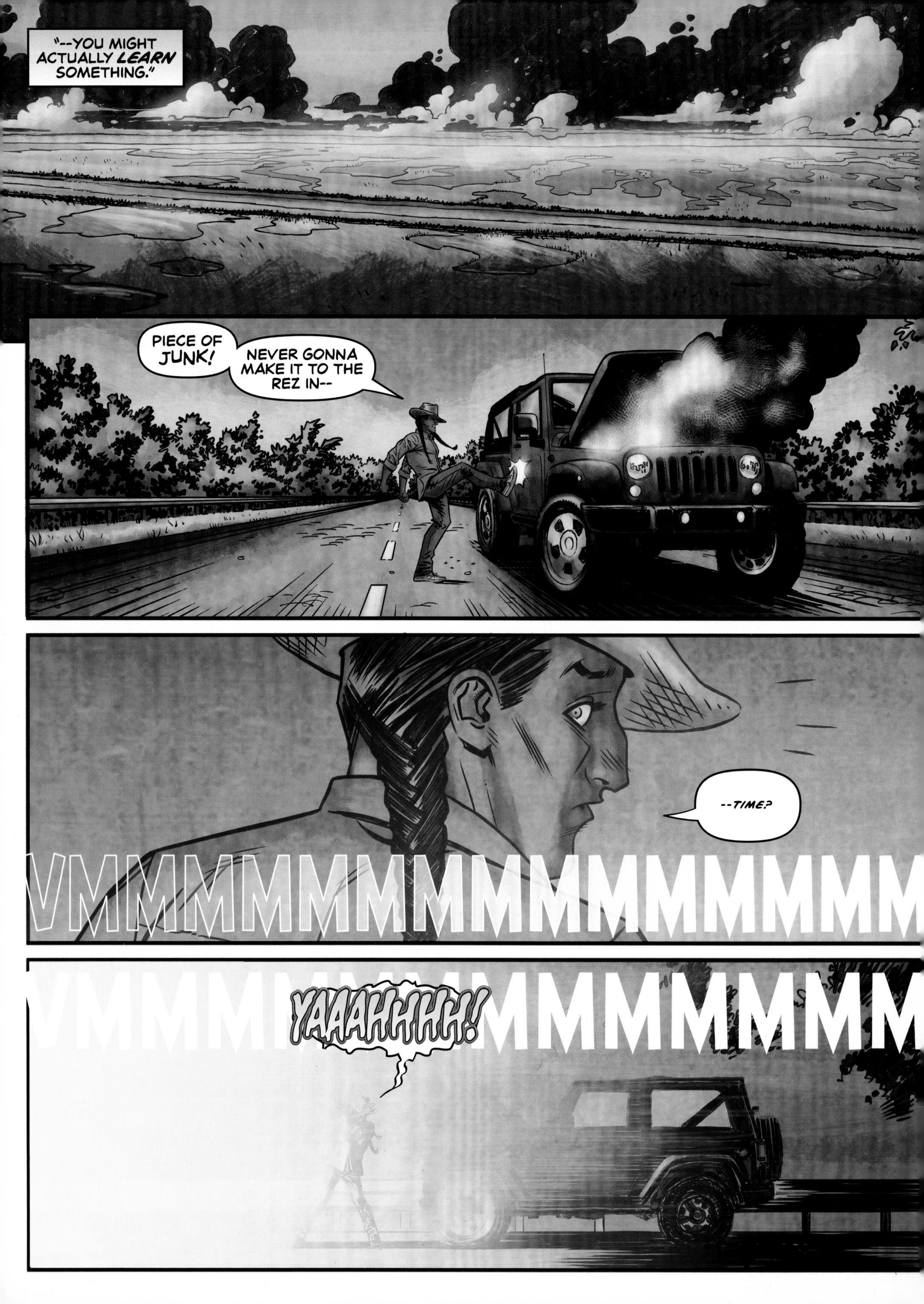
"--YOU MIGHT ACTUALLY LEARN SOMETHING."
PIECE OF JUNK!
NEVER GONNA MAKE IT TO THE REZ IN--
--TIME?
VMMMMMMMMMMMMMMM
VMMMMMMMMMMMMMMM
YAAAHHHH!

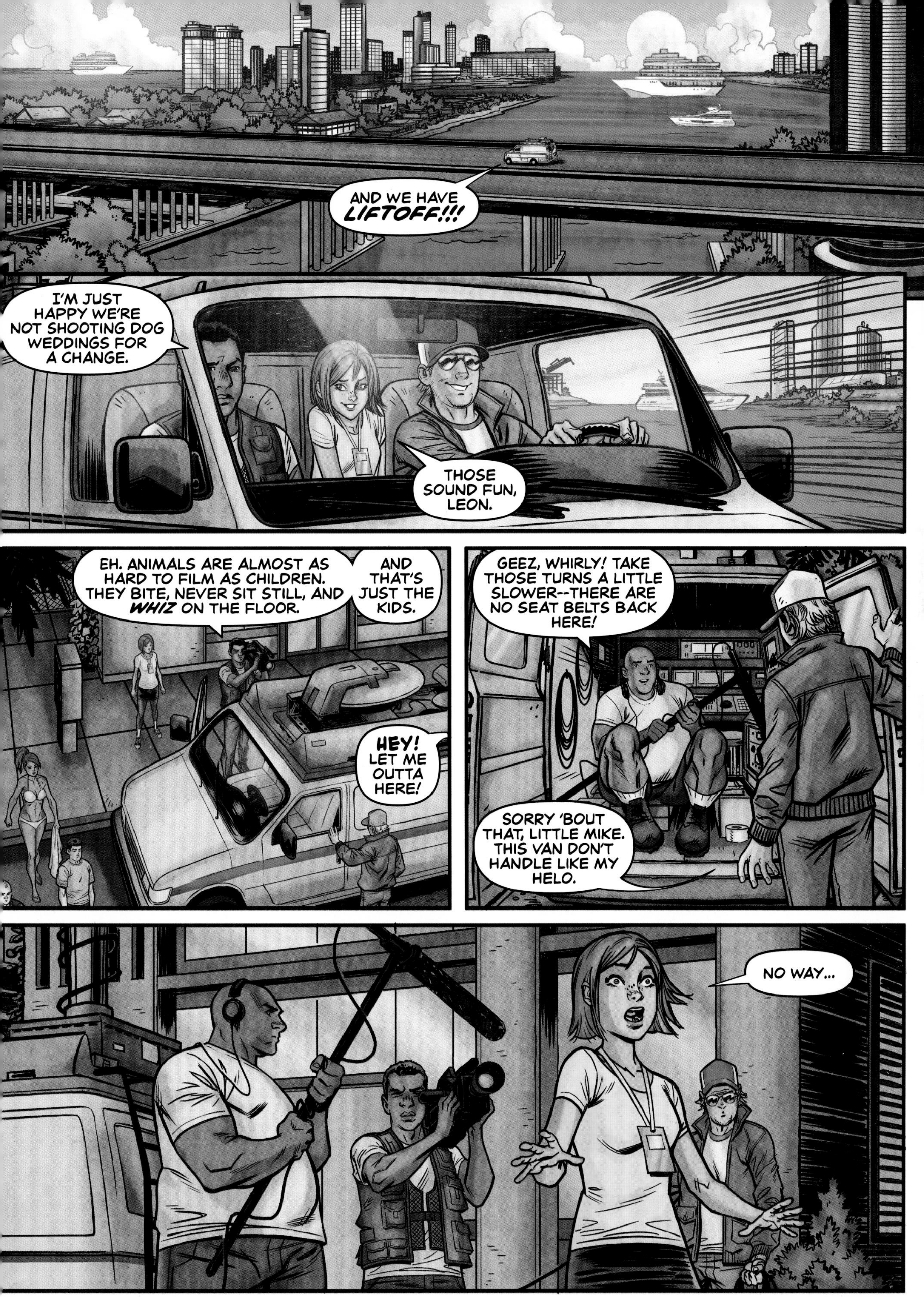

AND WE HAVE *LIFTOFF!!!*
I'M JUST HAPPY WE'RE NOT SHOOTING DOG WEDDINGS FOR A CHANGE.
THOSE SOUND FUN, LEON.
EH. ANIMALS ARE ALMOST AS HARD TO FILM AS CHILDREN. THEY BITE, NEVER SIT STILL, AND *WHIZ* ON THE FLOOR.
AND THAT'S JUST THE KIDS.
HEY! LET ME OUTTA HERE!
GEEZ, WHIRLY! TAKE THOSE TURNS A LITTLE SLOWER--THERE ARE NO SEAT BELTS BACK HERE!
SORRY 'BOUT THAT, LITTLE MIKE. THIS VAN DON'T HANDLE LIKE MY HELO.
NO WAY...

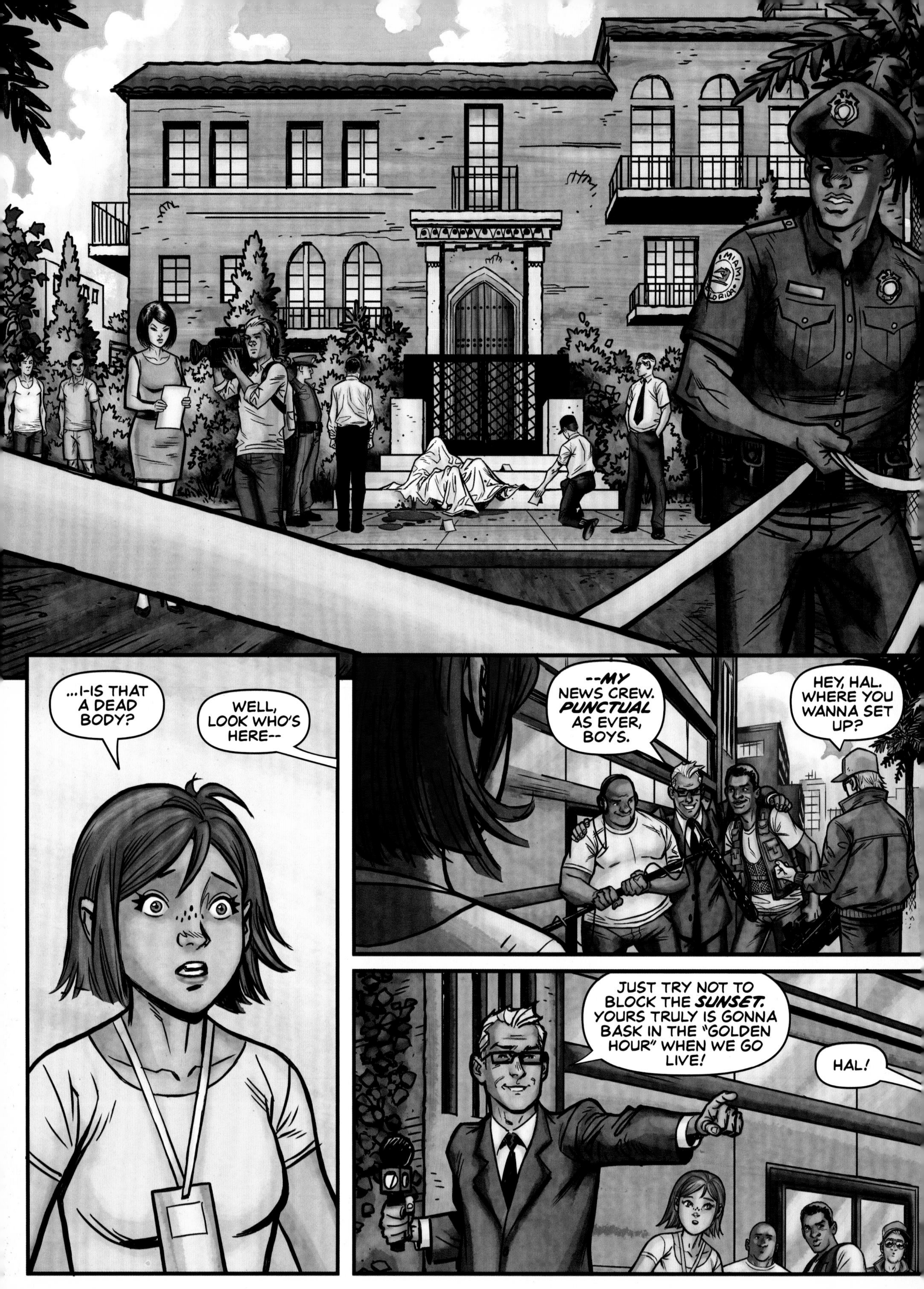
...I-IS THAT A DEAD BODY?
WELL, LOOK WHO'S HERE--
--MY NEWS CREW. PUNCTUAL AS EVER, BOYS.
HEY, HAL. WHERE YOU WANNA SET UP?
JUST TRY NOT TO BLOCK THE SUNSET. YOURS TRULY IS GONNA BASK IN THE "GOLDEN HOUR" WHEN WE GO LIVE!
HAL!

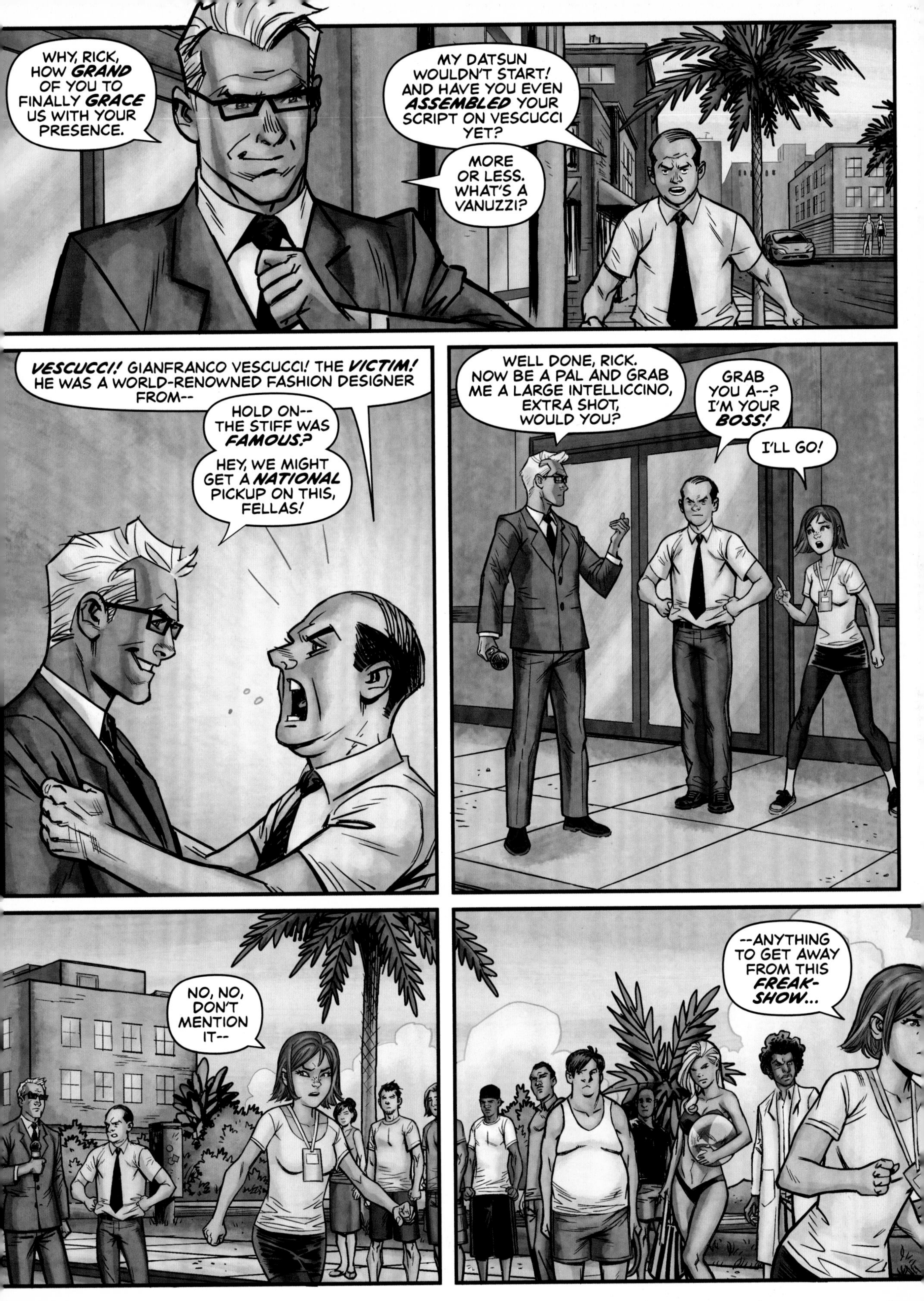
WHY, RICK, HOW GRAND OF YOU TO FINALLY GRACE US WITH YOUR PRESENCE.
MY DATSUN WOULDN'T START! AND HAVE YOU EVEN ASSEMBLED YOUR SCRIPT ON VESCUCCI YET?
MORE OR LESS. WHAT'S A VANUZZI?
VESCUCCI! GIANFRANCO VESCUCCI! THE VICTIM! HE WAS A WORLD-RENOWNED FASHION DESIGNER FROM--
HOLD ON-- THE STIFF WAS FAMOUS?
HEY, WE MIGHT GET A NATIONAL PICKUP ON THIS, FELLAS!
WELL DONE, RICK. NOW BE A PAL AND GRAB ME A LARGE INTELLICCINO, EXTRA SHOT, WOULD YOU?
GRAB YOU A--? I'M YOUR BOSS!
I'LL GO!
NO, NO, DON'T MENTION IT--
--ANYTHING TO GET AWAY FROM THIS FREAK-SHOW...

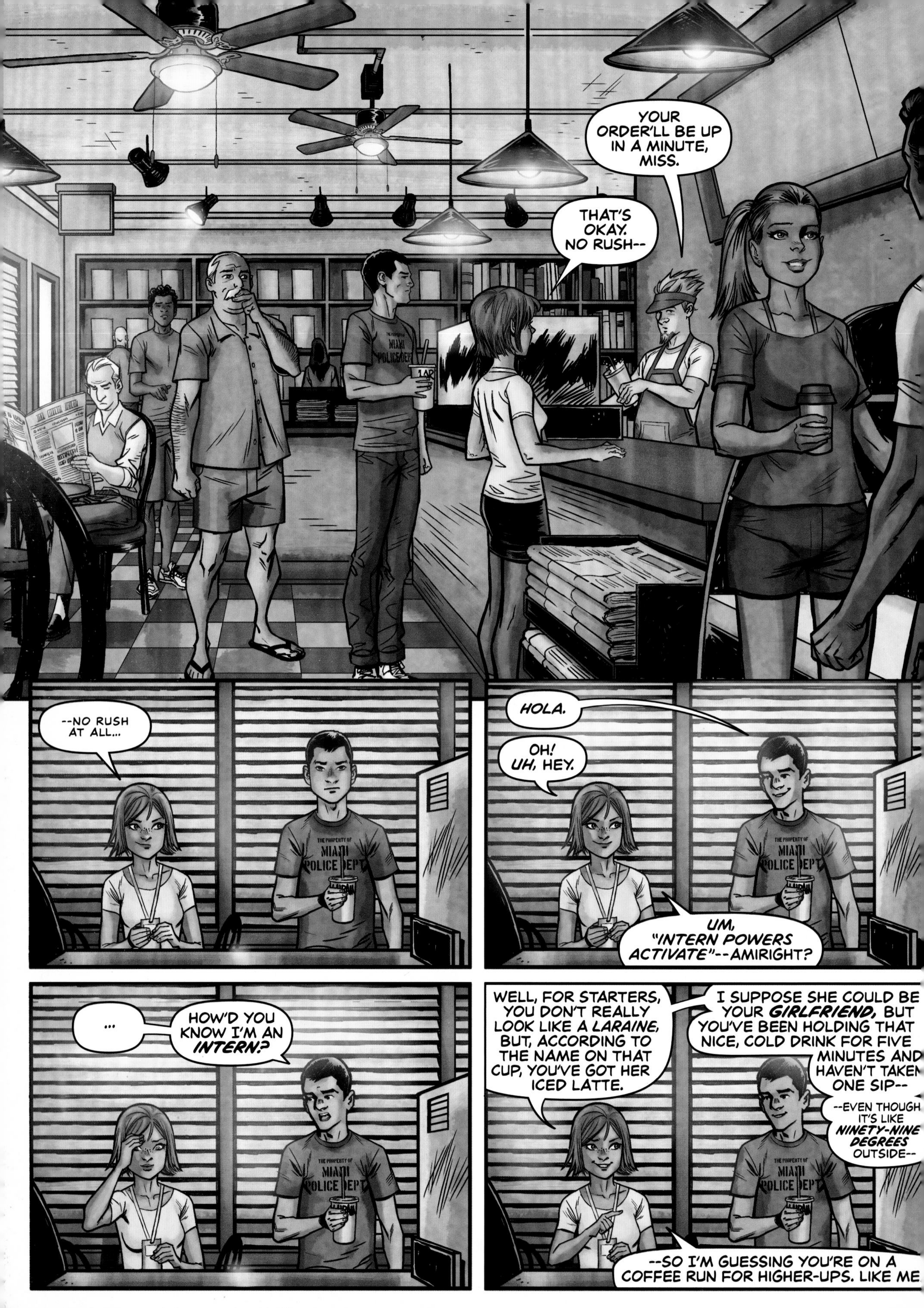
YOUR ORDER'LL BE UP IN A MINUTE, MISS.
THAT'S OKAY. NO RUSH--
--NO RUSH AT ALL...
HOLA.
OH! UH, HEY.
UM, "INTERN POWERS ACTIVATE"--AMIRIGHT?
...
HOW'D YOU KNOW I'M AN INTERN?
WELL, FOR STARTERS, YOU DON'T REALLY LOOK LIKE A LARAINE, BUT, ACCORDING TO THE NAME ON THAT CUP, YOU'VE GOT HER ICED LATTE.
I SUPPOSE SHE COULD BE YOUR GIRLFRIEND, BUT YOU'VE BEEN HOLDING THAT NICE, COLD DRINK FOR FIVE MINUTES AND HAVEN'T TAKEN ONE SIP--
--EVEN THOUGH IT'S LIKE NINETY-NINE DEGREES OUTSIDE--
--SO I'M GUESSING YOU'RE ON A COFFEE RUN FOR HIGHER-UPS. LIKE ME.

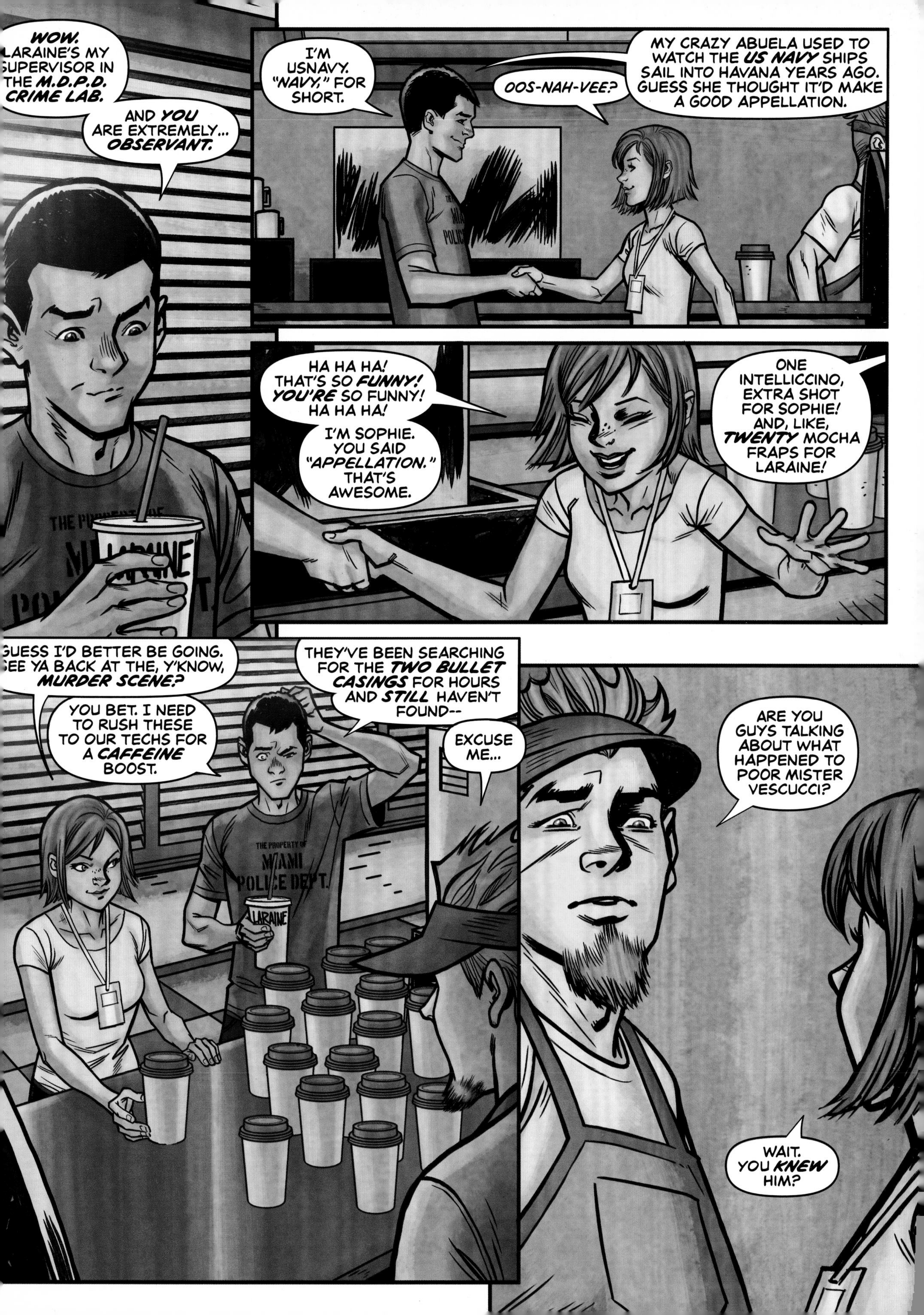
WOW. LARAINE'S MY SUPERVISOR IN THE M.D.P.D. CRIME LAB.
AND YOU ARE EXTREMELY... OBSERVANT.
I'M USNAVY. "NAVY," FOR SHORT.
OOS-NAH-VEE?
MY CRAZY ABUELA USED TO WATCH THE US NAVY SHIPS SAIL INTO HAVANA YEARS AGO. GUESS SHE THOUGHT IT'D MAKE A GOOD APPELLATION.
HA HA HA! THAT'S SO FUNNY! YOU'RE SO FUNNY! HA HA HA!
I'M SOPHIE. YOU SAID "APPELLATION." THAT'S AWESOME.
ONE INTELLICCINO, EXTRA SHOT FOR SOPHIE! AND, LIKE, TWENTY MOCHA FRAPS FOR LARAINE!
THE PROPERTY OF MIAMI POLICE DEPT.
LARAINE
GUESS I'D BETTER BE GOING. SEE YA BACK AT THE, Y'KNOW, MURDER SCENE?
YOU BET. I NEED TO RUSH THESE TO OUR TECHS FOR A CAFFEINE BOOST.
THEY'VE BEEN SEARCHING FOR THE TWO BULLET CASINGS FOR HOURS AND STILL HAVEN'T FOUND--
EXCUSE ME...
ARE YOU GUYS TALKING ABOUT WHAT HAPPENED TO POOR MISTER VESCUCCI?
WAIT. YOU KNEW HIM?

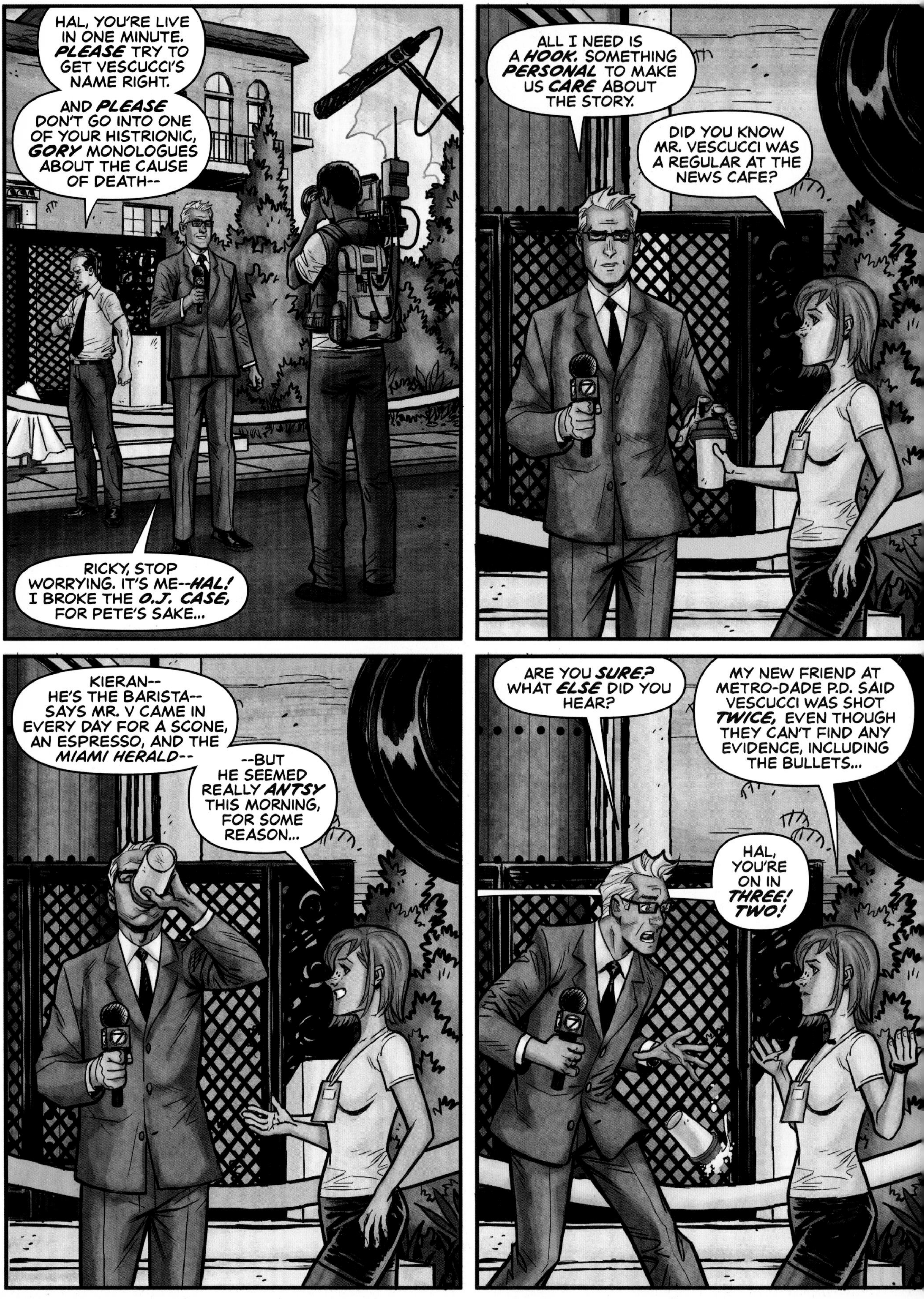
HAL, YOU'RE LIVE IN ONE MINUTE. PLEASE TRY TO GET VESCUCCI'S NAME RIGHT.
AND PLEASE DON'T GO INTO ONE OF YOUR HISTRIONIC, GORY MONOLOGUES ABOUT THE CAUSE OF DEATH--
RICKY, STOP WORRYING. IT'S ME--HAL! I BROKE THE O.J. CASE, FOR PETE'S SAKE...
ALL I NEED IS A HOOK. SOMETHING PERSONAL TO MAKE US CARE ABOUT THE STORY.
DID YOU KNOW MR. VESCUCCI WAS A REGULAR AT THE NEWS CAFE?
KIERAN-- HE'S THE BARISTA-- SAYS MR. V CAME IN EVERY DAY FOR A SCONE, AN ESPRESSO, AND THE MIAMI HERALD--
--BUT HE SEEMED REALLY ANTSY THIS MORNING, FOR SOME REASON...
ARE YOU SURE? WHAT ELSE DID YOU HEAR?
MY NEW FRIEND AT METRO-DADE P.D. SAID VESCUCCI WAS SHOT TWICE, EVEN THOUGH THEY CAN'T FIND ANY EVIDENCE, INCLUDING THE BULLETS...
HAL, YOU'RE ON IN THREE! TWO!

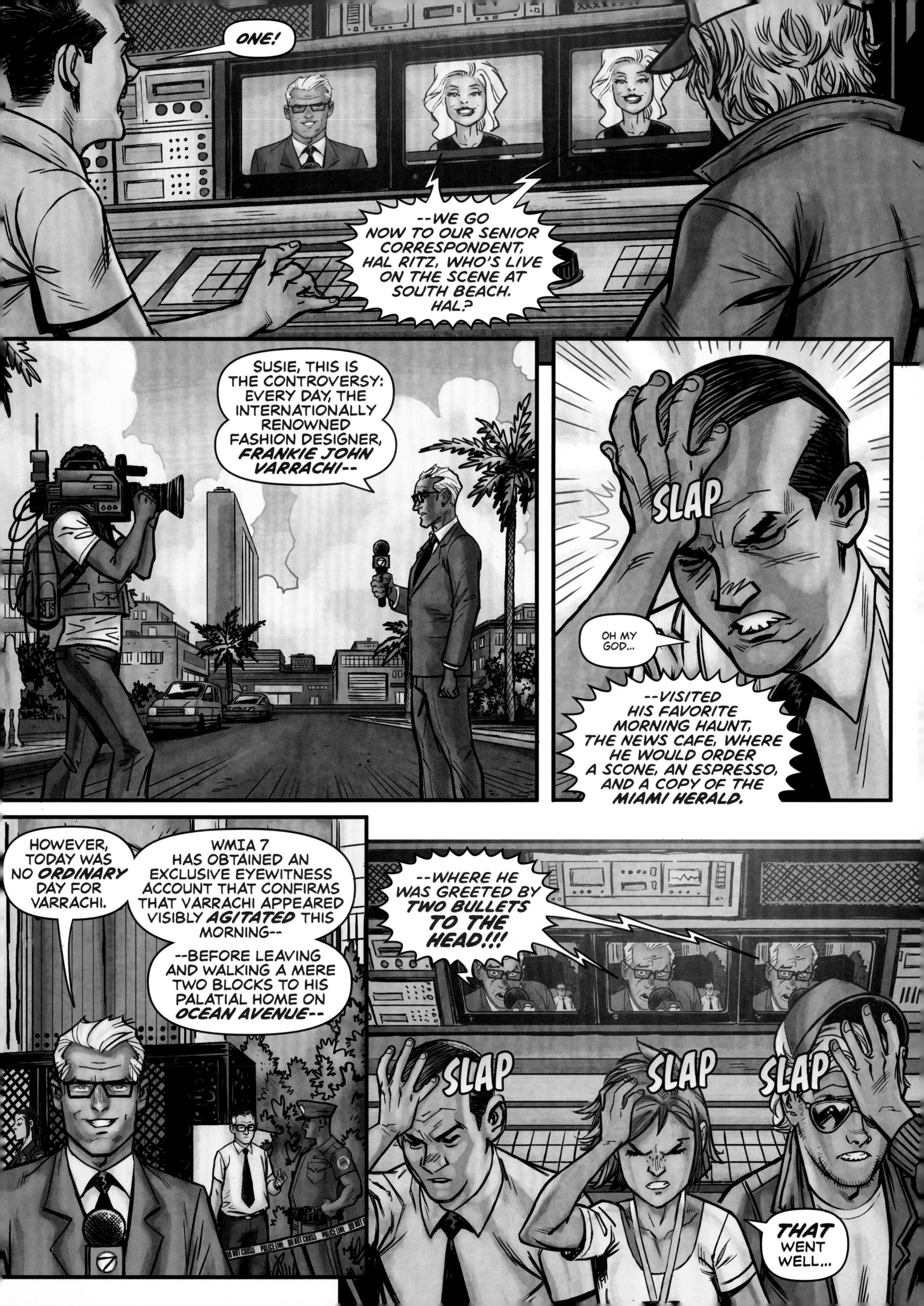
ONE!
--WE GO NOW TO OUR SENIOR CORRESPONDENT, HAL RITZ, WHO'S LIVE ON THE SCENE AT SOUTH BEACH. HAL?
SUSIE, THIS IS THE CONTROVERSY: EVERY DAY, THE INTERNATIONALLY RENOWNED FASHION DESIGNER, FRANKIE JOHN VARRACHI--
SLAP
OH MY GOD...
--VISITED HIS FAVORITE MORNING HAUNT, THE NEWS CAFE, WHERE HE WOULD ORDER A SCONE, AN ESPRESSO, AND A COPY OF THE MIAMI HERALD.
HOWEVER, TODAY WAS NO ORDINARY DAY FOR VARRACHI.
WMIA 7 HAS OBTAINED AN EXCLUSIVE EYEWITNESS ACCOUNT THAT CONFIRMS THAT VARRACHI APPEARED VISIBLY AGITATED THIS MORNING--
--BEFORE LEAVING AND WALKING A MERE TWO BLOCKS TO HIS PALATIAL HOME ON OCEAN AVENUE--
--WHERE HE WAS GREETED BY TWO BULLETS TO THE HEAD!!!
SLAP
SLAP
SLAP
THAT WENT WELL...

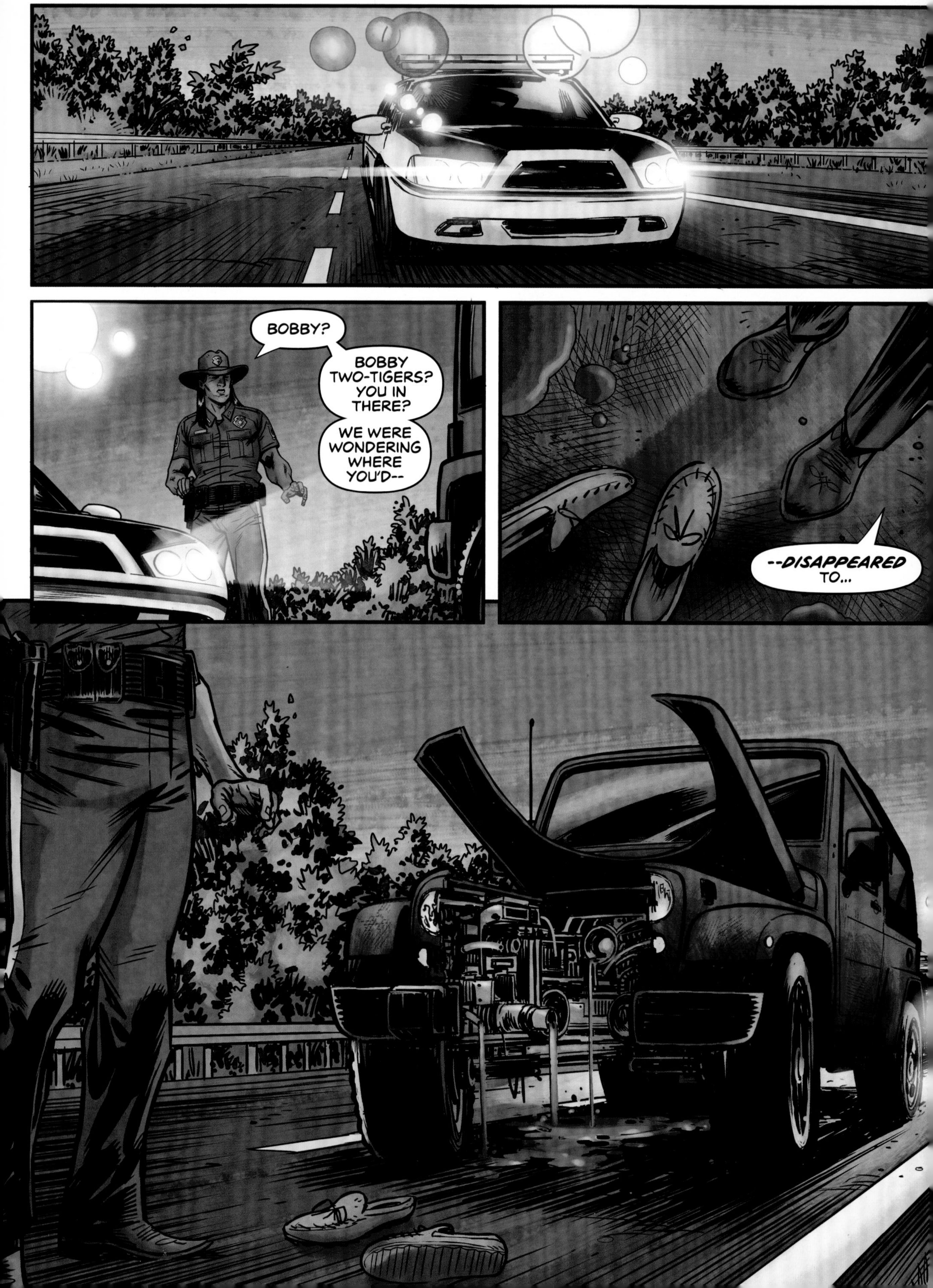
BOBBY?
BOBBY TWO-TIGERS? YOU IN THERE?
WE WERE WONDERING WHERE YOU'D--
--DISAPPEARED TO...

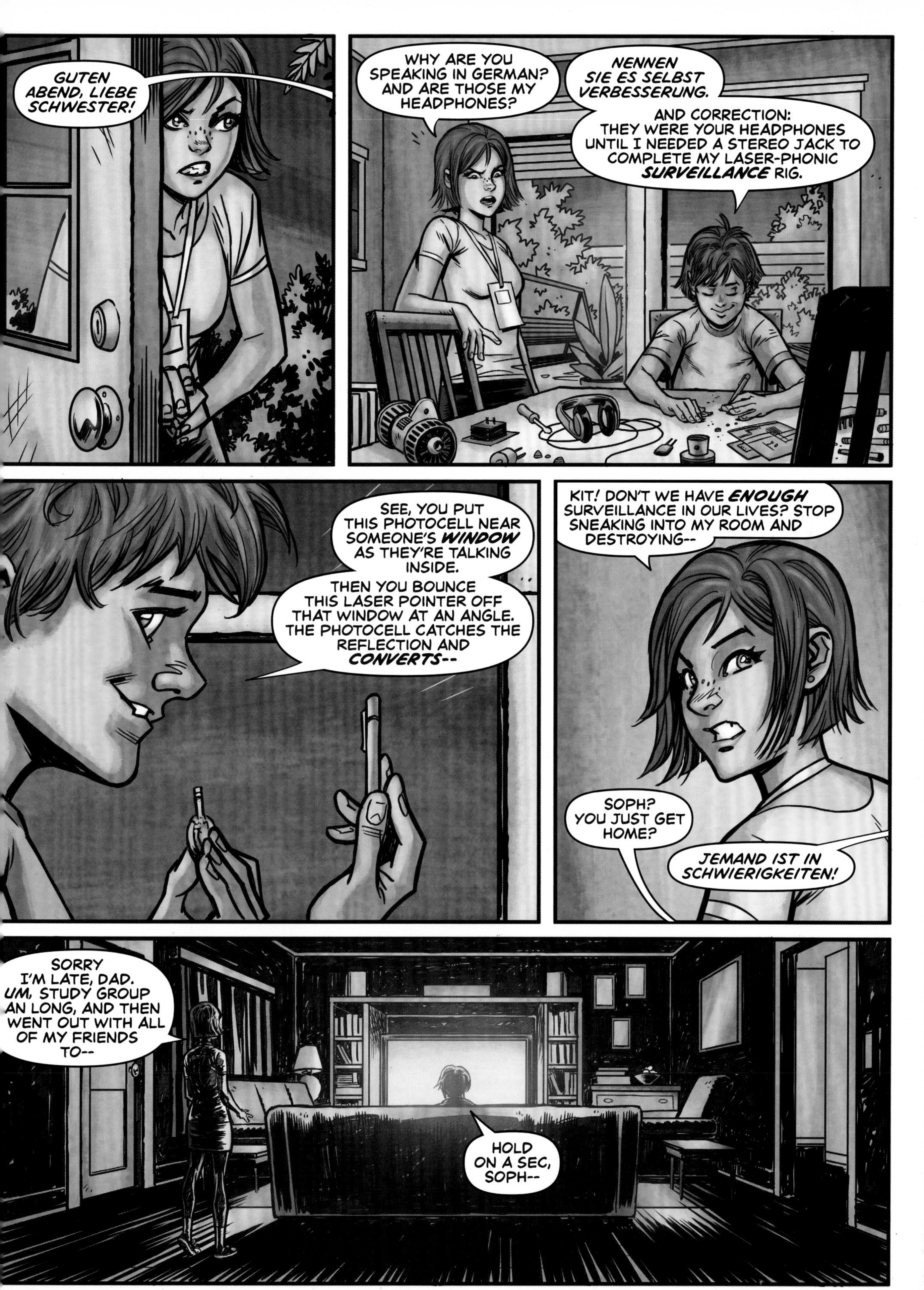
GUTEN ABEND, LIEBE SCHWESTER!
WHY ARE YOU SPEAKING IN GERMAN? AND ARE THOSE MY HEADPHONES?
NENNEN SIE ES SELBST VERBESSERUNG.
AND CORRECTION: THEY WERE YOUR HEADPHONES UNTIL I NEEDED A STEREO JACK TO COMPLETE MY LASER-PHONIC SURVEILLANCE RIG.
SEE, YOU PUT THIS PHOTOCELL NEAR SOMEONE'S WINDOW AS THEY'RE TALKING INSIDE.
THEN YOU BOUNCE THIS LASER POINTER OFF THAT WINDOW AT AN ANGLE. THE PHOTOCELL CATCHES THE REFLECTION AND CONVERTS--
KIT! DON'T WE HAVE ENOUGH SURVEILLANCE IN OUR LIVES? STOP SNEAKING INTO MY ROOM AND DESTROYING--
SOPH? YOU JUST GET HOME?
JEMAND IST IN SCHWIERIGKEITEN!
SORRY I'M LATE, DAD. UM, STUDY GROUP AN LONG, AND THEN WENT OUT WITH ALL OF MY FRIENDS TO--
HOLD ON A SEC, SOPH--

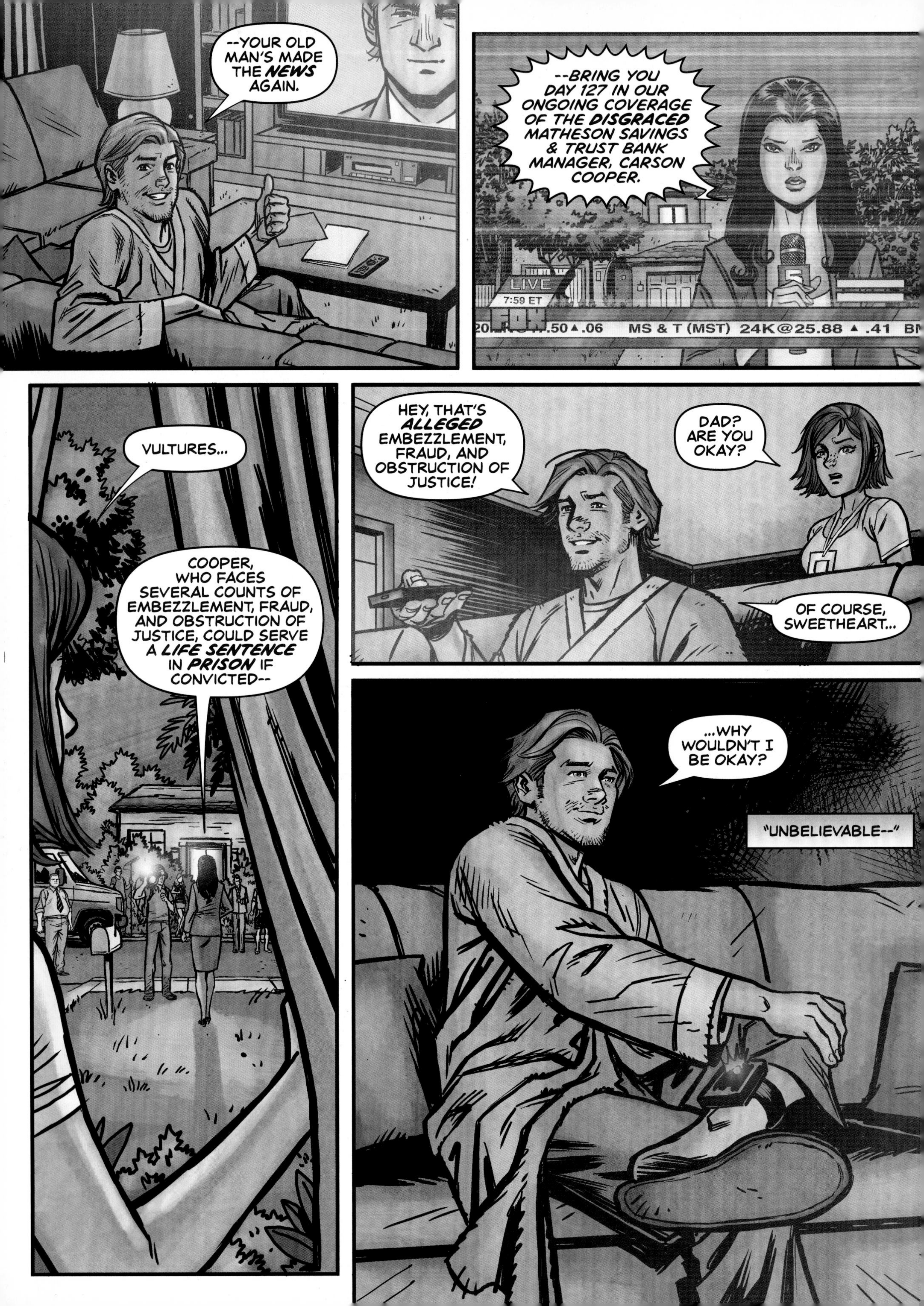
--YOUR OLD MAN'S MADE THE NEWS AGAIN.
--BRING YOU DAY 127 IN OUR ONGOING COVERAGE OF THE DISGRACED MATHESON SAVINGS & TRUST BANK MANAGER, CARSON COOPER.
LIVE
7:59 ET
FOX
MS & T (MST) 24K@25.88 ▲ .41
VULTURES...
COOPER, WHO FACES SEVERAL COUNTS OF EMBEZZLEMENT, FRAUD, AND OBSTRUCTION OF JUSTICE, COULD SERVE A LIFE SENTENCE IN PRISON IF CONVICTED--
HEY, THAT'S ALLEGED EMBEZZLEMENT, FRAUD, AND OBSTRUCTION OF JUSTICE!
DAD? ARE YOU OKAY?
OF COURSE, SWEETHEART...
...WHY WOULDN'T I BE OKAY?
"UNBELIEVABLE--"

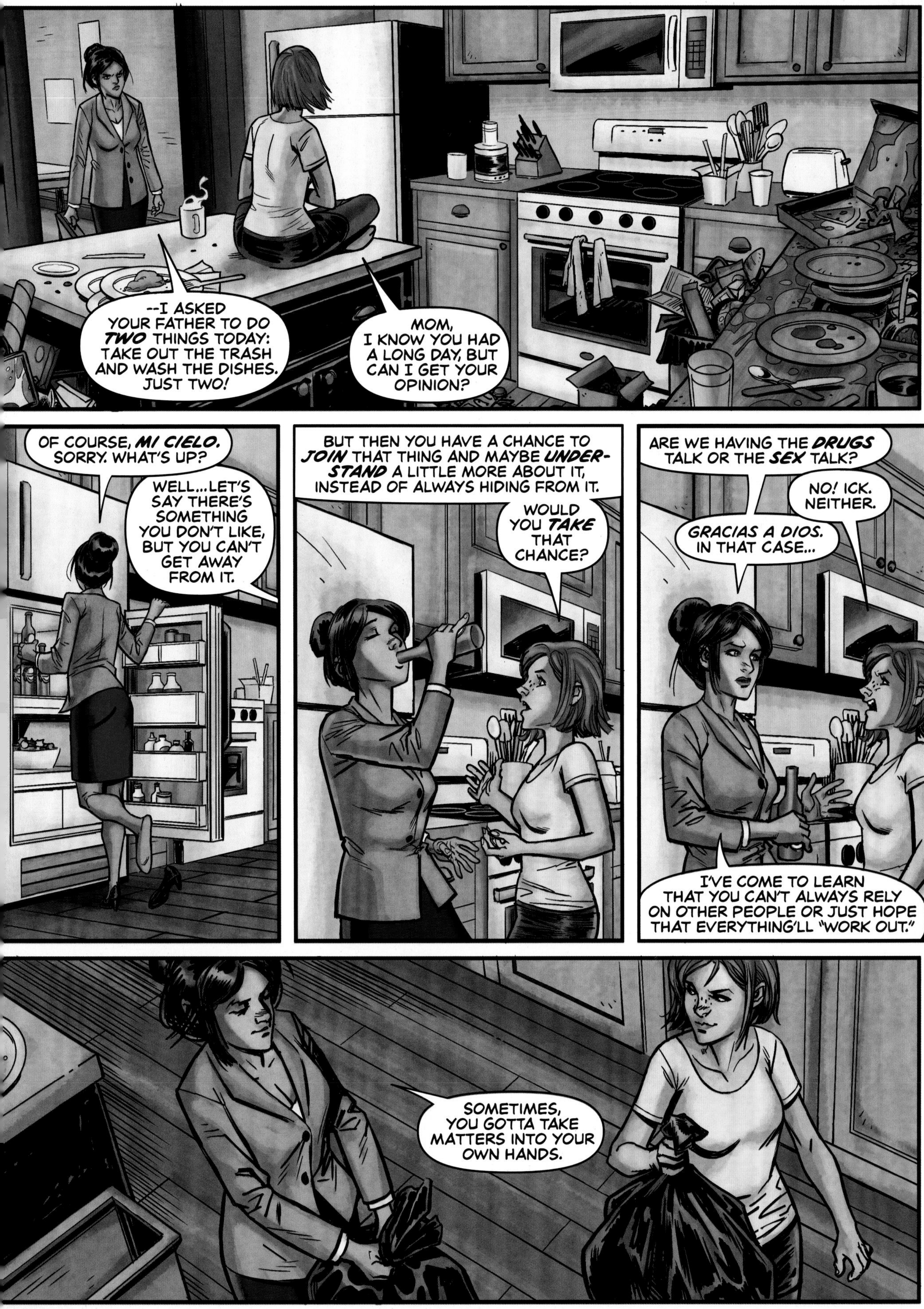
--I ASKED YOUR FATHER TO DO *TWO* THINGS TODAY: TAKE OUT THE TRASH AND WASH THE DISHES. JUST TWO!
MOM, I KNOW YOU HAD A LONG DAY, BUT CAN I GET YOUR OPINION?
OF COURSE, *MI CIELO.* SORRY. WHAT'S UP?
WELL...LET'S SAY THERE'S SOMETHING YOU DON'T LIKE, BUT YOU CAN'T GET AWAY FROM IT.
BUT THEN YOU HAVE A CHANCE TO *JOIN* THAT THING AND MAYBE *UNDERSTAND* A LITTLE MORE ABOUT IT, INSTEAD OF ALWAYS HIDING FROM IT.
WOULD YOU *TAKE* THAT CHANCE?
ARE WE HAVING THE *DRUGS* TALK OR THE *SEX* TALK?
NO! ICK. NEITHER.
GRACIAS A DIOS. IN THAT CASE...
I'VE COME TO LEARN THAT YOU CAN'T ALWAYS RELY ON OTHER PEOPLE OR JUST HOPE THAT EVERYTHING'LL "WORK OUT."
SOMETIMES, YOU GOTTA TAKE MATTERS INTO YOUR OWN HANDS.

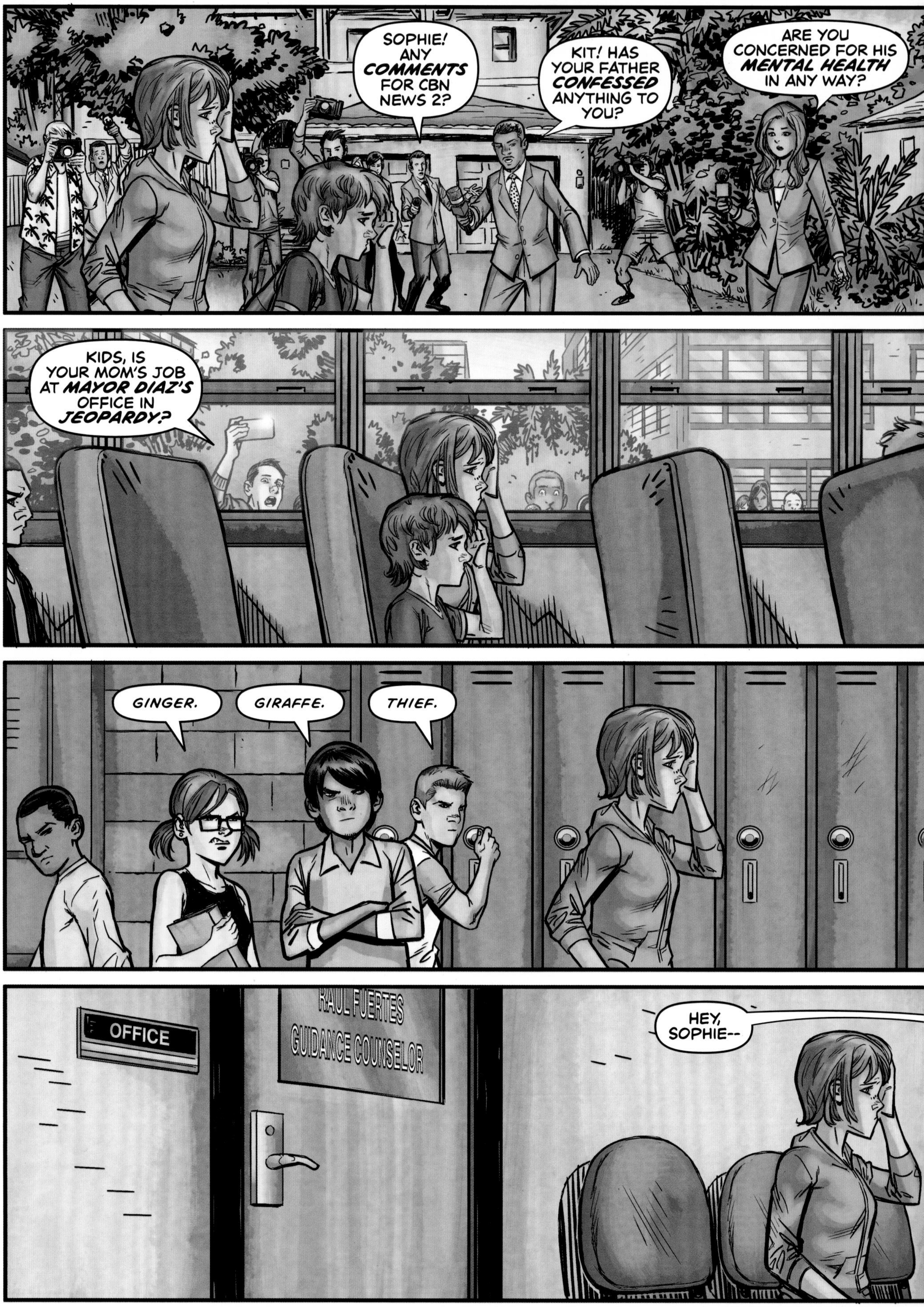
SOPHIE! ANY COMMENTS FOR CBN NEWS 2?
KIT! HAS YOUR FATHER CONFESSED ANYTHING TO YOU?
ARE YOU CONCERNED FOR HIS MENTAL HEALTH IN ANY WAY?
KIDS, IS YOUR MOM'S JOB AT MAYOR DIAZ'S OFFICE IN JEOPARDY?
GINGER.
GIRAFFE.
THIEF.
OFFICE
RAUL FUERTES
GUIDANCE COUNSELOR
HEY, SOPHIE--

--WHAT BRINGS YOU HERE? DIDJA *PUNCH* VERRUCA VERACRUZ IN THE NOSE AGAIN?

NAH. JUST NEED MR. FUERTES TO SIGN ANOTHER METRO RAIL *VOUCHER* SO I CAN GET TO MY INTERNSHIP.

OH. UH, WELL, SINCE YOU'RE NOT, Y'KNOW, GETTING *EXPELLED* AFTER ALL, MAYBE I CAN FINALLY CONVINCE YOU TO STAR IN MY LATEST MOVIE?

THE A.V. CLUB'S LETTING ME SERVICE THEIR CAMERAS THIS WEEKEND-- NO BIG DEAL--SO I THOUGHT, *"WHAT THE HEY? WHY NOT PUT 'EM TO GOOD USE ON MY NEXT PROJECT?"*

IT'S A SCI-FI THRILLER SET IN THE NOT-TOO-DISTANT FUTURE WITH THE WORKING TITLE OF *"DIE-BORG"*--

SENORITA COOPER... ¿SI ESTAS LISTA?

THANKS, MILO, BUT YOU KNOW HOW I FEEL ABOUT BEING *ON CAMERA*. I'LL CATCH YOU AND DIE-BURGER ON THE RED CARPET THOUGH!

SURE, SOPHIE. WE'LL DO LUNCH. AND IT'S, UH, DIE-*BORG*...

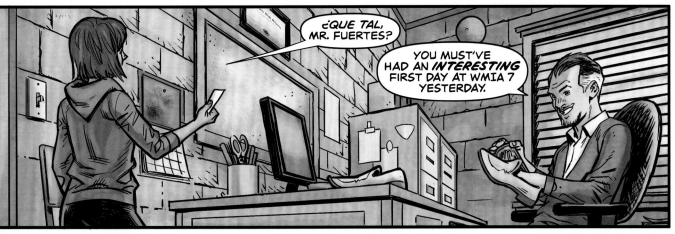

¿QUE TAL, MR. FUERTES?

YOU MUST'VE HAD AN *INTERESTING* FIRST DAY AT WMIA 7 YESTERDAY.

YEAH. THE VESCUCCI KILLING WAS THE *TOP STORY* LAST NIGHT. I THINK MY DAD MIGHT BE GETTING *JEALOUS*.

MURDER IS A PRETTY HEAVY SUBJECT, SOPHIE. YOU SURE THIS IS THE RIGHT INTERNSHIP FOR YOU?

THE NEWS REPORTING PROCESS HAS ALWAYS FASCINATED ME, AND I HAVE A DEEP AND ABIDING PASSION FOR THE TRUTH.

YOU SHOULD SAVE THAT FOR YOUR COLLEGE APPLICATIONS. LOOK, SOPHIE, I'LL JUST COME OUT AND SAY IT--

--I'M WORRIED YOU TOOK THIS INTERNSHIP TO SOMEHOW *PROVE* YOUR FATHER'S INNOCENCE ALL BY YOURSELF.

IT'S NOT LIKE I HAD MUCH OF A CHOICE, MR. FUERTES. YOU SAID I COULD EITHER VOLUNTEER FOR AN INTERNSHIP OR GET *SUSPENDED* FOR SOCKING VERRUCA-- EVEN THOUGH SHE TOTALLY *DESERVED* IT.

AND, SINCE IT'D BE KINDA EMBARRASSING TO HAVE *TWO* COOPERS UNDER *HOUSE ARREST*...

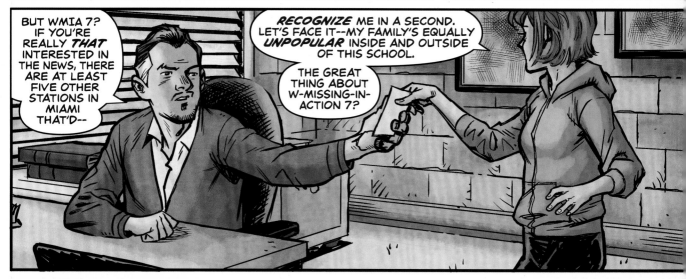

BUT WMIA 7? IF YOU'RE REALLY *THAT* INTERESTED IN THE NEWS, THERE ARE AT LEAST FIVE OTHER STATIONS IN MIAMI THAT'D--

RECOGNIZE ME IN A SECOND. LET'S FACE IT--MY FAMILY'S EQUALLY *UNPOPULAR* INSIDE AND OUTSIDE OF THIS SCHOOL.

THE GREAT THING ABOUT W-MISSING-IN-ACTION 7?

THOSE GUYS ARE *CLUELESS*...

HEY, KID--

--THANKS FOR THE COFFEE YESTERDAY.

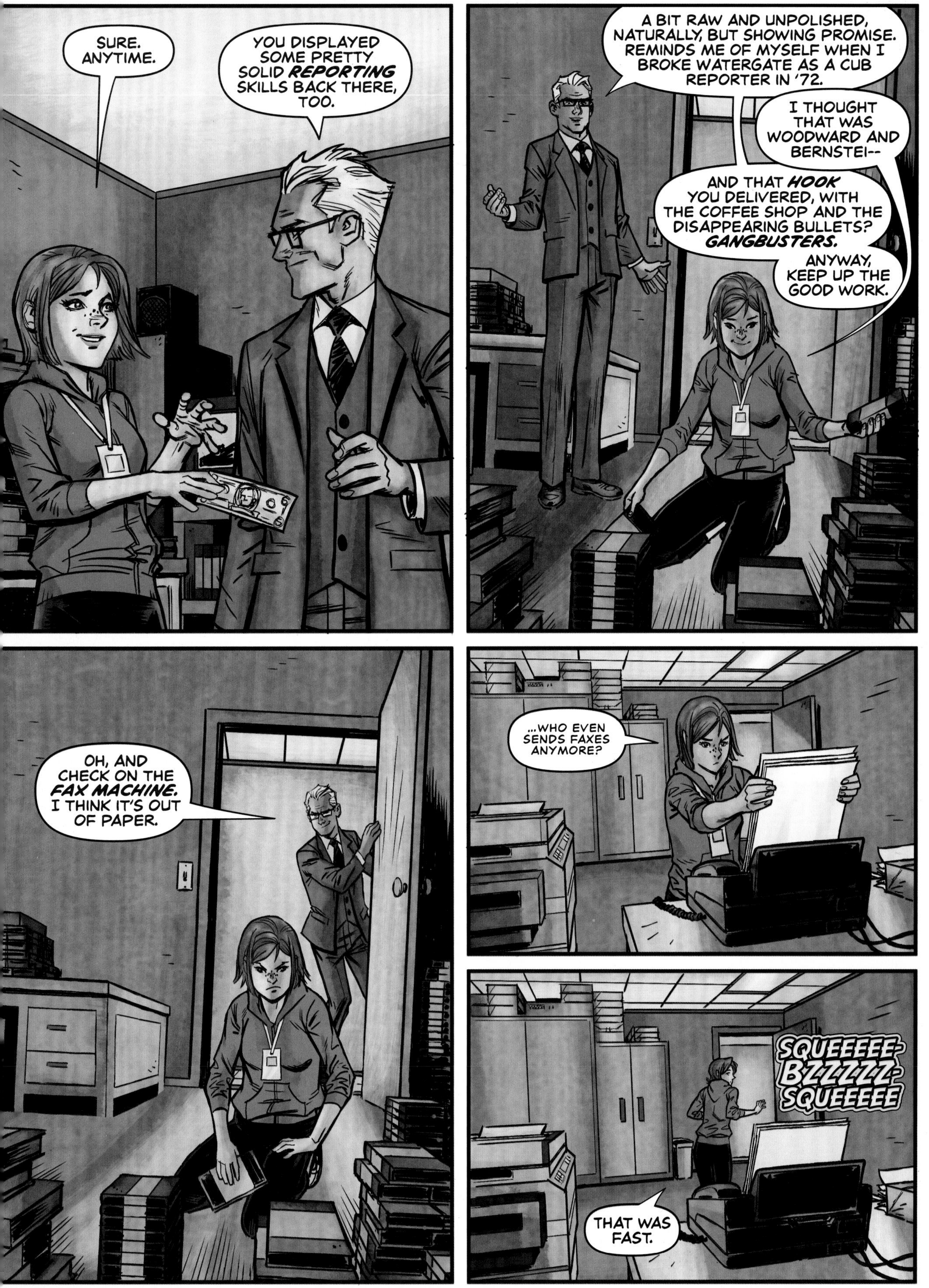
SURE. ANYTIME.
YOU DISPLAYED SOME PRETTY SOLID **REPORTING** SKILLS BACK THERE, TOO.
A BIT RAW AND UNPOLISHED, NATURALLY, BUT SHOWING PROMISE. REMINDS ME OF MYSELF WHEN I BROKE WATERGATE AS A CUB REPORTER IN '72.
I THOUGHT THAT WAS WOODWARD AND BERNSTEI--
AND THAT **HOOK** YOU DELIVERED, WITH THE COFFEE SHOP AND THE DISAPPEARING BULLETS? **GANGBUSTERS.**
ANYWAY, KEEP UP THE GOOD WORK.
OH, AND CHECK ON THE **FAX MACHINE.** I THINK IT'S OUT OF PAPER.
...WHO EVEN SENDS FAXES ANYMORE?
SQUEEEEEE-BZZZZZ-SQUEEEEEE
THAT WAS FAST.

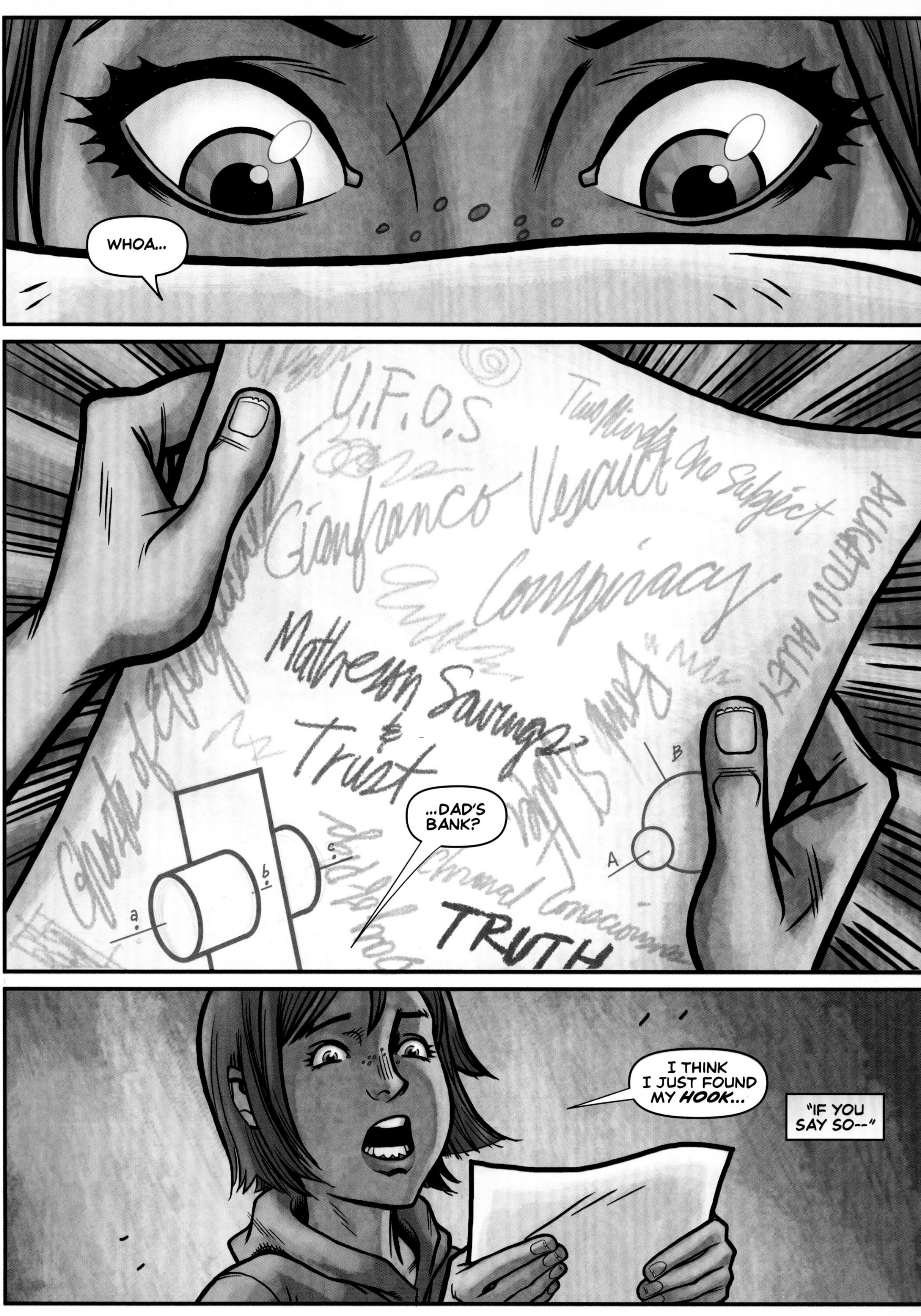
WHOA...
U.F.O.S
Conspiracy
TRUTH
...DAD'S BANK?
I THINK I JUST FOUND MY ***HOOK...***
"IF YOU SAY SO--"

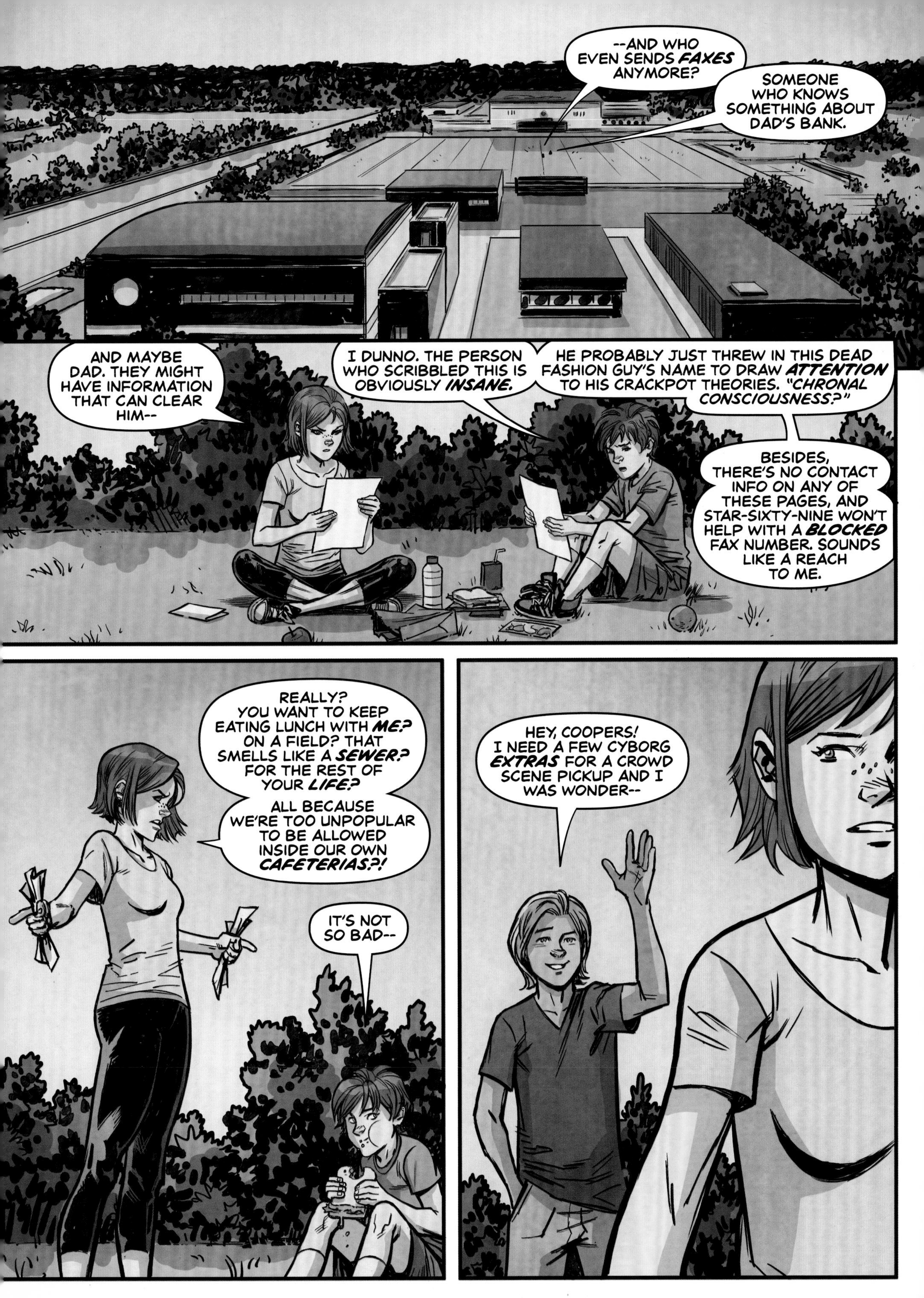
--AND WHO EVEN SENDS FAXES ANYMORE?
SOMEONE WHO KNOWS SOMETHING ABOUT DAD'S BANK.
AND MAYBE DAD. THEY MIGHT HAVE INFORMATION THAT CAN CLEAR HIM--
I DUNNO. THE PERSON WHO SCRIBBLED THIS IS OBVIOUSLY INSANE.
HE PROBABLY JUST THREW IN THIS DEAD FASHION GUY'S NAME TO DRAW ATTENTION TO HIS CRACKPOT THEORIES. "CHRONAL CONSCIOUSNESS?"
BESIDES, THERE'S NO CONTACT INFO ON ANY OF THESE PAGES, AND STAR-SIXTY-NINE WON'T HELP WITH A BLOCKED FAX NUMBER. SOUNDS LIKE A REACH TO ME.
REALLY? YOU WANT TO KEEP EATING LUNCH WITH ME? ON A FIELD? THAT SMELLS LIKE A SEWER? FOR THE REST OF YOUR LIFE?
ALL BECAUSE WE'RE TOO UNPOPULAR TO BE ALLOWED INSIDE OUR OWN CAFETERIAS?!
IT'S NOT SO BAD--
HEY, COOPERS! I NEED A FEW CYBORG EXTRAS FOR A CROWD SCENE PICKUP AND I WAS WONDER--

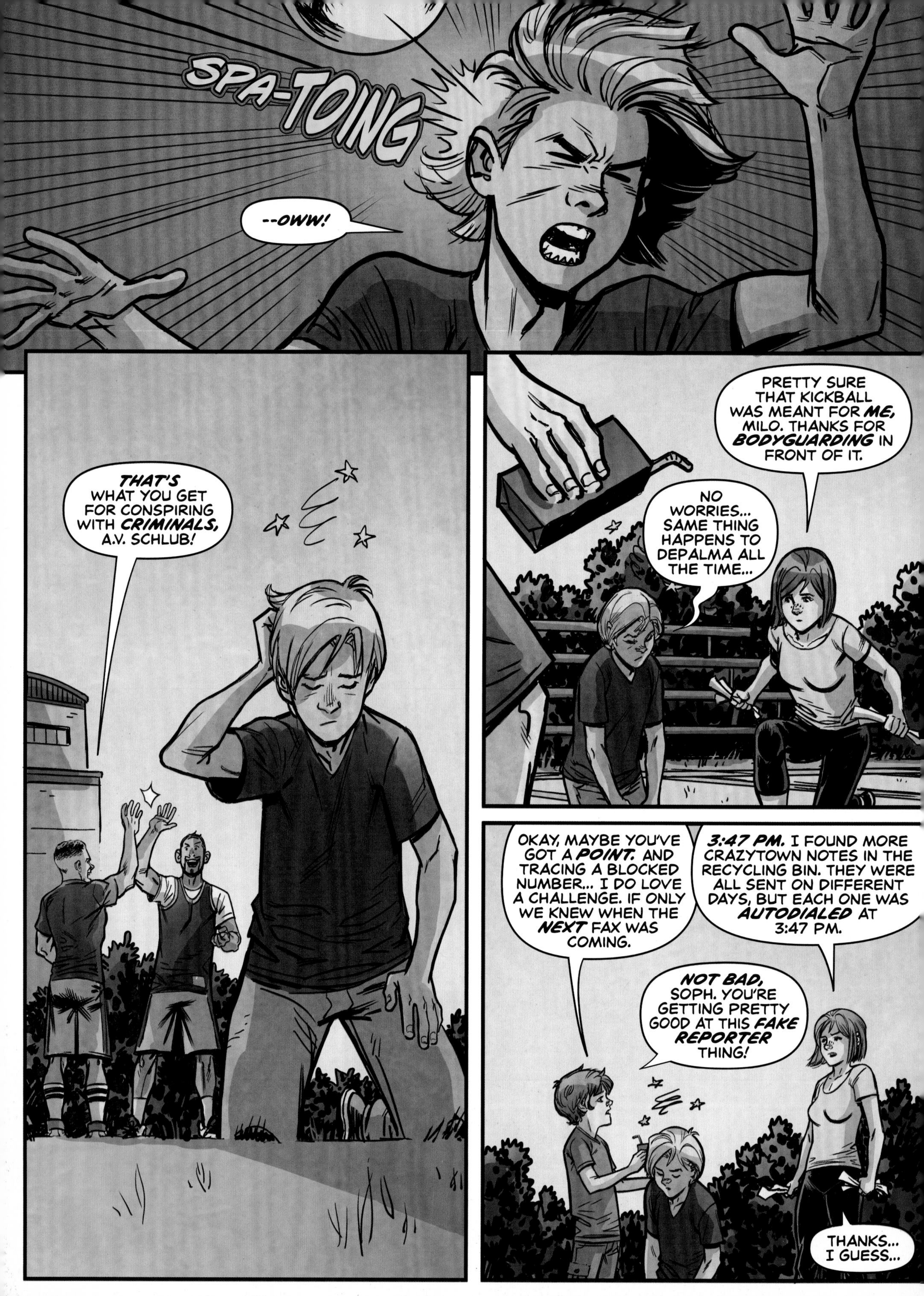
SPA-TONG
--OWW!
THAT'S WHAT YOU GET FOR CONSPIRING WITH CRIMINALS, A.V. SCHLUB!
PRETTY SURE THAT KICKBALL WAS MEANT FOR ME, MILO. THANKS FOR BODYGUARDING IN FRONT OF IT.
NO WORRIES... SAME THING HAPPENS TO DEPALMA ALL THE TIME...
OKAY, MAYBE YOU'VE GOT A POINT. AND TRACING A BLOCKED NUMBER... I DO LOVE A CHALLENGE. IF ONLY WE KNEW WHEN THE NEXT FAX WAS COMING.
3:47 PM. I FOUND MORE CRAZYTOWN NOTES IN THE RECYCLING BIN. THEY WERE ALL SENT ON DIFFERENT DAYS, BUT EACH ONE WAS AUTODIALED AT 3:47 PM.
NOT BAD, SOPH. YOU'RE GETTING PRETTY GOOD AT THIS FAKE REPORTER THING!
THANKS... I GUESS...

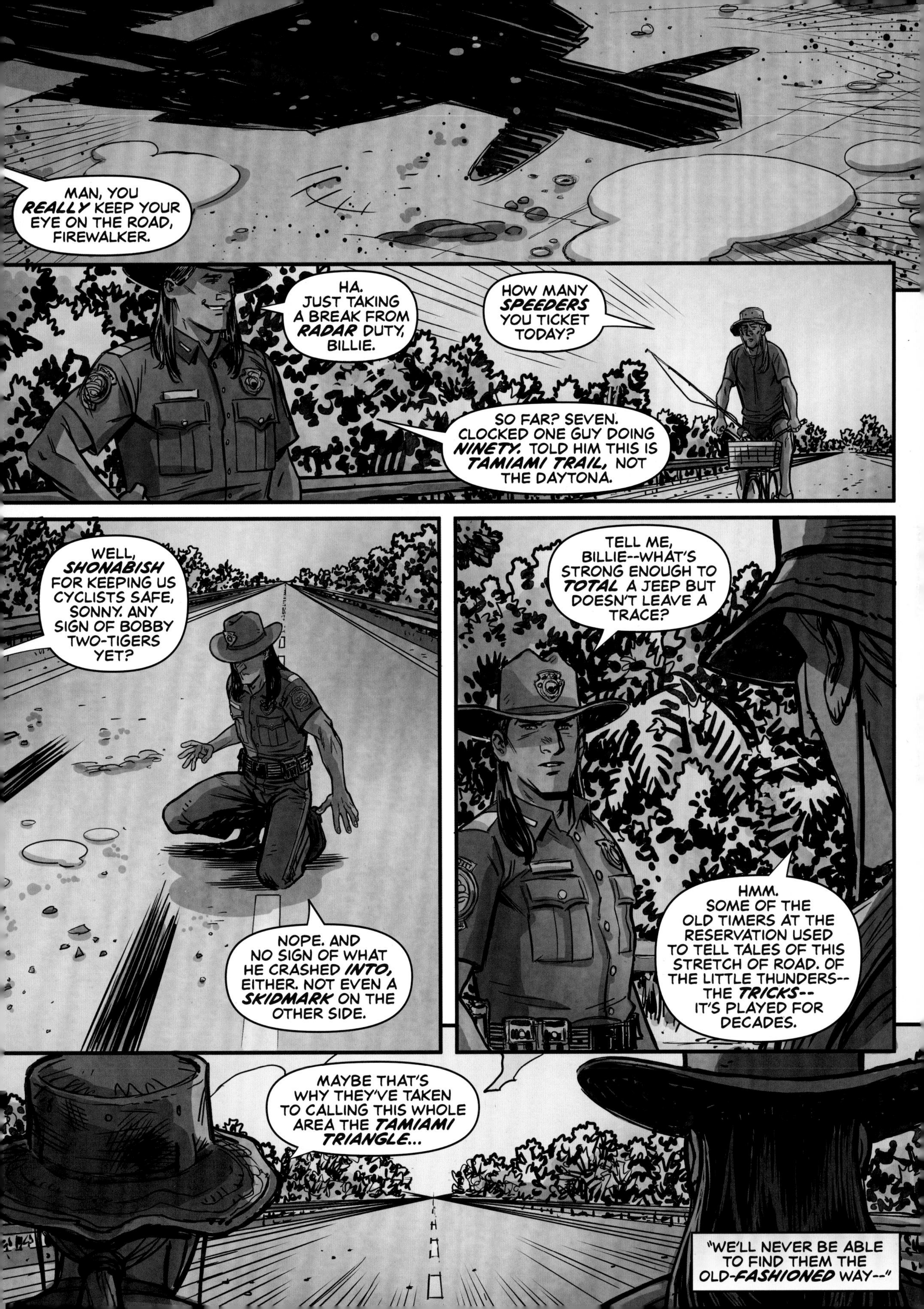
MAN, YOU REALLY KEEP YOUR EYE ON THE ROAD, FIREWALKER.
HA. JUST TAKING A BREAK FROM RADAR DUTY, BILLIE.
HOW MANY SPEEDERS YOU TICKET TODAY?
SO FAR? SEVEN. CLOCKED ONE GUY DOING NINETY. TOLD HIM THIS IS TAMIAMI TRAIL, NOT THE DAYTONA.
WELL, SHONABISH FOR KEEPING US CYCLISTS SAFE, SONNY. ANY SIGN OF BOBBY TWO-TIGERS YET?
NOPE. AND NO SIGN OF WHAT HE CRASHED INTO, EITHER. NOT EVEN A SKIDMARK ON THE OTHER SIDE.
TELL ME, BILLIE--WHAT'S STRONG ENOUGH TO TOTAL A JEEP BUT DOESN'T LEAVE A TRACE?
HMM. SOME OF THE OLD TIMERS AT THE RESERVATION USED TO TELL TALES OF THIS STRETCH OF ROAD. OF THE LITTLE THUNDERS-- THE TRICKS-- IT'S PLAYED FOR DECADES.
MAYBE THAT'S WHY THEY'VE TAKEN TO CALLING THIS WHOLE AREA THE TAMIAMI TRIANGLE...
"WE'LL NEVER BE ABLE TO FIND THEM THE OLD-FASHIONED WAY--"

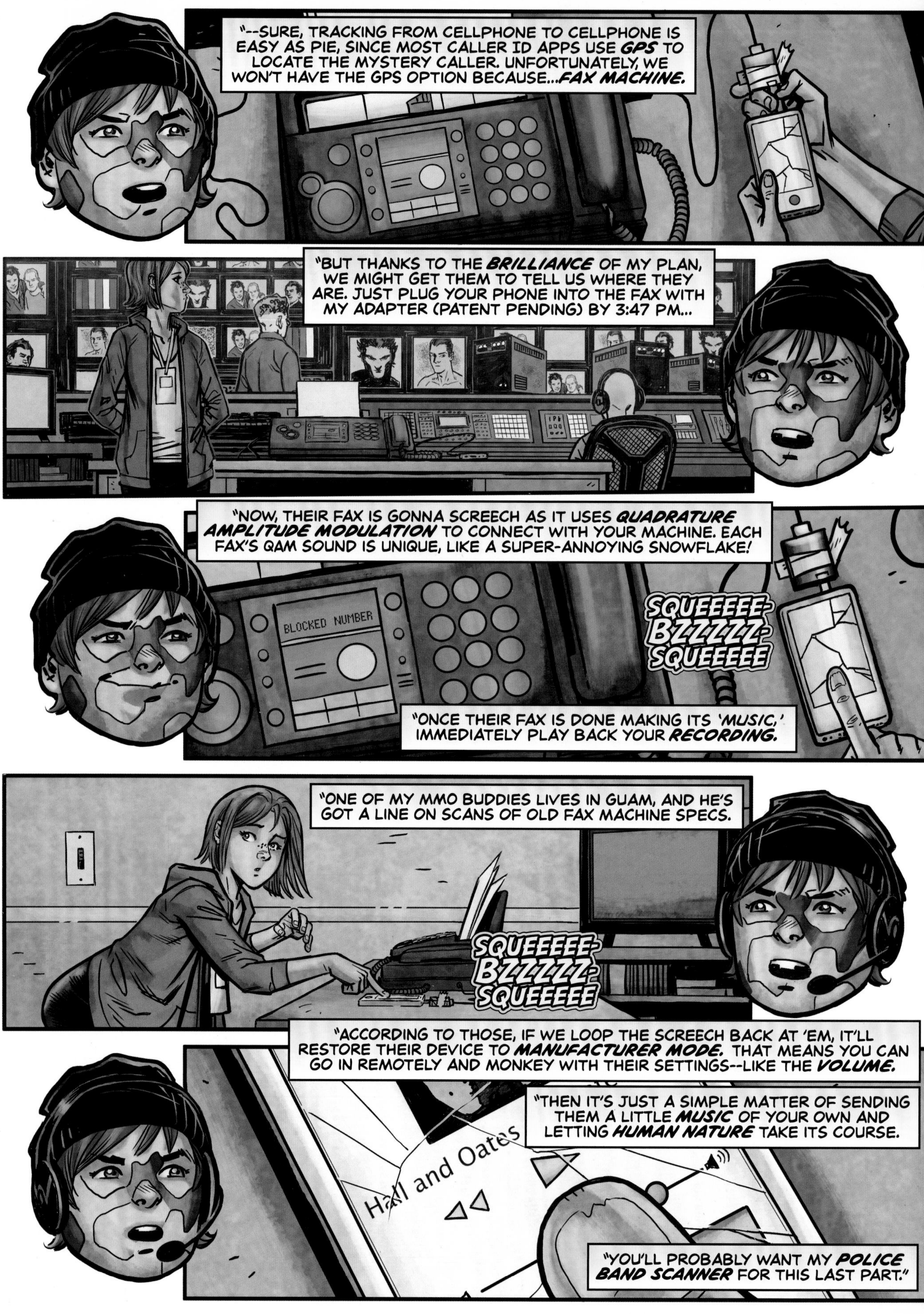
"--SURE, TRACKING FROM CELLPHONE TO CELLPHONE IS EASY AS PIE, SINCE MOST CALLER ID APPS USE GPS TO LOCATE THE MYSTERY CALLER. UNFORTUNATELY, WE WON'T HAVE THE GPS OPTION BECAUSE...FAX MACHINE.
"BUT THANKS TO THE BRILLIANCE OF MY PLAN, WE MIGHT GET THEM TO TELL US WHERE THEY ARE. JUST PLUG YOUR PHONE INTO THE FAX WITH MY ADAPTER (PATENT PENDING) BY 3:47 PM...
"NOW, THEIR FAX IS GONNA SCREECH AS IT USES QUADRATURE AMPLITUDE MODULATION TO CONNECT WITH YOUR MACHINE. EACH FAX'S QAM SOUND IS UNIQUE, LIKE A SUPER-ANNOYING SNOWFLAKE!
BLOCKED NUMBER
SQUEEEEE-BZZZZZ-SQUEEEEE
"ONCE THEIR FAX IS DONE MAKING ITS 'MUSIC,' IMMEDIATELY PLAY BACK YOUR RECORDING.
"ONE OF MY MMO BUDDIES LIVES IN GUAM, AND HE'S GOT A LINE ON SCANS OF OLD FAX MACHINE SPECS.
SQUEEEEE-BZZZZZ-SQUEEEEE
"ACCORDING TO THOSE, IF WE LOOP THE SCREECH BACK AT 'EM, IT'LL RESTORE THEIR DEVICE TO MANUFACTURER MODE. THAT MEANS YOU CAN GO IN REMOTELY AND MONKEY WITH THEIR SETTINGS--LIKE THE VOLUME.
"THEN IT'S JUST A SIMPLE MATTER OF SENDING THEM A LITTLE MUSIC OF YOUR OWN AND LETTING HUMAN NATURE TAKE ITS COURSE.
Hall and Oates
"YOU'LL PROBABLY WANT MY POLICE BAND SCANNER FOR THIS LAST PART."

...SENDING CRUISER FOR A 288 DOMESTIC DISTURBANCE, OVER...

WHY DOES A NINE-YEAR-OLD HAVE A POLICE SCANNER?

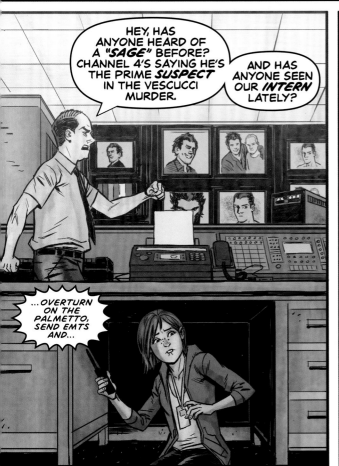

HEY, HAS ANYONE HEARD OF A *"SAGE"* BEFORE? CHANNEL 4'S SAYING HE'S THE PRIME *SUSPECT* IN THE VESCUCCI MURDER.

AND HAS ANYONE SEEN OUR *INTERN* LATELY?

...OVERTURN ON THE PALMETTO, SEND EMTS AND...

...-ING GUY NEXT DOOR BE PLAYIN' *MUTHA-- -- -- HALL AND OATES FULL BLAST,* GOD-- -- --...

NO WAY...

WHAT ABOUT HAL? ANYONE SEEN *HIM?*

WE'VE REGISTERED YOUR NOISE COMPLAINT, SIR. JUST GIVE US YOUR *ADDRESS,* AND WE'LL SEND A--

WHY WON'T SOMEBODY *ANSWER* ME?! I'M YOUR *BOSS,* PEOPLE!

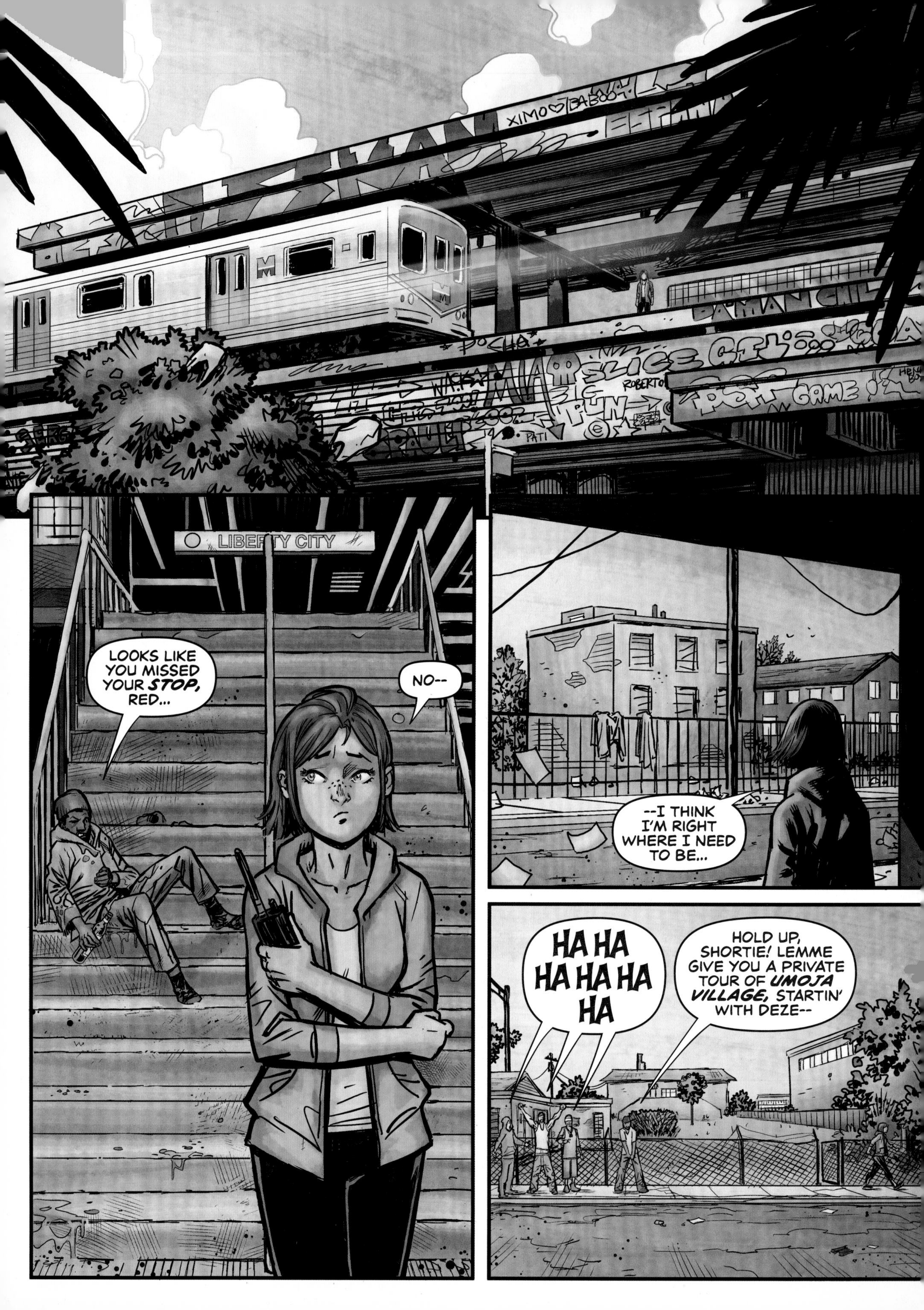
LIBERTY CITY
LOOKS LIKE YOU MISSED YOUR *STOP,* RED...
NO--
--I THINK I'M RIGHT WHERE I NEED TO BE...
HA HA HA HA HA HA
HOLD UP, SHORTIE! LEMME GIVE YOU A PRIVATE TOUR OF *UMOJA VILLAGE,* STARTIN' WITH DEZE--

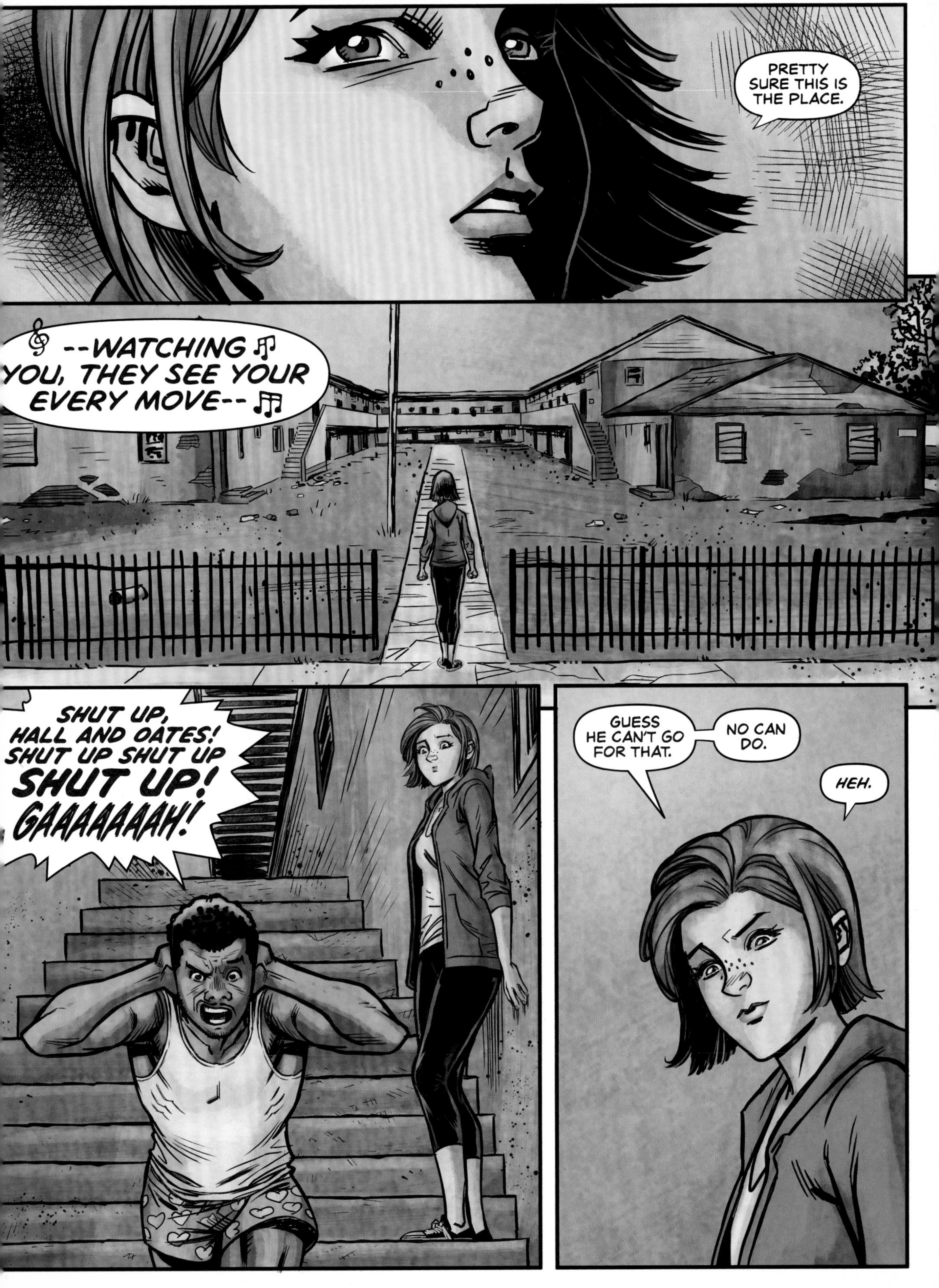
PRETTY SURE THIS IS THE PLACE.
--WATCHING YOU, THEY SEE YOUR EVERY MOVE--
SHUT UP, HALL AND OATES! SHUT UP SHUT UP SHUT UP! GAAAAAAAH!
GUESS HE CAN'T GO FOR THAT.
NO CAN DO.
HEH.

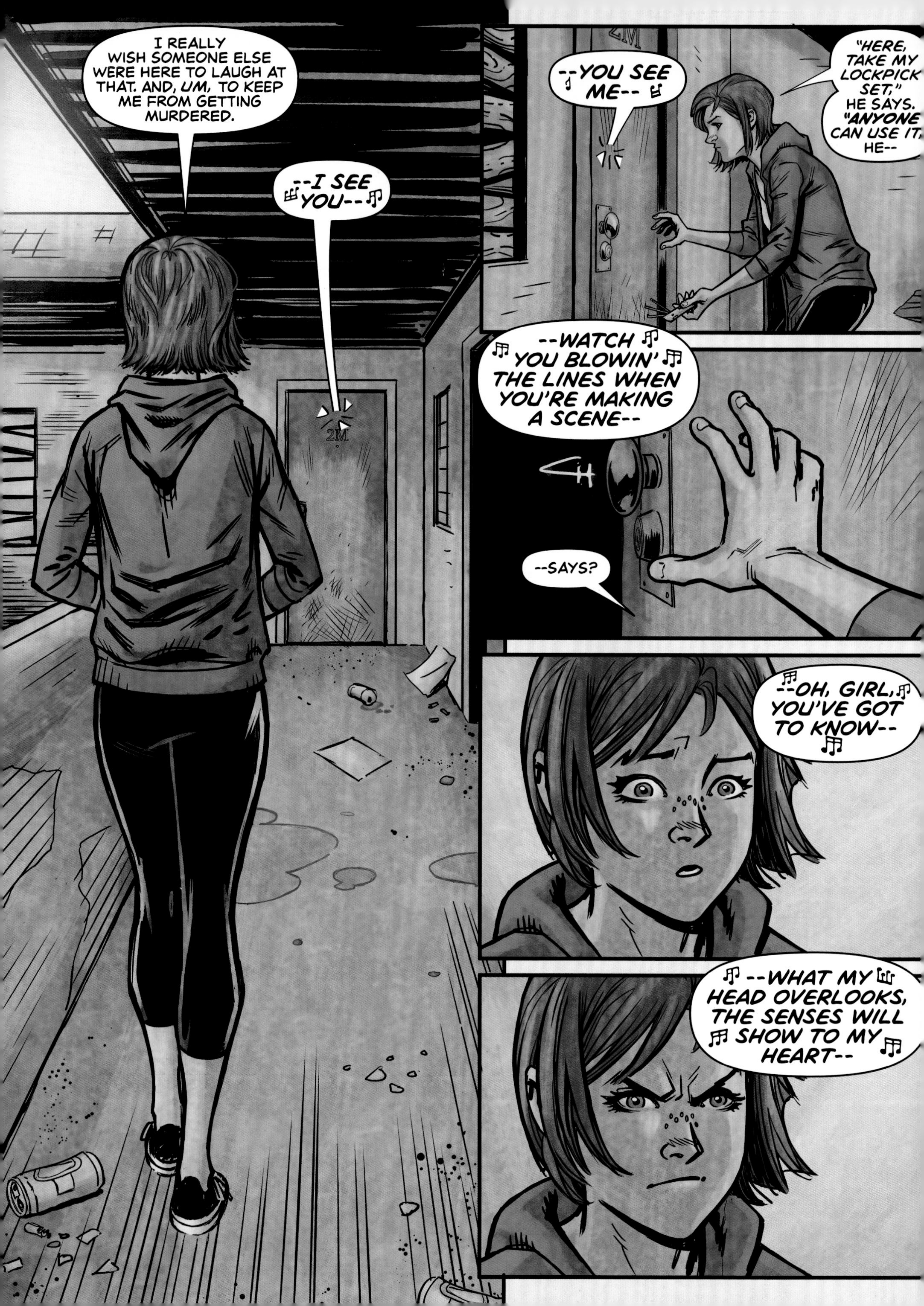

I REALLY WISH SOMEONE ELSE WERE HERE TO LAUGH AT THAT. AND, *UM,* TO KEEP ME FROM GETTING MURDERED.
--I SEE YOU--
--YOU SEE ME--
"HERE, TAKE MY LOCKPICK SET," HE SAYS. "ANYONE CAN USE IT," HE--
--WATCH YOU BLOWIN' THE LINES WHEN YOU'RE MAKING A SCENE--
--SAYS?
--OH, GIRL, YOU'VE GOT TO KNOW--
--WHAT MY HEAD OVERLOOKS, THE SENSES WILL SHOW TO MY HEART--

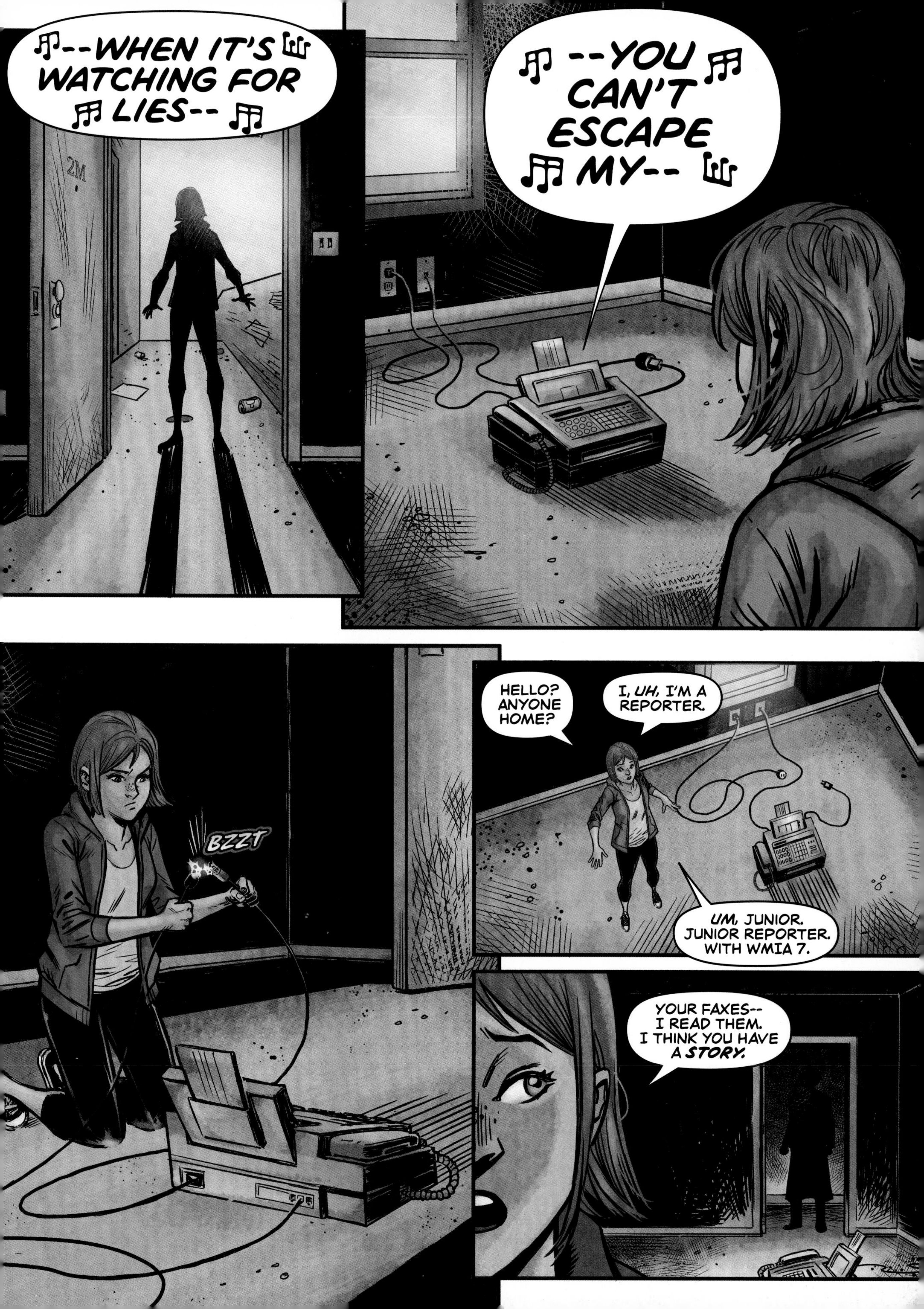

--WHEN IT'S WATCHING FOR LIES--
--YOU CAN'T ESCAPE MY--
BZZT
HELLO? ANYONE HOME?
I, *UH,* I'M A REPORTER.
UM, JUNIOR. JUNIOR REPORTER. WITH WMIA 7.
YOUR FAXES-- I READ THEM. I THINK YOU HAVE A *STORY.*

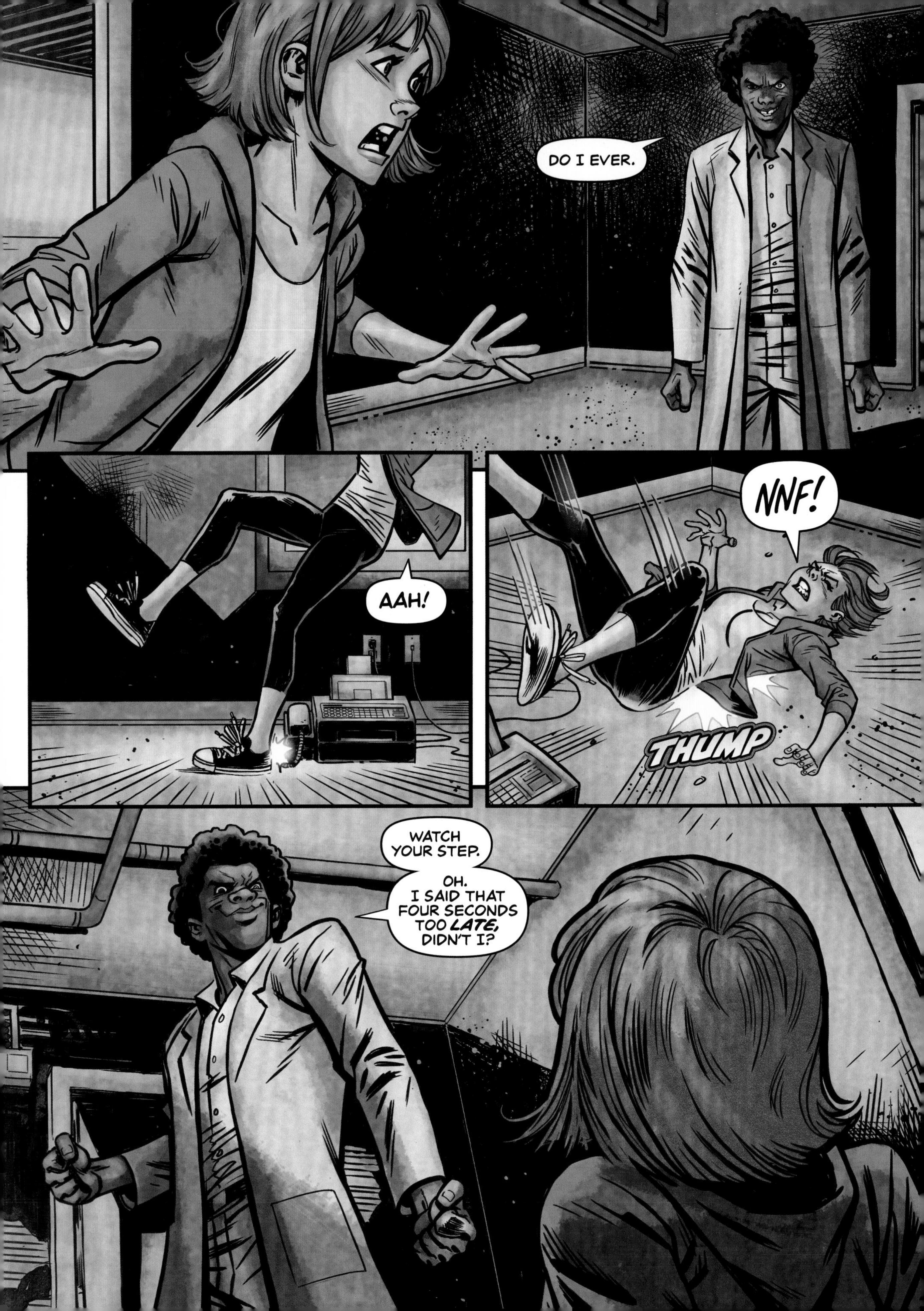
DO I EVER.
AAH!
NNF!
THUMP
WATCH YOUR STEP.
OH. I SAID THAT FOUR SECONDS TOO *LATE,* DIDN'T I?

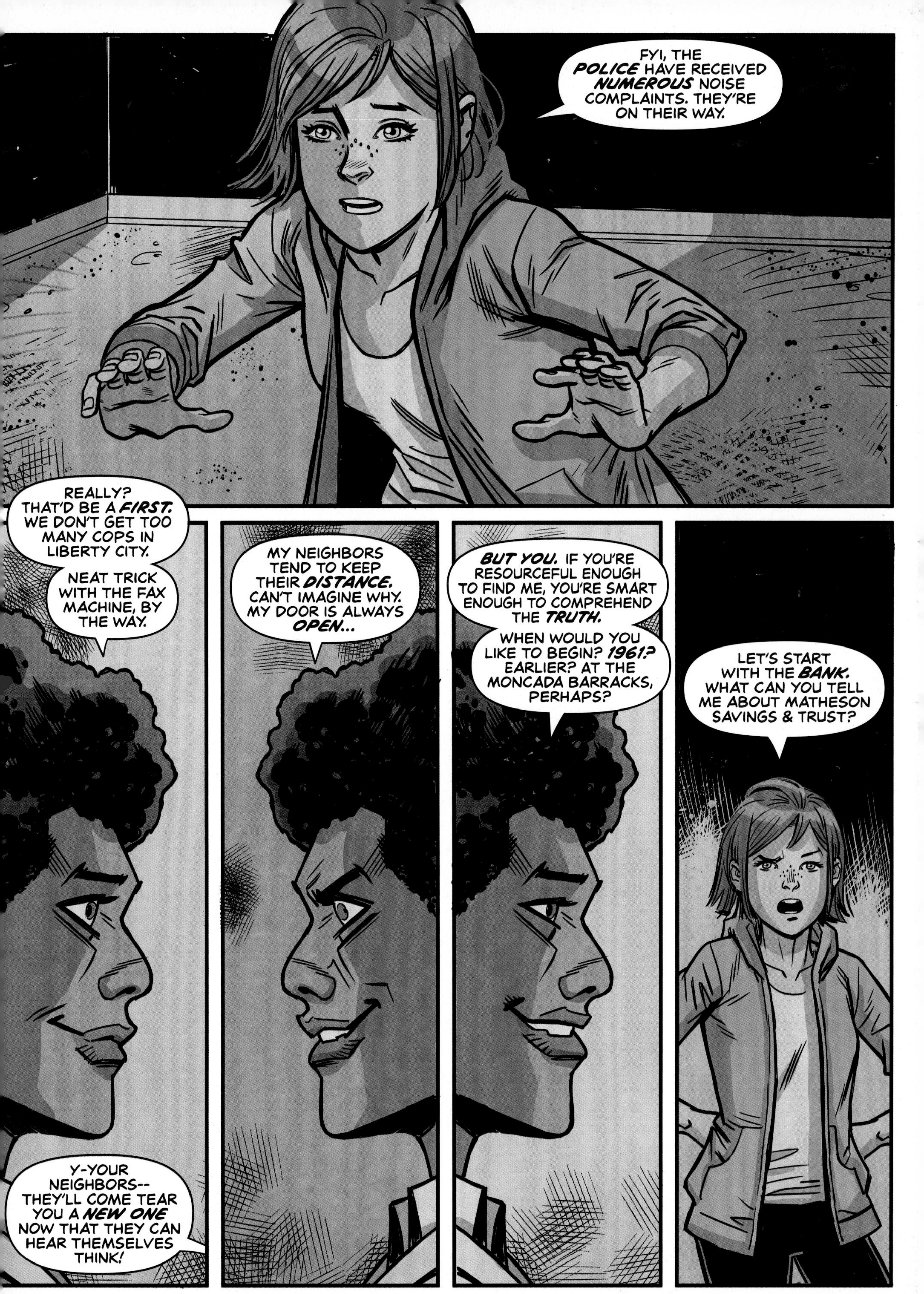
FYI, THE POLICE HAVE RECEIVED NUMEROUS NOISE COMPLAINTS. THEY'RE ON THEIR WAY.
REALLY? THAT'D BE A FIRST. WE DON'T GET TOO MANY COPS IN LIBERTY CITY.
NEAT TRICK WITH THE FAX MACHINE, BY THE WAY.
Y-YOUR NEIGHBORS-- THEY'LL COME TEAR YOU A NEW ONE NOW THAT THEY CAN HEAR THEMSELVES THINK!
MY NEIGHBORS TEND TO KEEP THEIR DISTANCE. CAN'T IMAGINE WHY. MY DOOR IS ALWAYS OPEN...
BUT YOU. IF YOU'RE RESOURCEFUL ENOUGH TO FIND ME, YOU'RE SMART ENOUGH TO COMPREHEND THE TRUTH.
WHEN WOULD YOU LIKE TO BEGIN? 1961? EARLIER? AT THE MONCADA BARRACKS, PERHAPS?
LET'S START WITH THE BANK. WHAT CAN YOU TELL ME ABOUT MATHESON SAVINGS & TRUST?

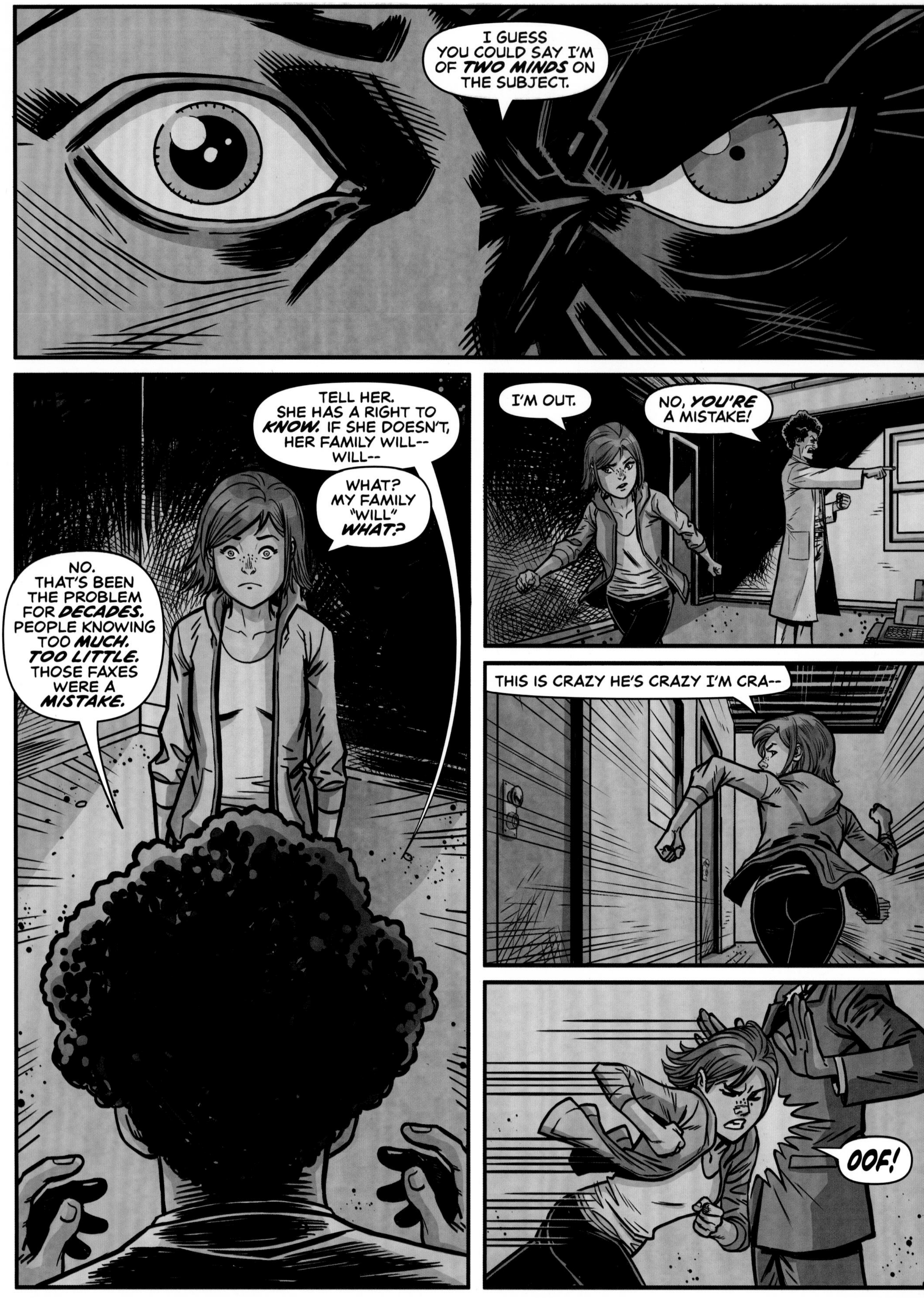
I GUESS YOU COULD SAY I'M OF TWO MINDS ON THE SUBJECT.
TELL HER. SHE HAS A RIGHT TO KNOW. IF SHE DOESN'T, HER FAMILY WILL-- WILL--
WHAT? MY FAMILY "WILL" WHAT?
NO. THAT'S BEEN THE PROBLEM FOR DECADES. PEOPLE KNOWING TOO MUCH. TOO LITTLE. THOSE FAXES WERE A MISTAKE.
I'M OUT.
NO, YOU'RE A MISTAKE!
THIS IS CRAZY HE'S CRAZY I'M CRA--
OOF!

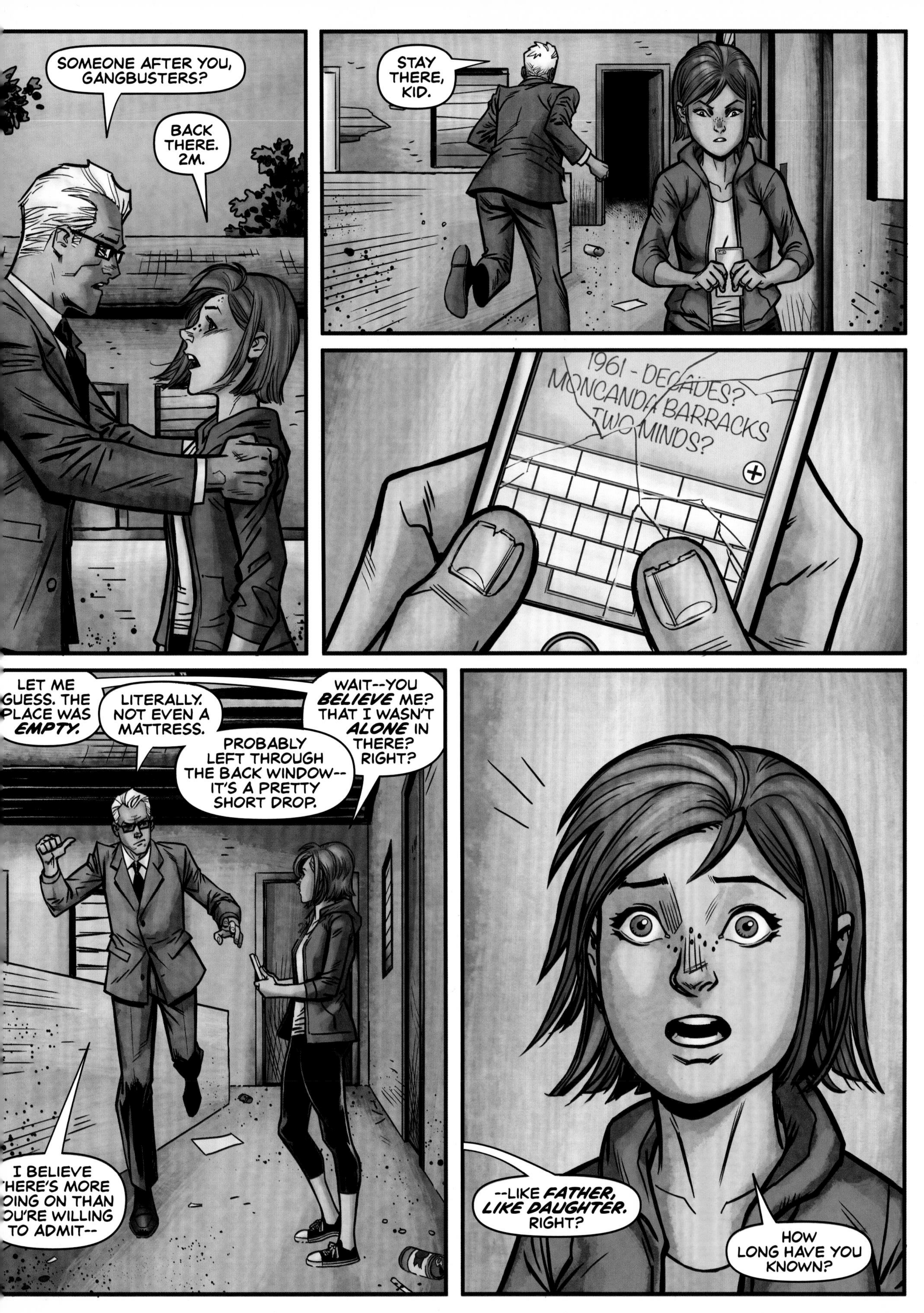

SOMEONE AFTER YOU, GANGBUSTERS?
BACK THERE. 2M.
STAY THERE, KID.
1961 - DECADES? MONCANDA BARRACKS TWO MINDS?
LET ME GUESS. THE PLACE WAS *EMPTY.*
LITERALLY. NOT EVEN A MATTRESS.
PROBABLY LEFT THROUGH THE BACK WINDOW-- IT'S A PRETTY SHORT DROP.
WAIT--YOU *BELIEVE* ME? THAT I WASN'T *ALONE* IN THERE? RIGHT?
I BELIEVE 'HERE'S MORE OING ON THAN OU'RE WILLING TO ADMIT--
--LIKE *FATHER, LIKE DAUGHTER.* RIGHT?
HOW LONG HAVE YOU KNOWN?

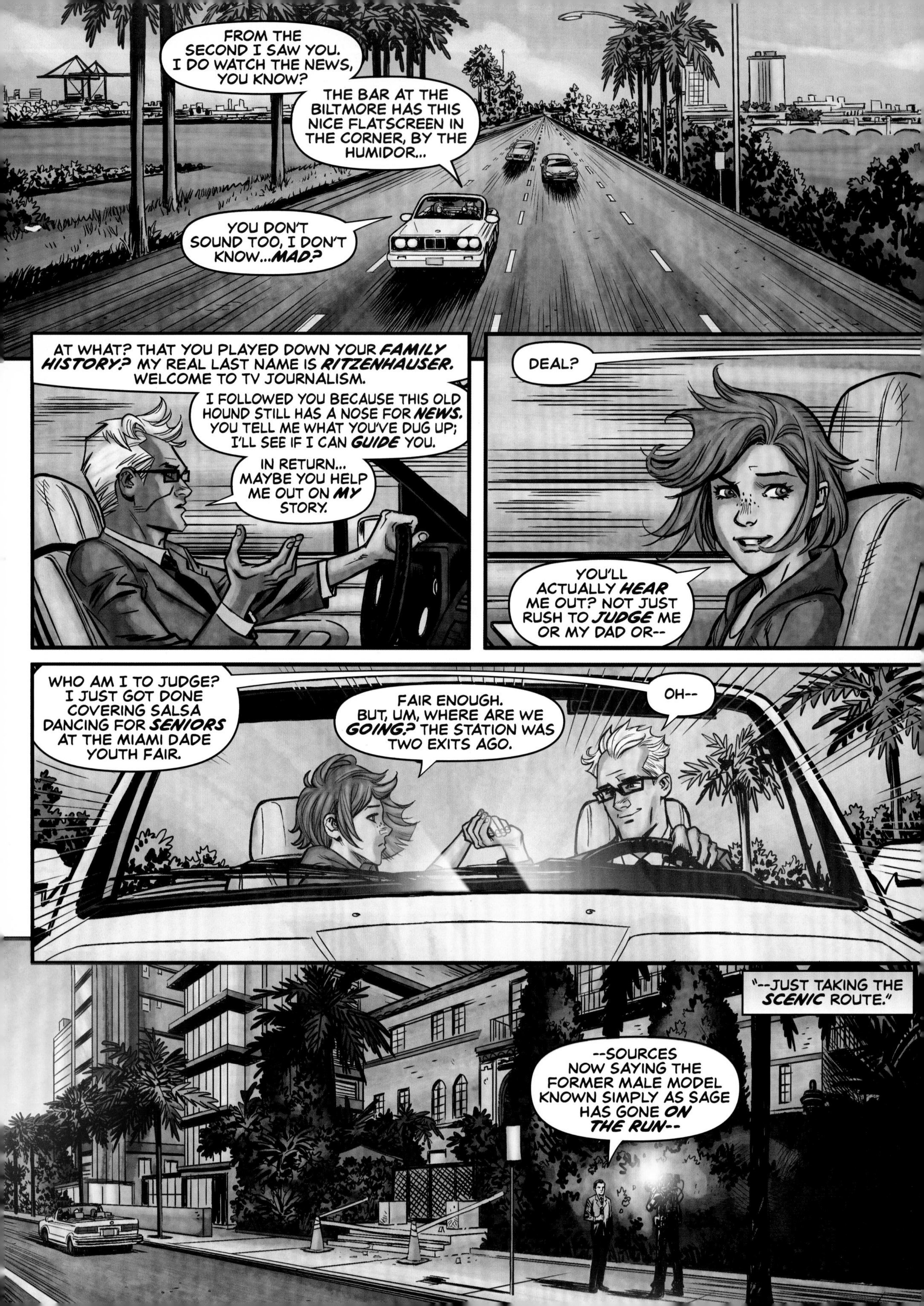

FROM THE SECOND I SAW YOU. I DO WATCH THE NEWS, YOU KNOW?
THE BAR AT THE BILTMORE HAS THIS NICE FLATSCREEN IN THE CORNER, BY THE HUMIDOR...
YOU DON'T SOUND TOO, I DON'T KNOW...*MAD?*
AT WHAT? THAT YOU PLAYED DOWN YOUR *FAMILY HISTORY?* MY REAL LAST NAME IS *RITZENHAUSER.* WELCOME TO TV JOURNALISM.
I FOLLOWED YOU BECAUSE THIS OLD HOUND STILL HAS A NOSE FOR *NEWS.* YOU TELL ME WHAT YOU'VE DUG UP; I'LL SEE IF I CAN *GUIDE* YOU.
IN RETURN... MAYBE YOU HELP ME OUT ON *MY* STORY.
DEAL?
YOU'LL ACTUALLY *HEAR* ME OUT? NOT JUST RUSH TO *JUDGE* ME OR MY DAD OR--
WHO AM I TO JUDGE? I JUST GOT DONE COVERING SALSA DANCING FOR *SENIORS* AT THE MIAMI DADE YOUTH FAIR.
FAIR ENOUGH. BUT, UM, WHERE ARE WE *GOING?* THE STATION WAS TWO EXITS AGO.
OH--
"--JUST TAKING THE *SCENIC* ROUTE."
--SOURCES NOW SAYING THE FORMER MALE MODEL KNOWN SIMPLY AS SAGE HAS GONE *ON THE RUN*--

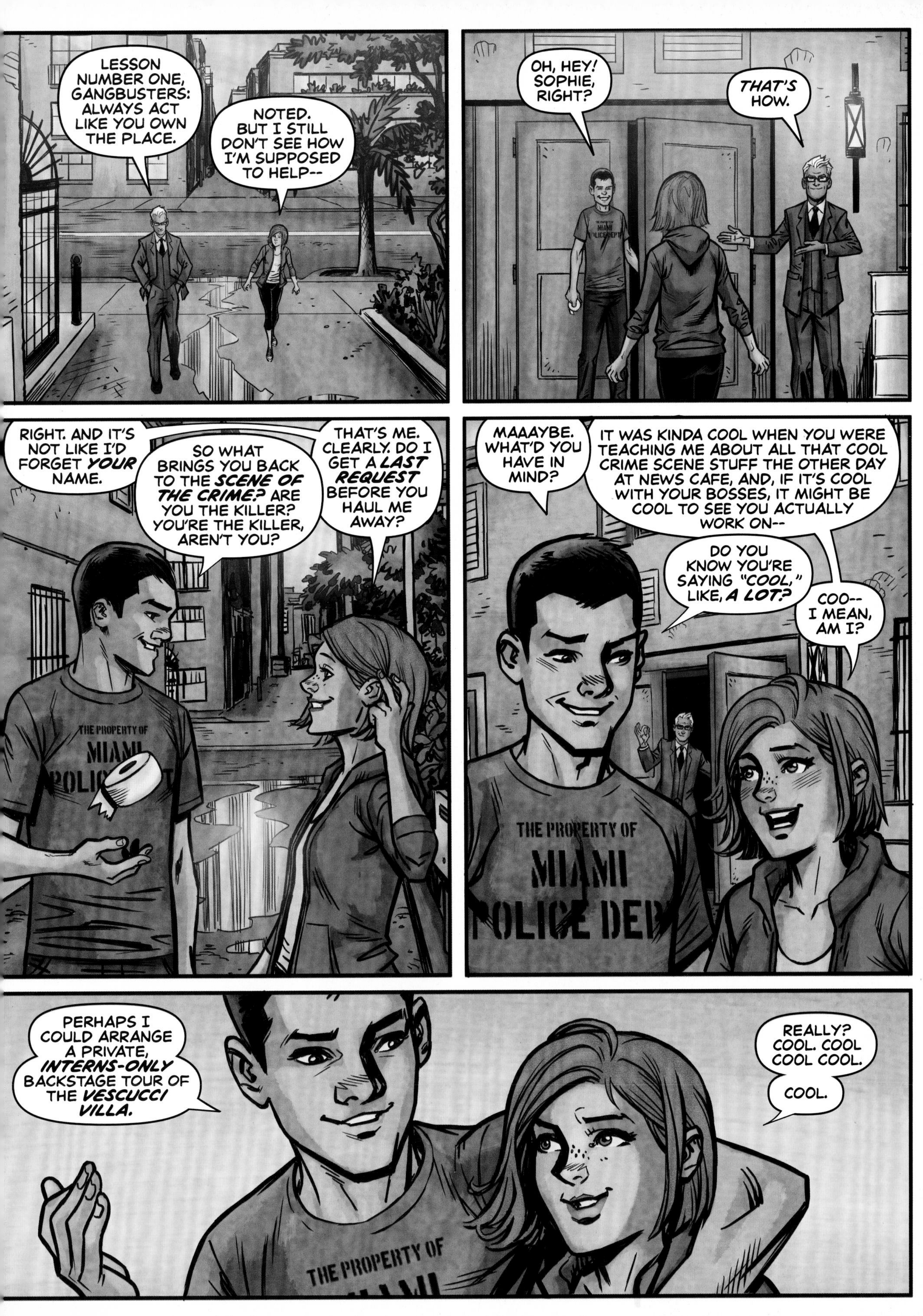
LESSON NUMBER ONE, GANGBUSTERS: ALWAYS ACT LIKE YOU OWN THE PLACE.
NOTED. BUT I STILL DON'T SEE HOW I'M SUPPOSED TO HELP--
OH, HEY! SOPHIE, RIGHT?
THAT'S HOW.
THE PROPERTY OF MIAMI POLICE DEPT
RIGHT. AND IT'S NOT LIKE I'D FORGET YOUR NAME.
SO WHAT BRINGS YOU BACK TO THE SCENE OF THE CRIME? ARE YOU THE KILLER? YOU'RE THE KILLER, AREN'T YOU?
THAT'S ME. CLEARLY. DO I GET A LAST REQUEST BEFORE YOU HAUL ME AWAY?
THE PROPERTY OF MIAMI
MAAAYBE. WHAT'D YOU HAVE IN MIND?
IT WAS KINDA COOL WHEN YOU WERE TEACHING ME ABOUT ALL THAT COOL CRIME SCENE STUFF THE OTHER DAY AT NEWS CAFE, AND, IF IT'S COOL WITH YOUR BOSSES, IT MIGHT BE COOL TO SEE YOU ACTUALLY WORK ON--
DO YOU KNOW YOU'RE SAYING "COOL," LIKE, A LOT?
COO-- I MEAN, AM I?
THE PROPERTY OF MIAMI POLICE DEP
PERHAPS I COULD ARRANGE A PRIVATE, INTERNS-ONLY BACKSTAGE TOUR OF THE VESCUCCI VILLA.
REALLY? COOL. COOL COOL COOL.
COOL.
THE PROPERTY OF

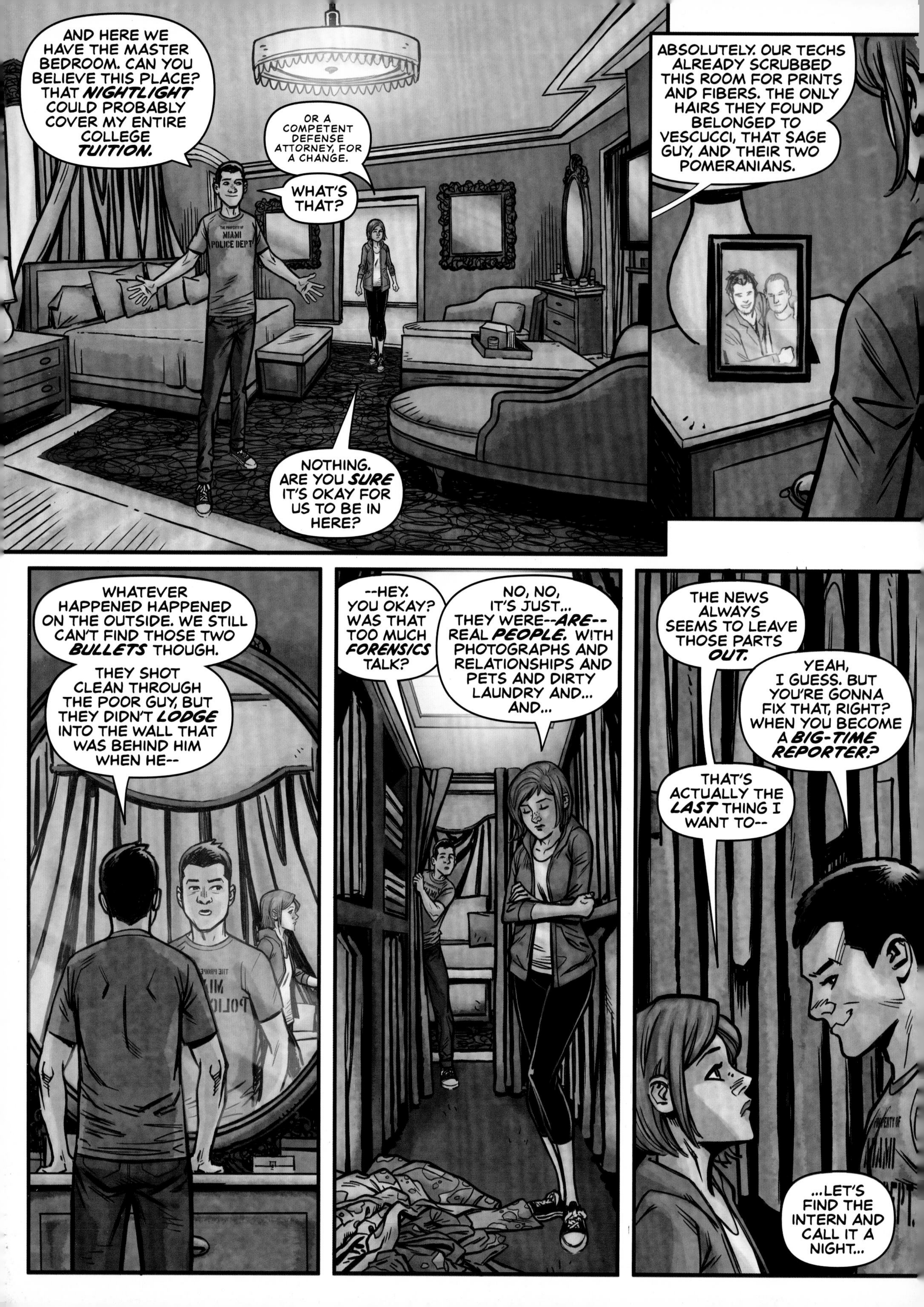
AND HERE WE HAVE THE MASTER BEDROOM. CAN YOU BELIEVE THIS PLACE? THAT NIGHTLIGHT COULD PROBABLY COVER MY ENTIRE COLLEGE TUITION.
OR A COMPETENT DEFENSE ATTORNEY, FOR A CHANGE.
WHAT'S THAT?
NOTHING. ARE YOU SURE IT'S OKAY FOR US TO BE IN HERE?
THE PROPERTY OF MIAMI POLICE DEPT
ABSOLUTELY. OUR TECHS ALREADY SCRUBBED THIS ROOM FOR PRINTS AND FIBERS. THE ONLY HAIRS THEY FOUND BELONGED TO VESCUCCI, THAT SAGE GUY, AND THEIR TWO POMERANIANS.
WHATEVER HAPPENED HAPPENED ON THE OUTSIDE. WE STILL CAN'T FIND THOSE TWO BULLETS THOUGH.
THEY SHOT CLEAN THROUGH THE POOR GUY, BUT THEY DIDN'T LODGE INTO THE WALL THAT WAS BEHIND HIM WHEN HE--
--HEY. YOU OKAY? WAS THAT TOO MUCH FORENSICS TALK?
NO, NO, IT'S JUST... THEY WERE--ARE--REAL PEOPLE. WITH PHOTOGRAPHS AND RELATIONSHIPS AND PETS AND DIRTY LAUNDRY AND... AND...
THE NEWS ALWAYS SEEMS TO LEAVE THOSE PARTS OUT.
YEAH, I GUESS. BUT YOU'RE GONNA FIX THAT, RIGHT? WHEN YOU BECOME A BIG-TIME REPORTER?
THAT'S ACTUALLY THE LAST THING I WANT TO--
...LET'S FIND THE INTERN AND CALL IT A NIGHT...

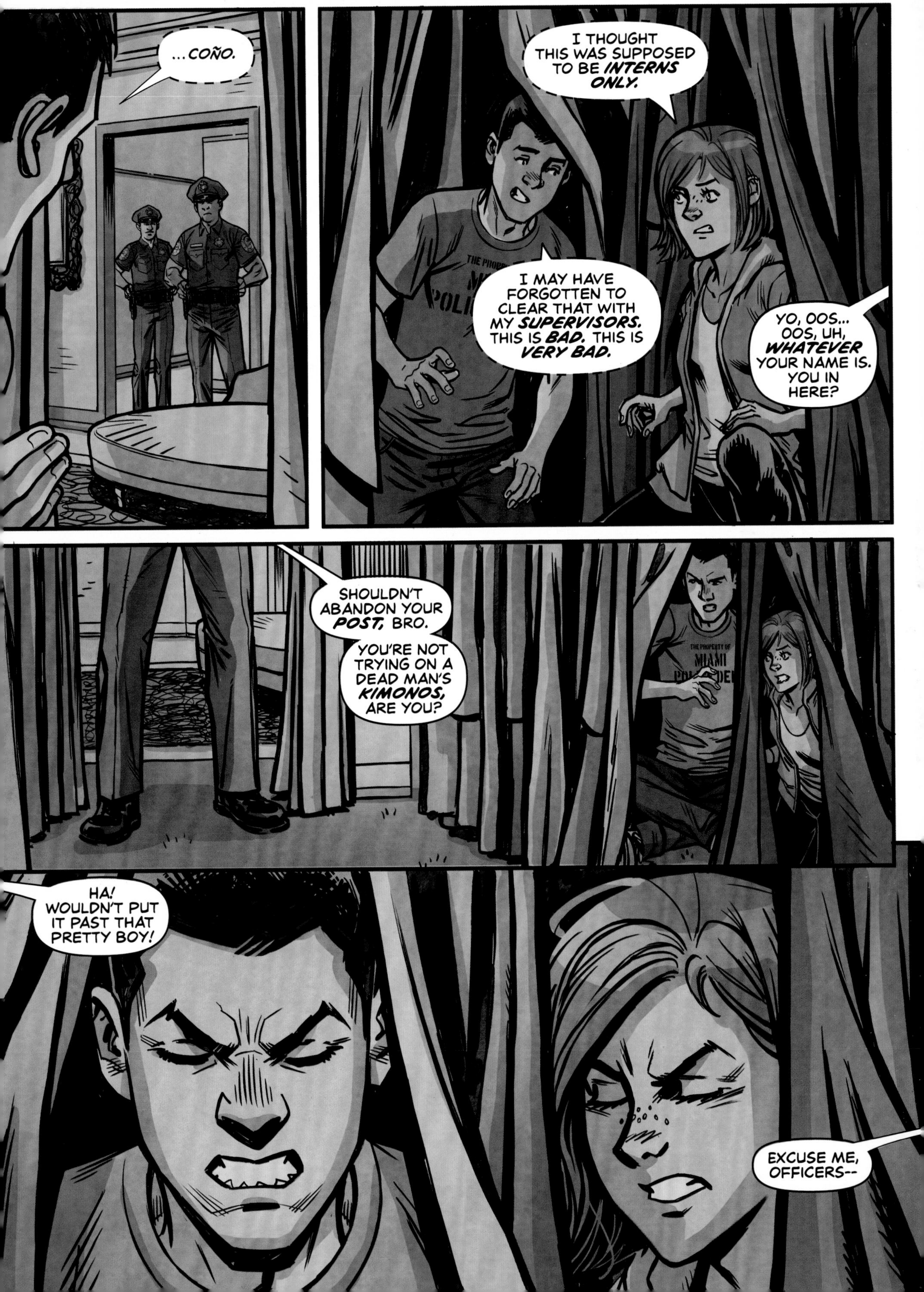
...COÑO.
I THOUGHT THIS WAS SUPPOSED TO BE INTERNS ONLY.
I MAY HAVE FORGOTTEN TO CLEAR THAT WITH MY SUPERVISORS. THIS IS BAD. THIS IS VERY BAD.
YO, OOS... OOS, UH, WHATEVER YOUR NAME IS. YOU IN HERE?
SHOULDN'T ABANDON YOUR POST, BRO.
YOU'RE NOT TRYING ON A DEAD MAN'S KIMONOS, ARE YOU?
HA! WOULDN'T PUT IT PAST THAT PRETTY BOY!
EXCUSE ME, OFFICERS--

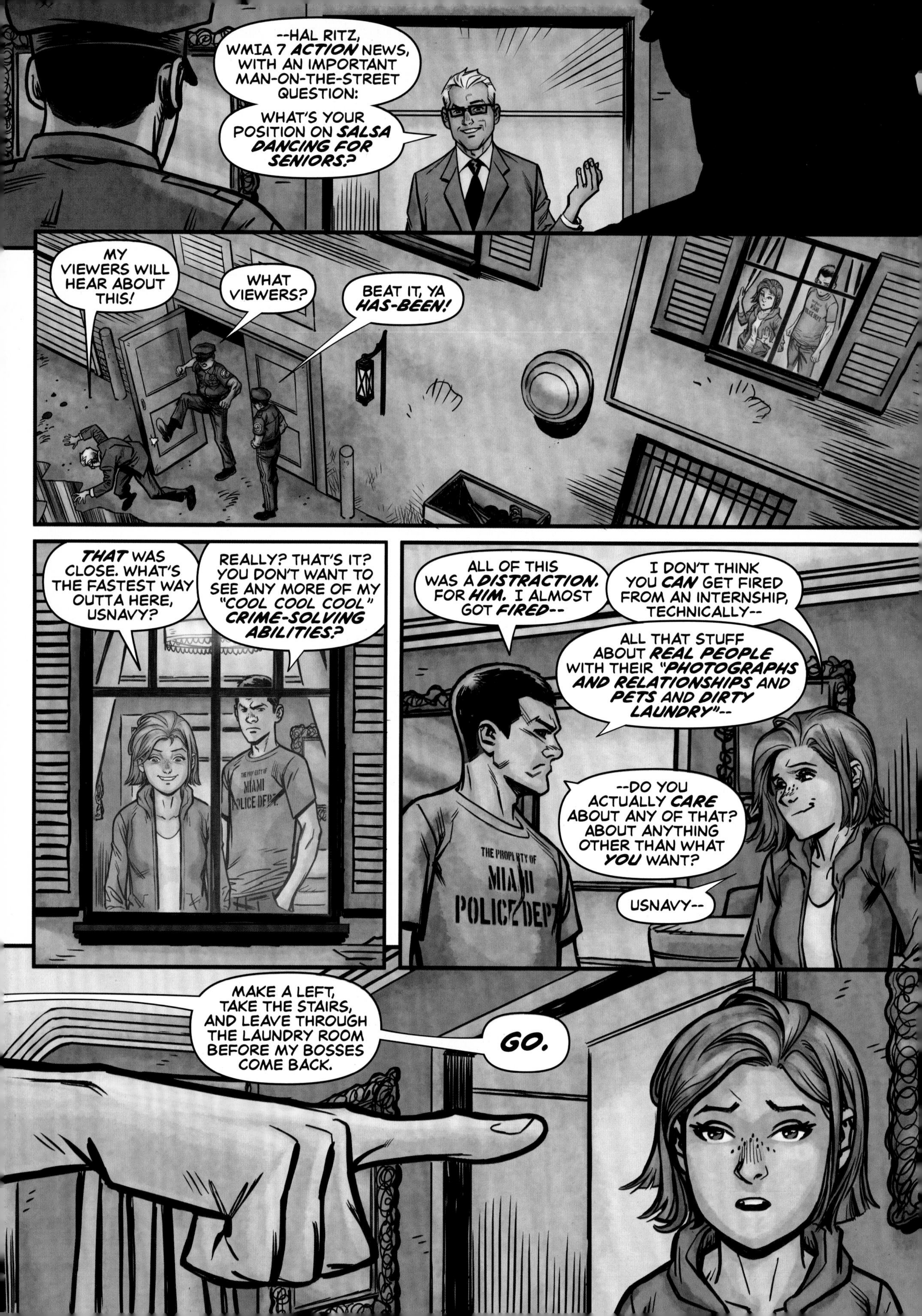

--HAL RITZ, WMIA 7 *ACTION* NEWS, WITH AN IMPORTANT MAN-ON-THE-STREET QUESTION:
WHAT'S YOUR POSITION ON *SALSA DANCING FOR SENIORS?*
MY VIEWERS WILL HEAR ABOUT THIS!
WHAT VIEWERS?
BEAT IT, YA *HAS-BEEN!*
THAT WAS CLOSE. WHAT'S THE FASTEST WAY OUTTA HERE, USNAVY?
REALLY? THAT'S IT? YOU DON'T WANT TO SEE ANY MORE OF MY *"COOL COOL COOL" CRIME-SOLVING ABILITIES?*
ALL OF THIS WAS A *DISTRACTION.* FOR *HIM.* I ALMOST GOT *FIRED*--
I DON'T THINK YOU *CAN* GET FIRED FROM AN INTERNSHIP, TECHNICALLY--
ALL THAT STUFF ABOUT *REAL PEOPLE* WITH THEIR *"PHOTOGRAPHS AND RELATIONSHIPS* AND *PETS* AND *DIRTY LAUNDRY"*--
--DO YOU ACTUALLY *CARE* ABOUT ANY OF THAT? ABOUT ANYTHING OTHER THAN WHAT *YOU* WANT?
USNAVY--
THE PROPERTY OF MIAMI POLICE DEPT
MAKE A LEFT, TAKE THE STAIRS, AND LEAVE THROUGH THE LAUNDRY ROOM BEFORE MY BOSSES COME BACK.
GO.

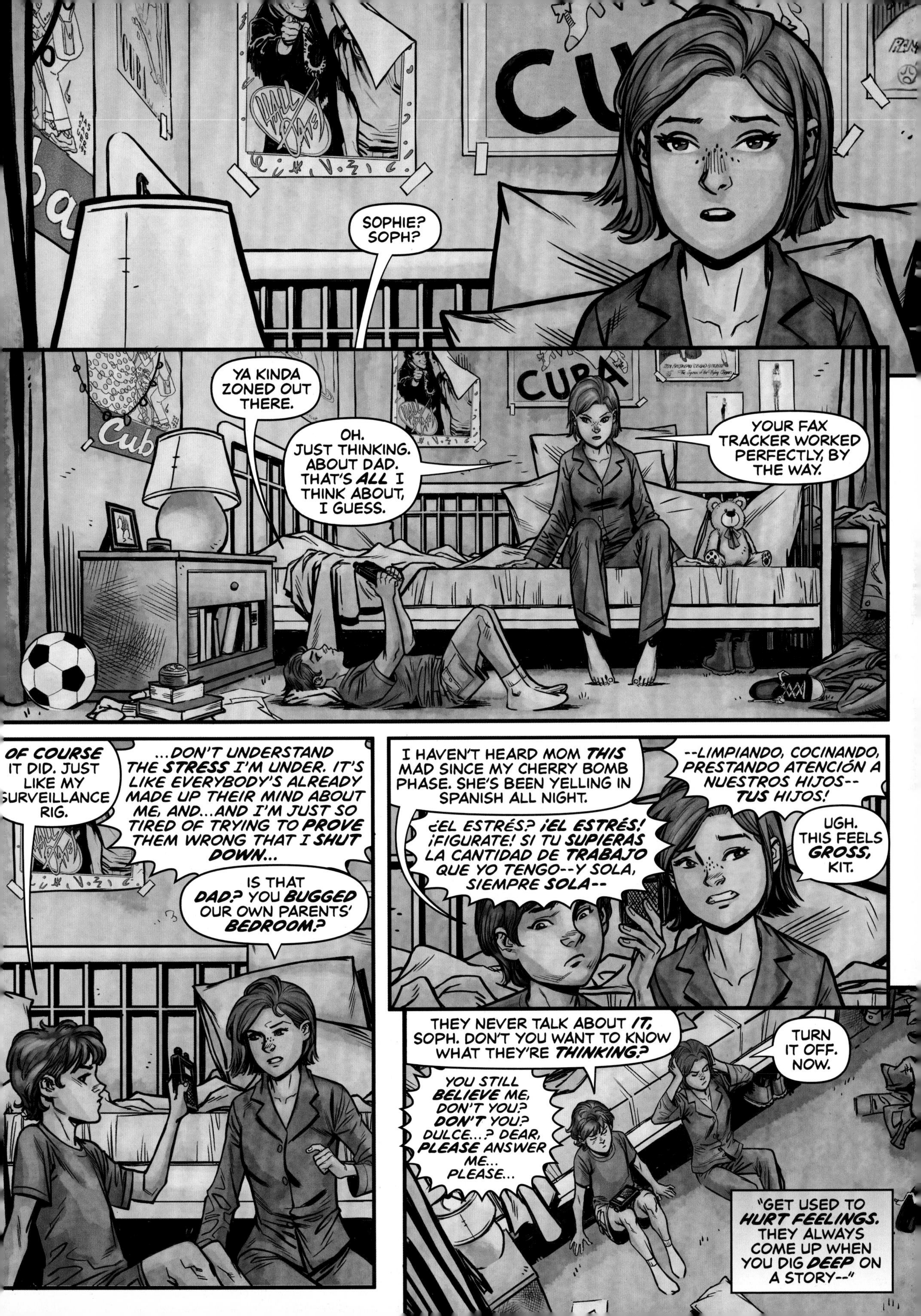
SOPHIE? SOPH?
YA KINDA ZONED OUT THERE.
OH. JUST THINKING. ABOUT DAD. THAT'S ALL I THINK ABOUT, I GUESS.
YOUR FAX TRACKER WORKED PERFECTLY, BY THE WAY.
CUBA
OF COURSE IT DID. JUST LIKE MY SURVEILLANCE RIG.
...DON'T UNDERSTAND THE STRESS I'M UNDER. IT'S LIKE EVERYBODY'S ALREADY MADE UP THEIR MIND ABOUT ME, AND...AND I'M JUST SO TIRED OF TRYING TO PROVE THEM WRONG THAT I SHUT DOWN...
IS THAT DAD? YOU BUGGED OUR OWN PARENTS' BEDROOM?
I HAVEN'T HEARD MOM THIS MAD SINCE MY CHERRY BOMB PHASE. SHE'S BEEN YELLING IN SPANISH ALL NIGHT.
--LIMPIANDO, COCINANDO, PRESTANDO ATENCIÓN A NUESTROS HIJOS-- TUS HIJOS!
¿EL ESTRÉS? ¡EL ESTRÉS! ¡FIGURATE! SI TU SUPIERAS LA CANTIDAD DE TRABAJO QUE YO TENGO--Y SOLA, SIEMPRE SOLA--
UGH. THIS FEELS GROSS, KIT.
THEY NEVER TALK ABOUT IT, SOPH. DON'T YOU WANT TO KNOW WHAT THEY'RE THINKING?
TURN IT OFF. NOW.
YOU STILL BELIEVE ME, DON'T YOU? DON'T YOU? DULCE...? DEAR, PLEASE ANSWER ME... PLEASE...
"GET USED TO HURT FEELINGS. THEY ALWAYS COME UP WHEN YOU DIG DEEP ON A STORY--"

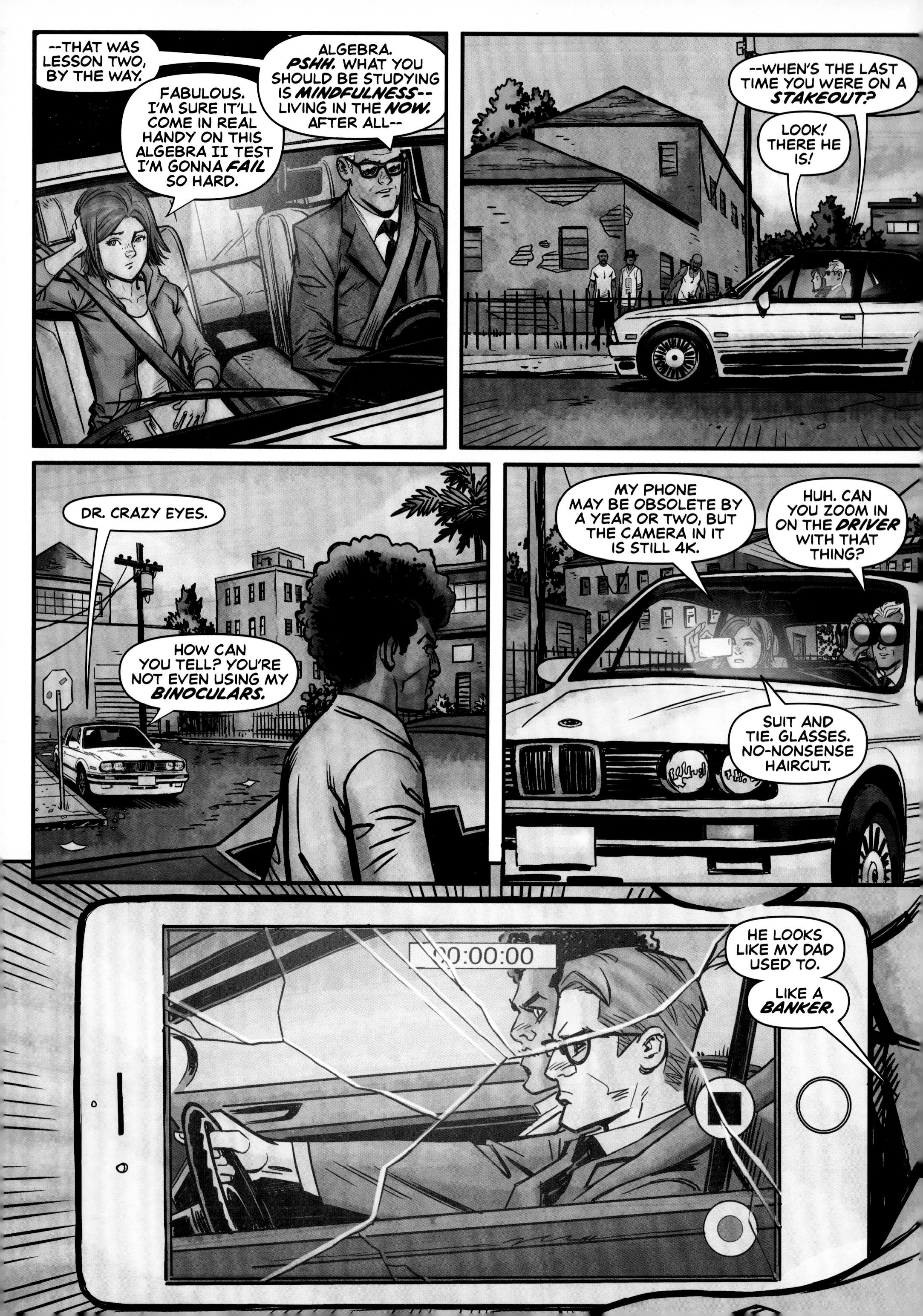
--THAT WAS LESSON TWO, BY THE WAY.
ALGEBRA. PSHH. WHAT YOU SHOULD BE STUDYING IS MINDFULNESS-- LIVING IN THE NOW. AFTER ALL--
FABULOUS. I'M SURE IT'LL COME IN REAL HANDY ON THIS ALGEBRA II TEST I'M GONNA FAIL SO HARD.
--WHEN'S THE LAST TIME YOU WERE ON A STAKEOUT?
LOOK! THERE HE IS!
DR. CRAZY EYES.
HOW CAN YOU TELL? YOU'RE NOT EVEN USING MY BINOCULARS.
MY PHONE MAY BE OBSOLETE BY A YEAR OR TWO, BUT THE CAMERA IN IT IS STILL 4K.
HUH. CAN YOU ZOOM IN ON THE DRIVER WITH THAT THING?
SUIT AND TIE. GLASSES. NO-NONSENSE HAIRCUT.
00:00:00
HE LOOKS LIKE MY DAD USED TO.
LIKE A BANKER.

YOU FEEL THAT?

THE HUMIDITY?

NO--THAT *ELECTRICITY.* THAT SENSATION THAT YOU'RE *ONTO* SOMETHING. SOMETHING *BIG.*

THIS IS THE THRILL THAT SURGES THROUGH A REPORTER WHEN HE-- OR *SHE*--GETS THE *SCOOP.*

THE LAST TIME I FELT THIS ALIVE, I WAS BREAKING THE TONYA HARDING ATTACK...

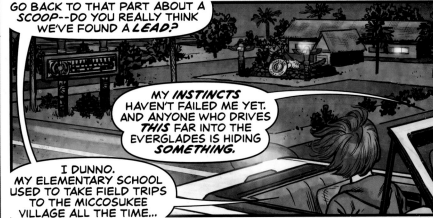

GO BACK TO THAT PART ABOUT A *SCOOP*--DO YOU REALLY THINK WE'VE FOUND A *LEAD?*

MY *INSTINCTS* HAVEN'T FAILED ME YET. AND ANYONE WHO DRIVES *THIS* FAR INTO THE EVERGLADES IS HIDING *SOMETHING.*

I DUNNO. MY ELEMENTARY SCHOOL USED TO TAKE FIELD TRIPS TO THE MICCOSUKEE VILLAGE ALL THE TIME...

DID YOUR SCHOOL ALSO TAKE FIELD TRIPS ONTO UNMARKED, BLINK-AND-YOU'LL-MISS-'EM *SERVICE ROADS?*

UM. NO.

FEELING THE ELECTRICITY YET, GANGBUSTERS?

MORE LIKE THAT HOLLOWNESS IN MY STOMACH BEFORE I GET *BAD NEWS.* WHERE'D THEY GO?

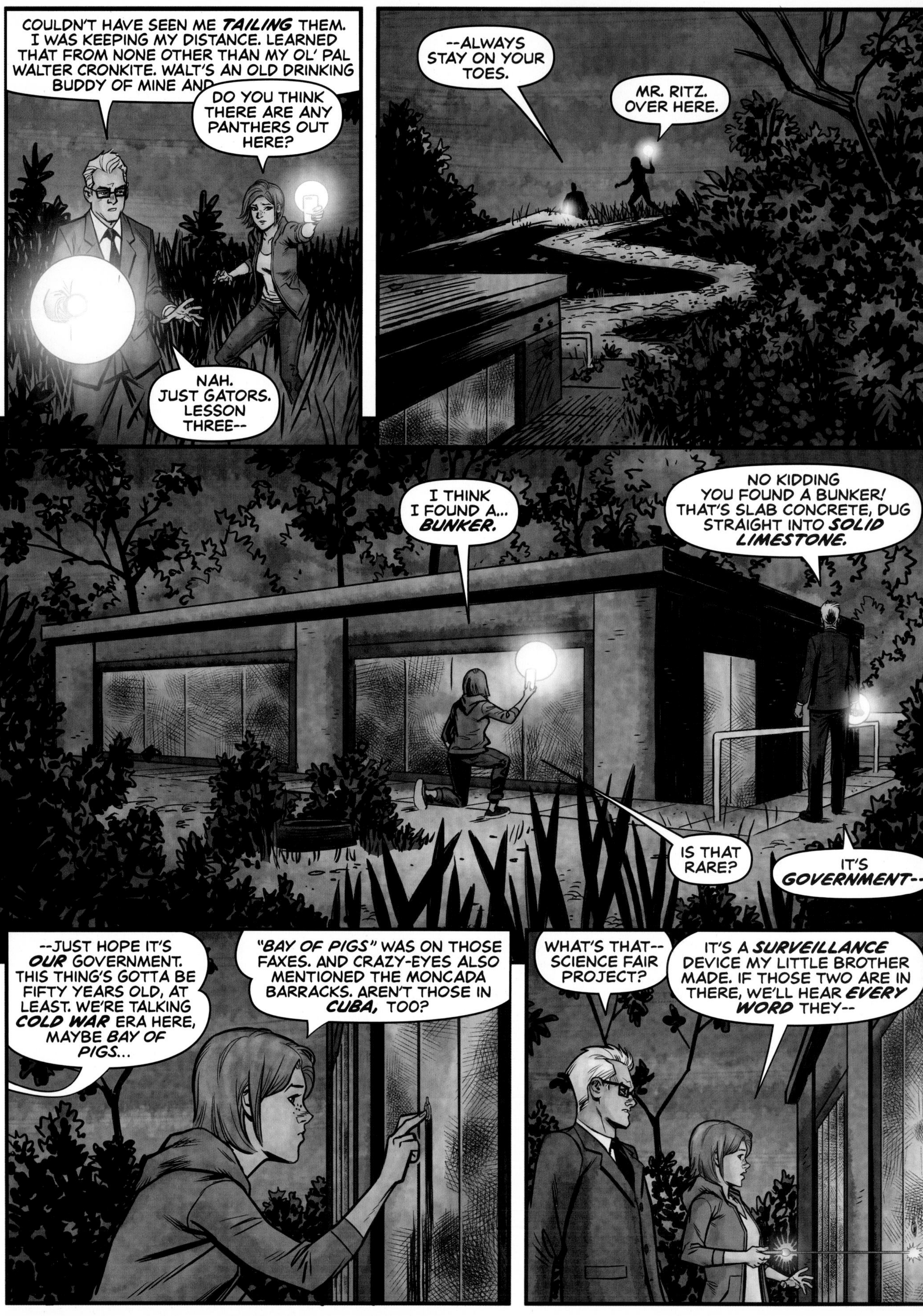
COULDN'T HAVE SEEN ME TAILING THEM. I WAS KEEPING MY DISTANCE. LEARNED THAT FROM NONE OTHER THAN MY OL' PAL WALTER CRONKITE. WALT'S AN OLD DRINKING BUDDY OF MINE AND
DO YOU THINK THERE ARE ANY PANTHERS OUT HERE?
NAH. JUST GATORS. LESSON THREE--
--ALWAYS STAY ON YOUR TOES.
MR. RITZ. OVER HERE.
I THINK I FOUND A... BUNKER.
NO KIDDING YOU FOUND A BUNKER! THAT'S SLAB CONCRETE, DUG STRAIGHT INTO SOLID LIMESTONE.
IS THAT RARE?
IT'S GOVERNMENT--
--JUST HOPE IT'S OUR GOVERNMENT. THIS THING'S GOTTA BE FIFTY YEARS OLD, AT LEAST. WE'RE TALKING COLD WAR ERA HERE, MAYBE BAY OF PIGS...
"BAY OF PIGS" WAS ON THOSE FAXES. AND CRAZY-EYES ALSO MENTIONED THE MONCADA BARRACKS. AREN'T THOSE IN CUBA, TOO?
WHAT'S THAT-- SCIENCE FAIR PROJECT?
IT'S A SURVEILLANCE DEVICE MY LITTLE BROTHER MADE. IF THOSE TWO ARE IN THERE, WE'LL HEAR EVERY WORD THEY--

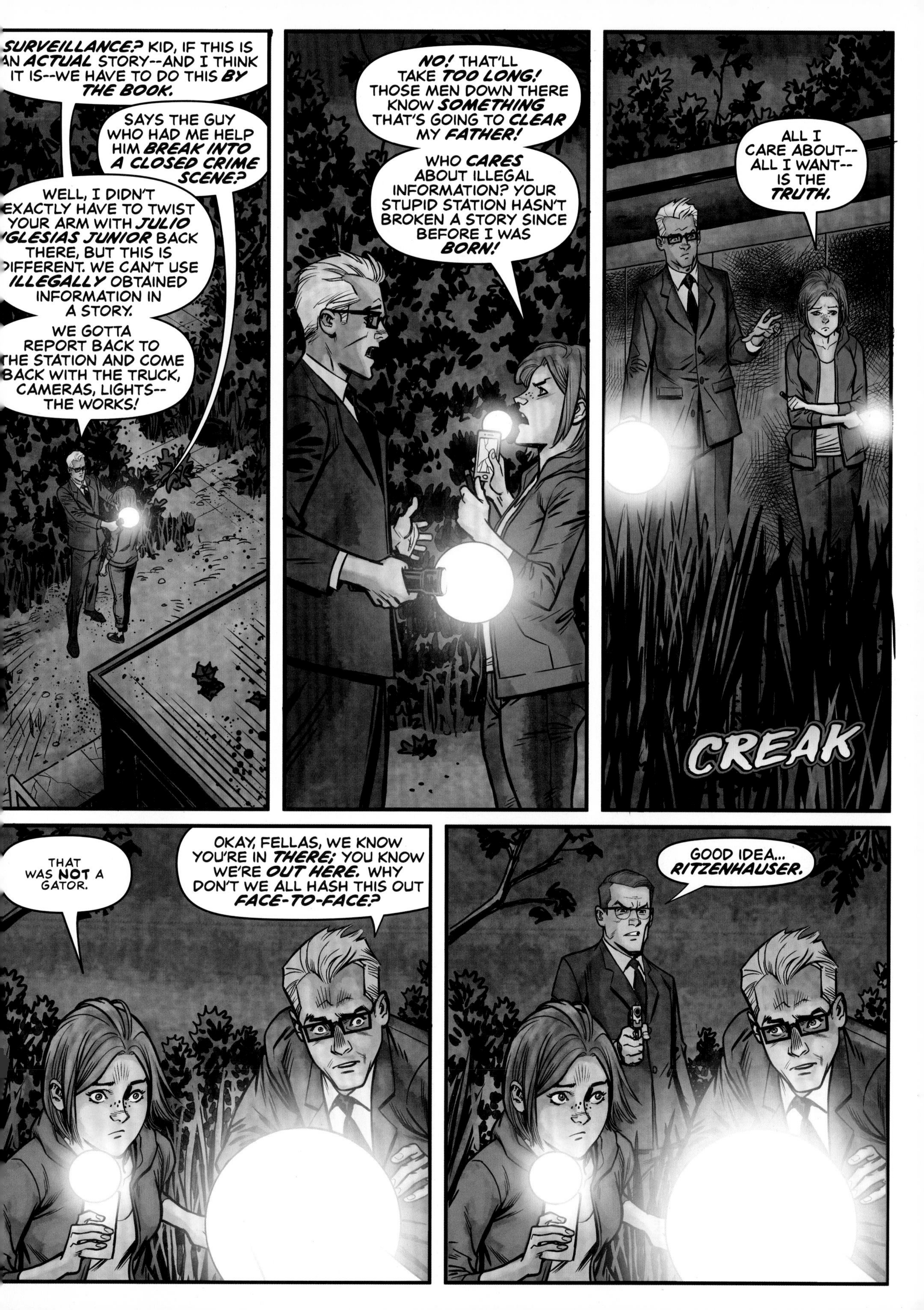
SURVEILLANCE? KID, IF THIS IS AN ACTUAL STORY--AND I THINK IT IS--WE HAVE TO DO THIS BY THE BOOK.
SAYS THE GUY WHO HAD ME HELP HIM BREAK INTO A CLOSED CRIME SCENE?
WELL, I DIDN'T EXACTLY HAVE TO TWIST YOUR ARM WITH JULIO IGLESIAS JUNIOR BACK THERE, BUT THIS IS DIFFERENT. WE CAN'T USE ILLEGALLY OBTAINED INFORMATION IN A STORY.
WE GOTTA REPORT BACK TO THE STATION AND COME BACK WITH THE TRUCK, CAMERAS, LIGHTS-- THE WORKS!
NO! THAT'LL TAKE TOO LONG! THOSE MEN DOWN THERE KNOW SOMETHING THAT'S GOING TO CLEAR MY FATHER!
WHO CARES ABOUT ILLEGAL INFORMATION? YOUR STUPID STATION HASN'T BROKEN A STORY SINCE BEFORE I WAS BORN!
ALL I CARE ABOUT-- ALL I WANT-- IS THE TRUTH.
CREAK
THAT WAS NOT A GATOR.
OKAY, FELLAS, WE KNOW YOU'RE IN THERE; YOU KNOW WE'RE OUT HERE. WHY DON'T WE ALL HASH THIS OUT FACE-TO-FACE?
GOOD IDEA... RITZENHAUSER.

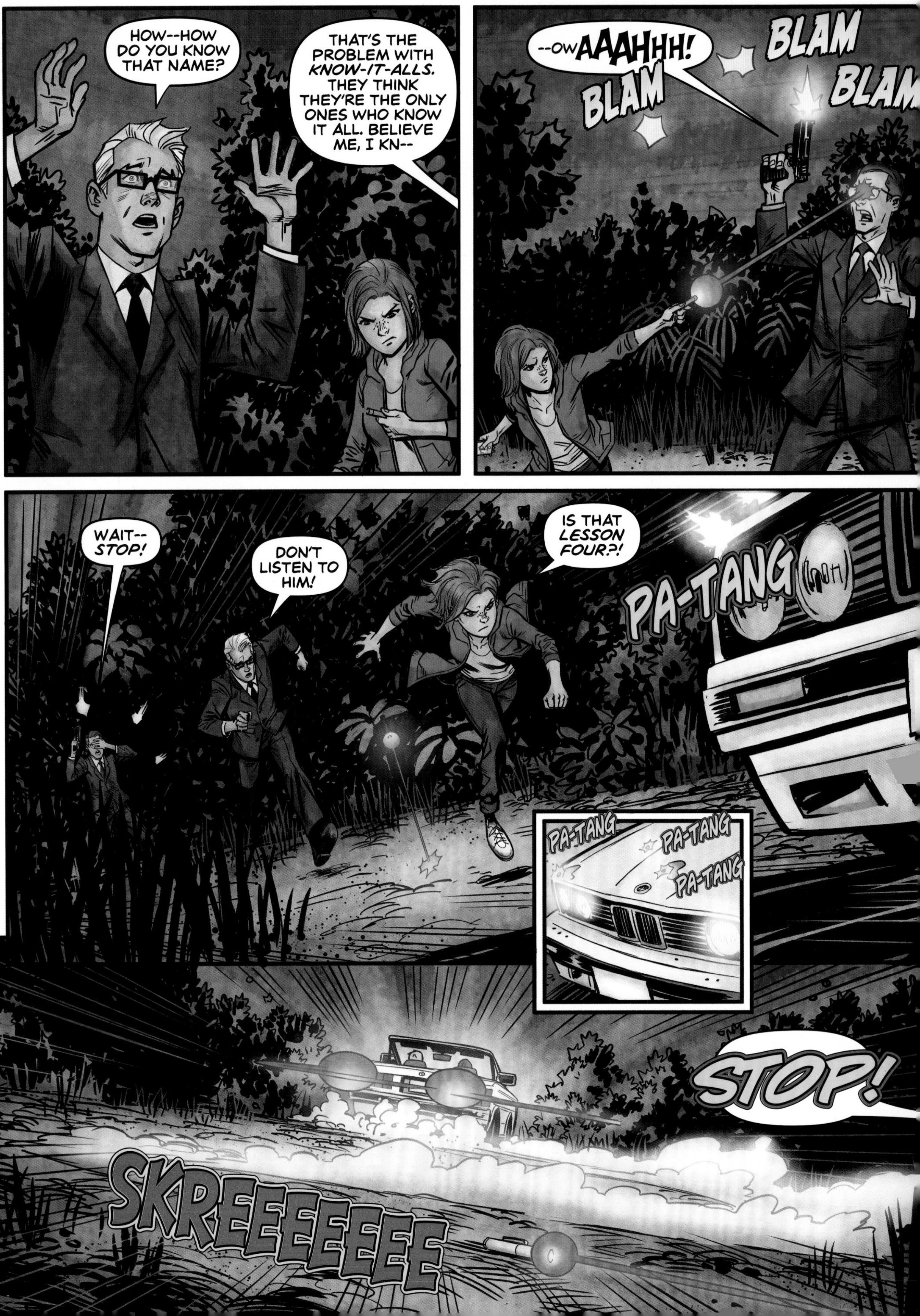
HOW--HOW DO YOU KNOW THAT NAME?
THAT'S THE PROBLEM WITH *KNOW-IT-ALLS.* THEY THINK THEY'RE THE ONLY ONES WHO KNOW IT ALL. BELIEVE ME, I KN--
--OWAAAHHH!
BLAM
BLAM
BLAM
WAIT-- *STOP!*
DON'T LISTEN TO HIM!
IS THAT *LESSON FOUR?!*
PA-TANG
PA-TANG
PA-TANG
PA-TANG
STOP!
SKREEEEEEEE

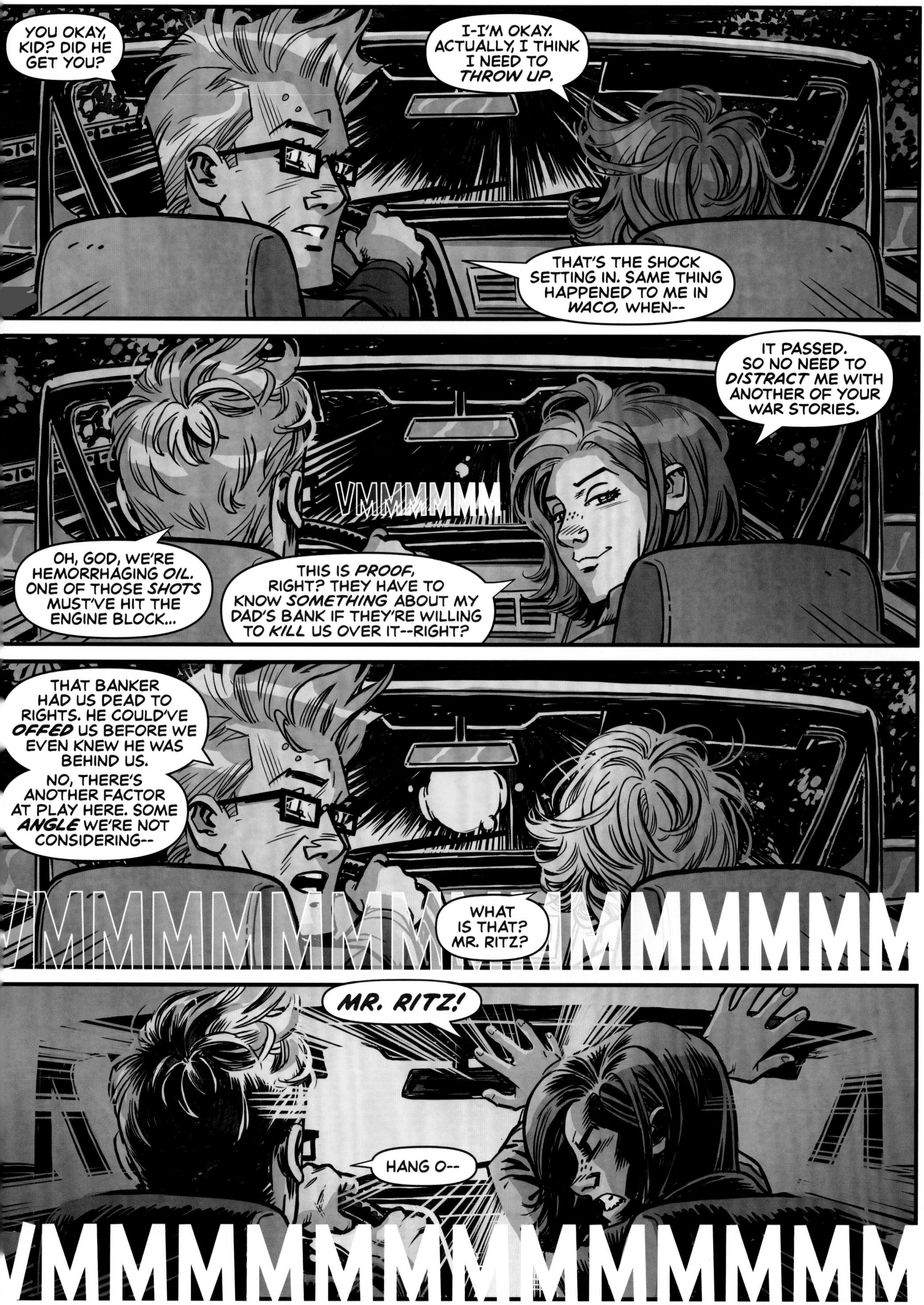

YOU OKAY, KID? DID HE GET YOU?
I-I'M OKAY. ACTUALLY, I THINK I NEED TO THROW UP.
THAT'S THE SHOCK SETTING IN. SAME THING HAPPENED TO ME IN WACO, WHEN--
IT PASSED. SO NO NEED TO DISTRACT ME WITH ANOTHER OF YOUR WAR STORIES.
VMMMMMM
OH, GOD, WE'RE HEMORRHAGING OIL. ONE OF THOSE SHOTS MUST'VE HIT THE ENGINE BLOCK...
THIS IS PROOF, RIGHT? THEY HAVE TO KNOW SOMETHING ABOUT MY DAD'S BANK IF THEY'RE WILLING TO KILL US OVER IT--RIGHT?
THAT BANKER HAD US DEAD TO RIGHTS. HE COULD'VE OFFED US BEFORE WE EVEN KNEW HE WAS BEHIND US.
NO, THERE'S ANOTHER FACTOR AT PLAY HERE. SOME ANGLE WE'RE NOT CONSIDERING--
WHAT IS THAT? MR. RITZ?
MR. RITZ!
HANG O--
VMMMMMMMMMMMMM

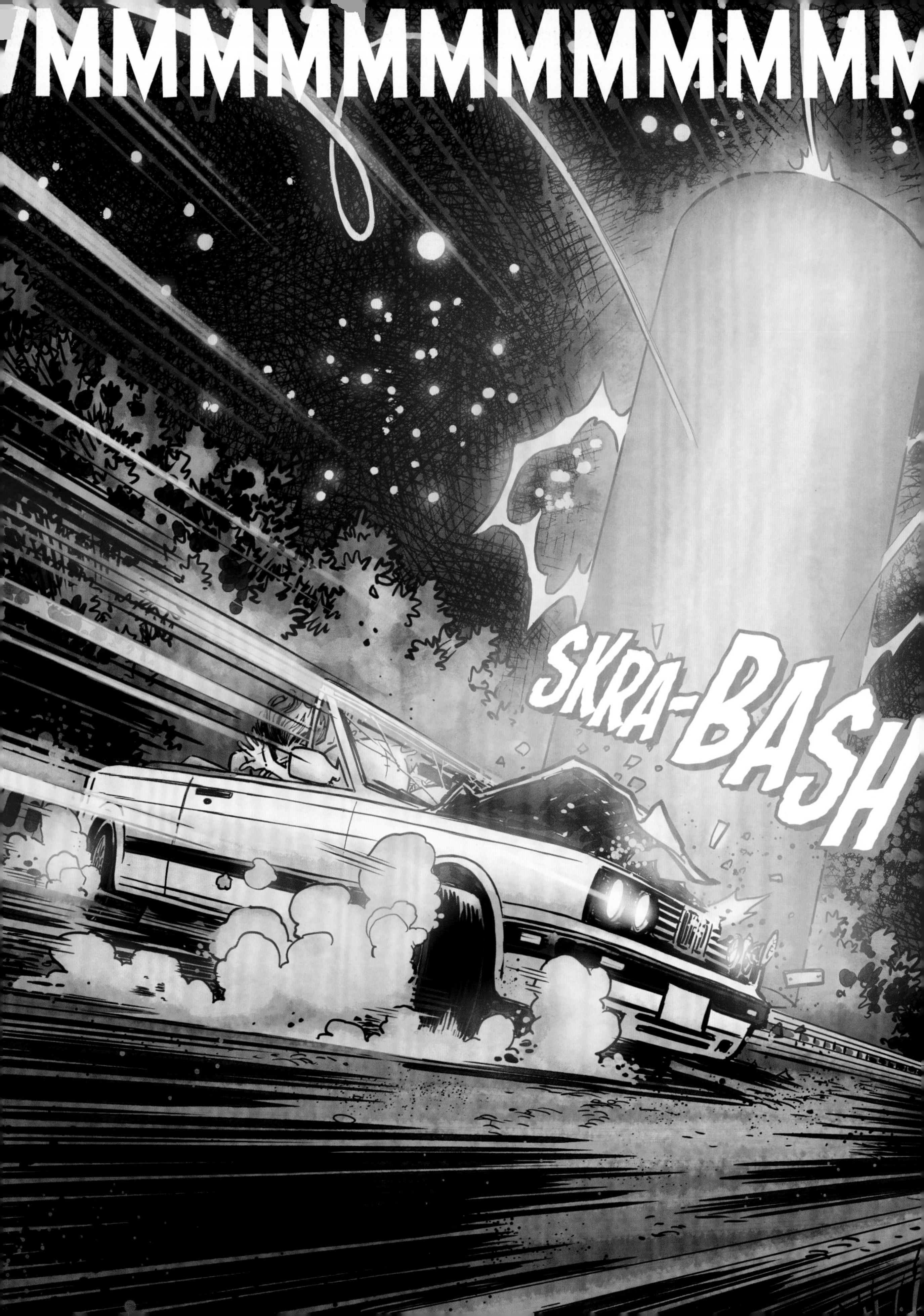
MMMMMMMMMMMMMM
SKRA-BASH

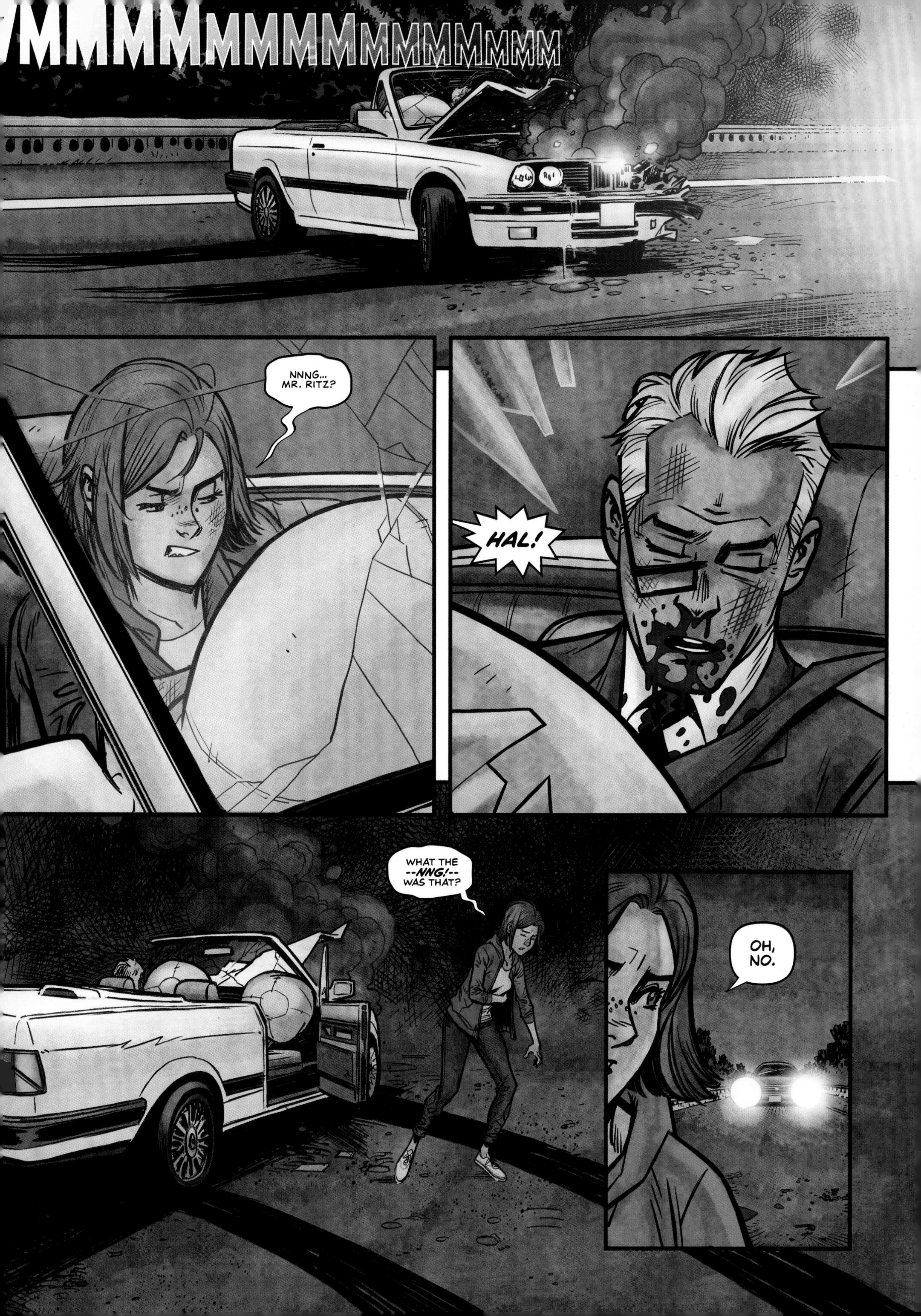
VMMMMMMMMMMMMMMMMM
NNNG... MR. RITZ?
HAL!
WHAT THE --NNG!-- WAS THAT?
OH, NO.

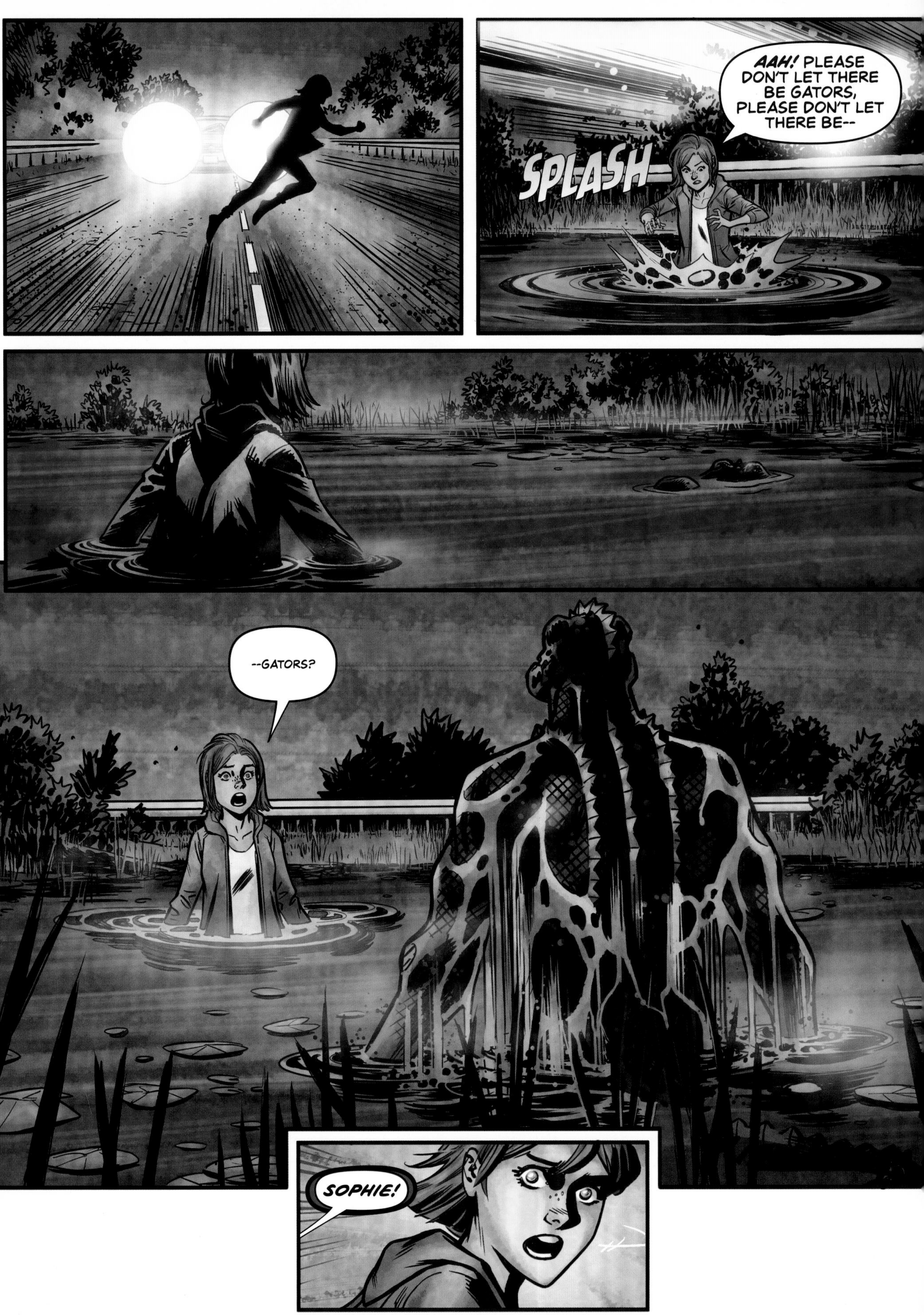
AAH! PLEASE DON'T LET THERE BE GATORS, PLEASE DON'T LET THERE BE--
SPLASH
--GATORS?
SOPHIE!

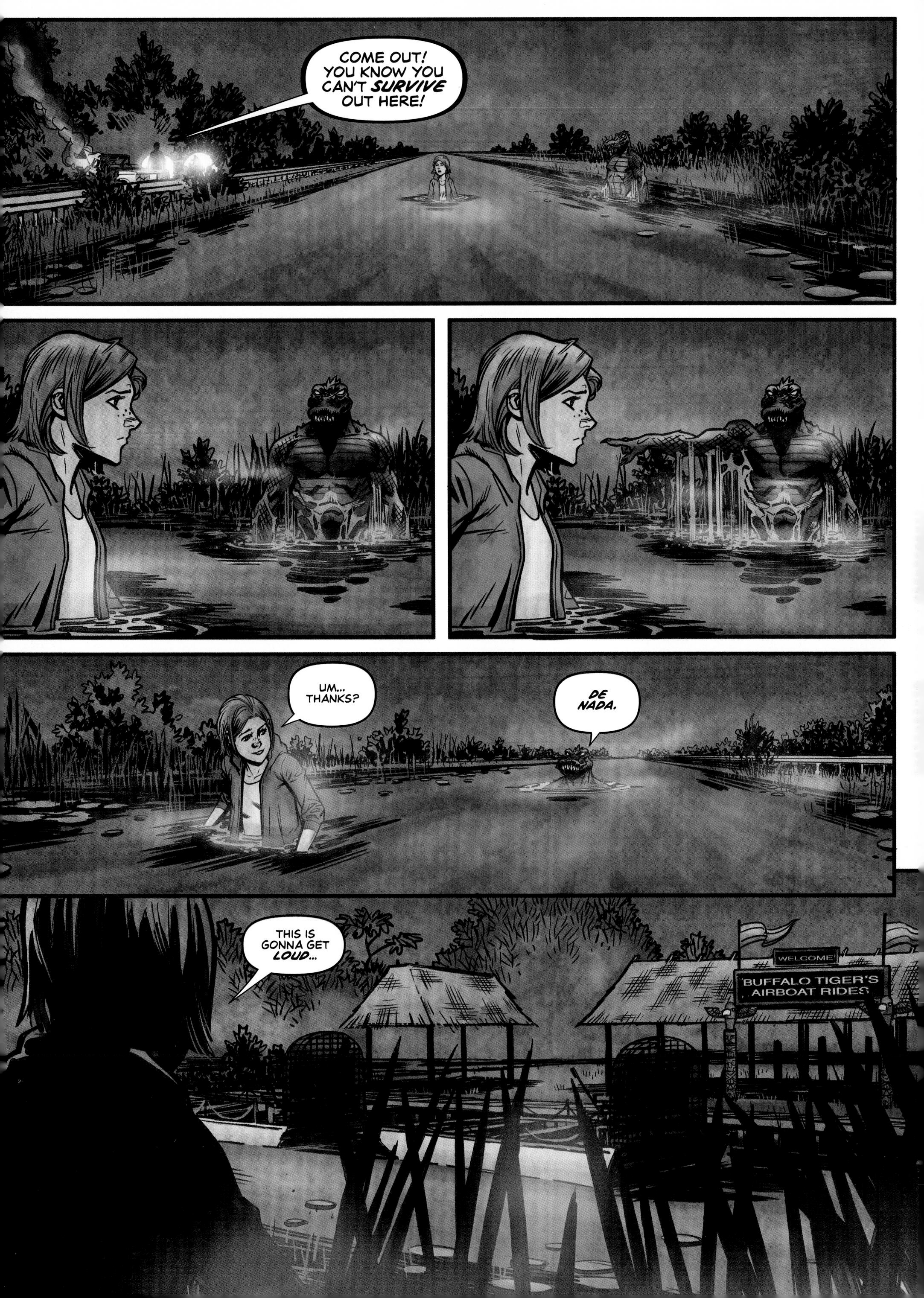
COME OUT! YOU KNOW YOU CAN'T SURVIVE OUT HERE!
UM... THANKS?
DE NADA.
THIS IS GONNA GET LOUD...
WELCOME
BUFFALO TIGER'S AIRBOAT RIDES

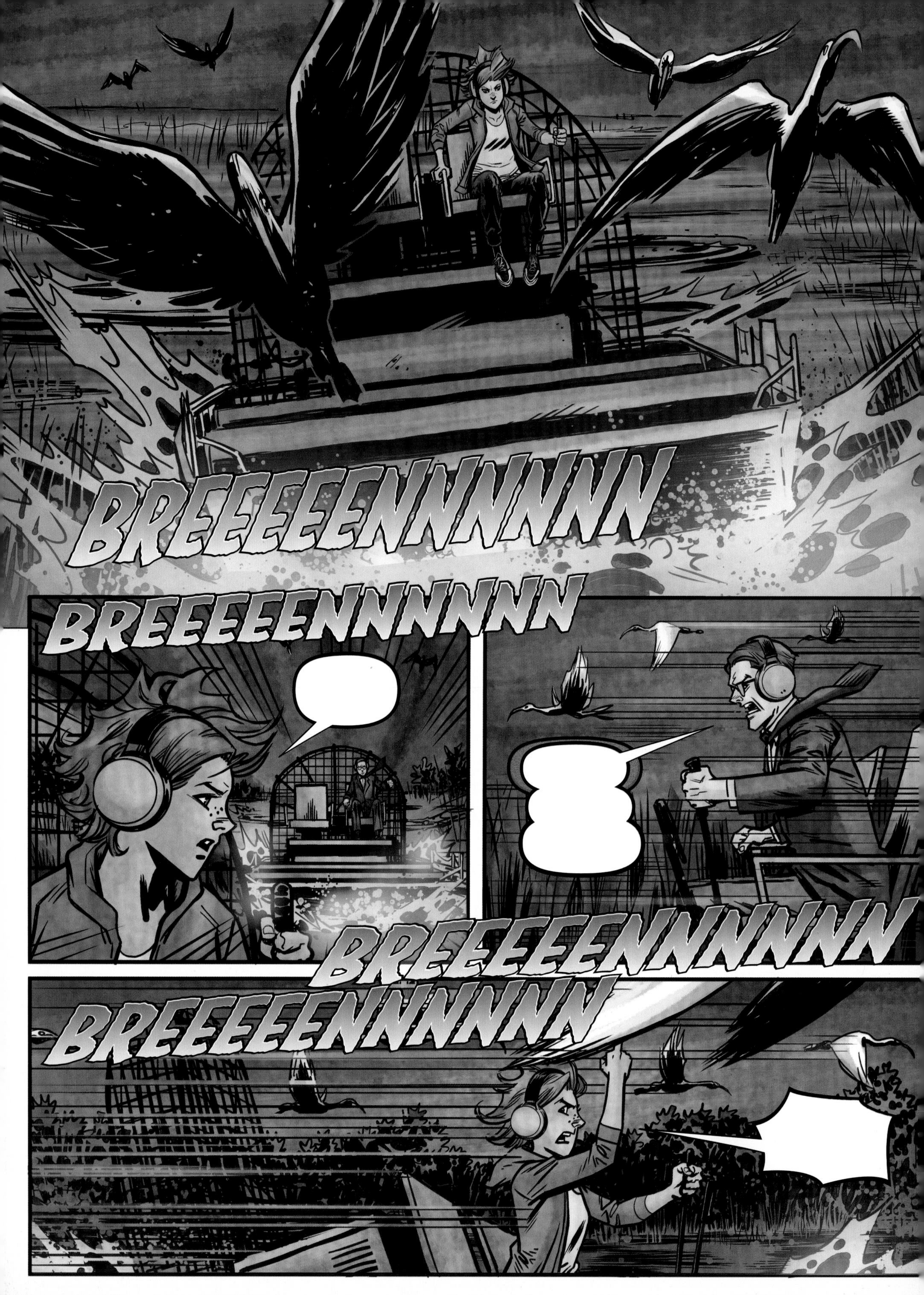
BREEEEEENNNNNNN
BREEEEEENNNNNNN
BREEEEEENNNNNNN
BREEEEEENNNNNNN

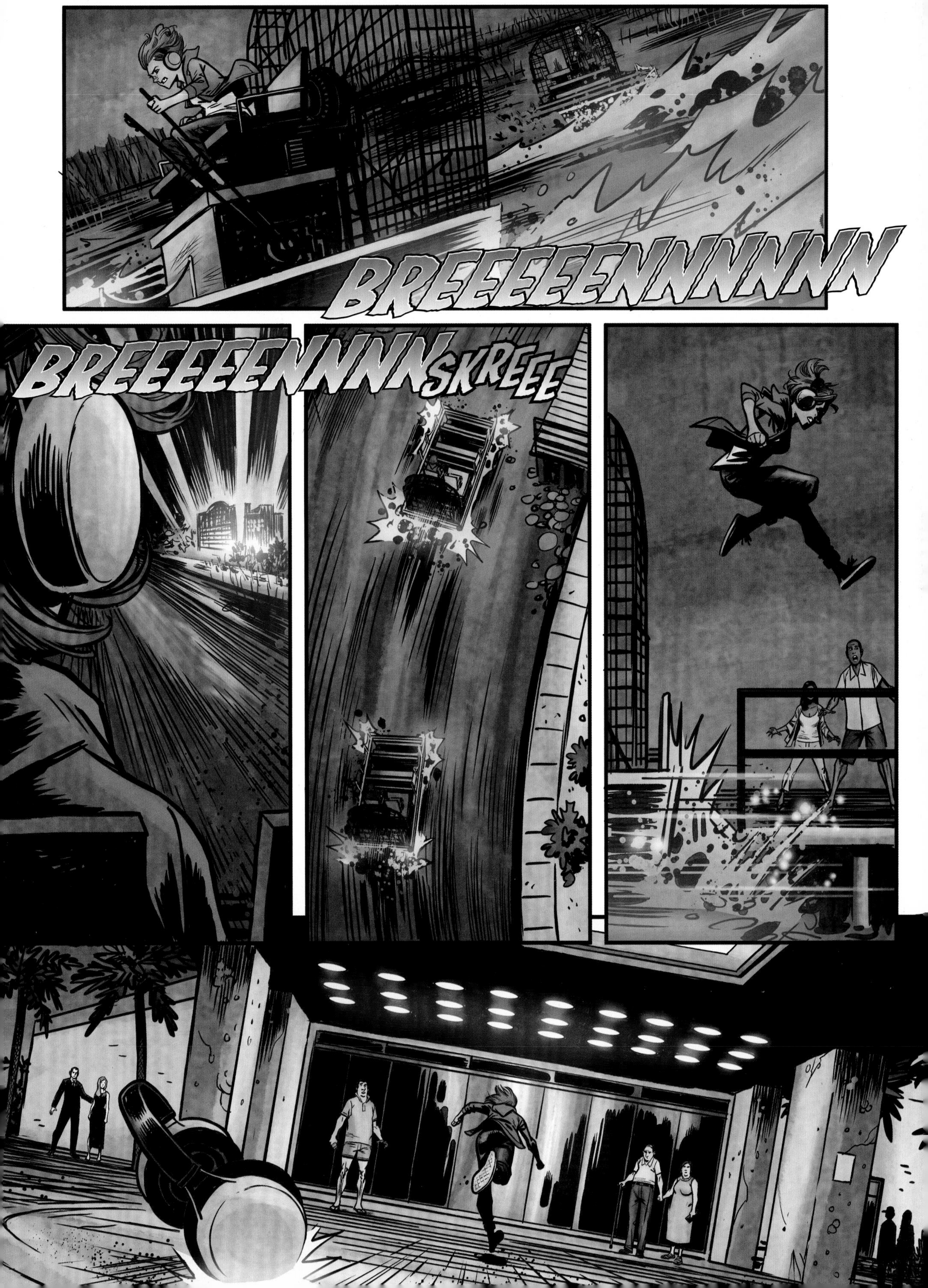
BREEEEEENNNNNNN
BREEEEEENNNNN
SKREEE

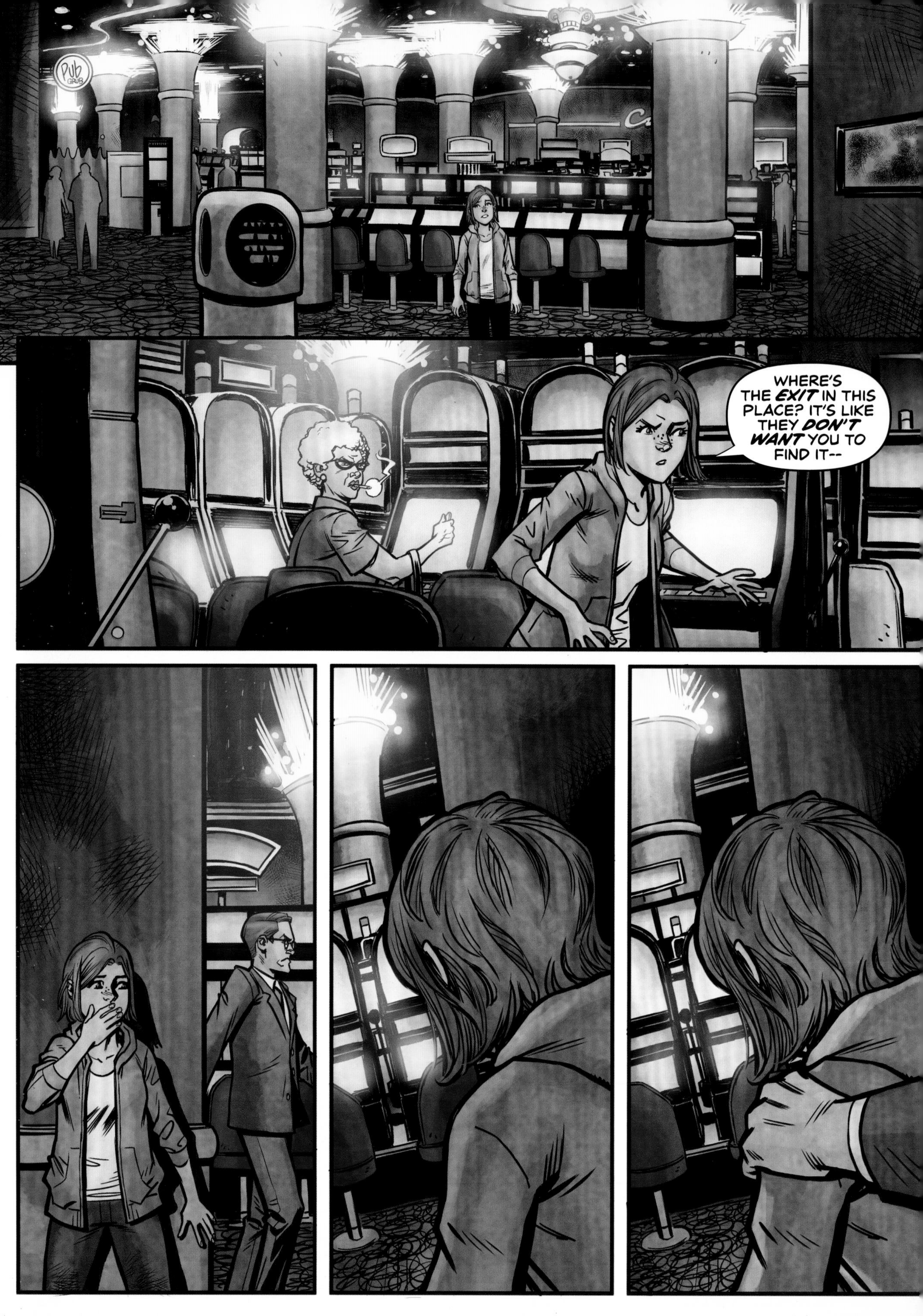
WHERE'S THE *EXIT* IN THIS PLACE? IT'S LIKE THEY *DON'T WANT* YOU TO FIND IT--

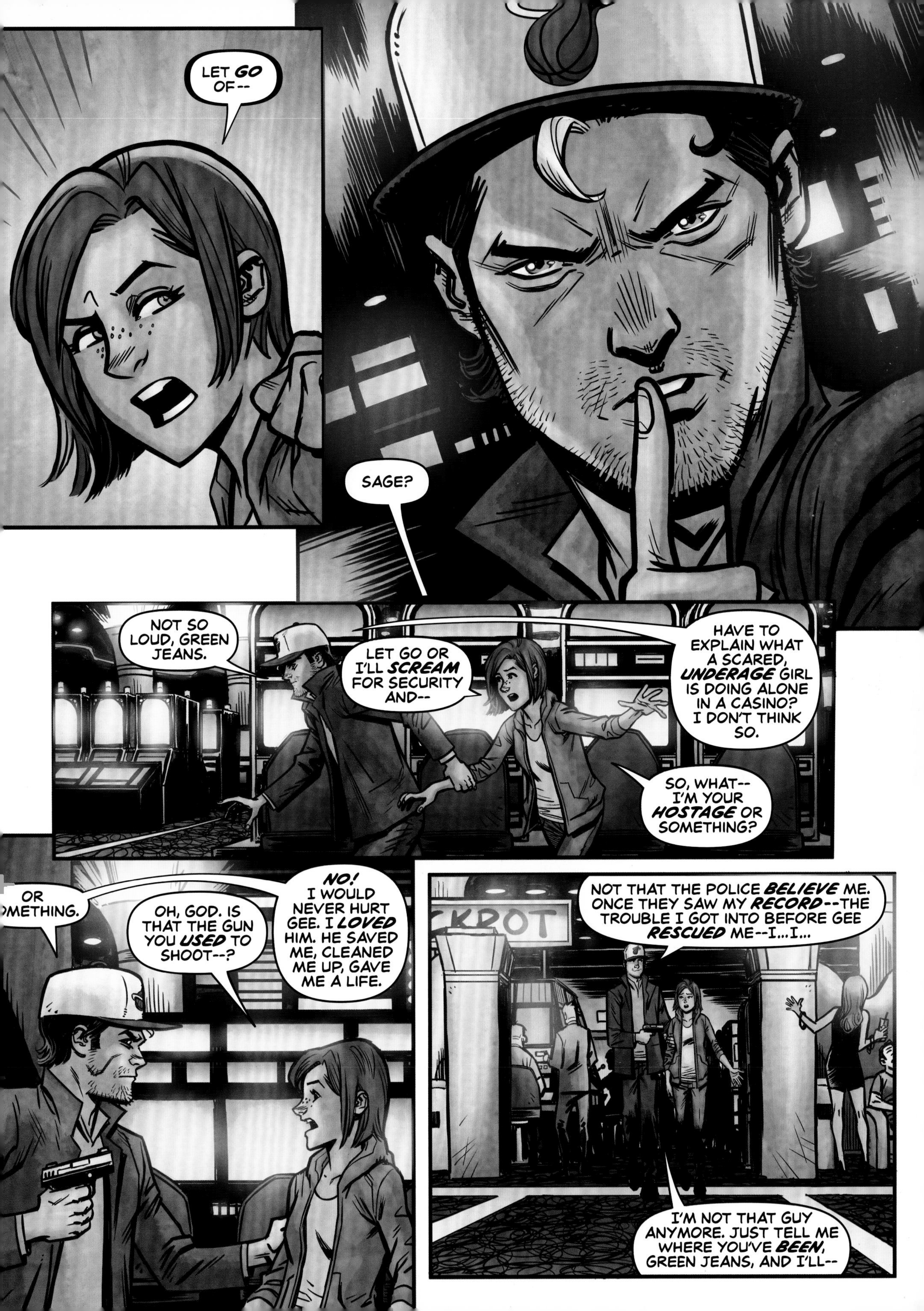
LET GO OF--
SAGE?
NOT SO LOUD, GREEN JEANS.
LET GO OR I'LL SCREAM FOR SECURITY AND--
HAVE TO EXPLAIN WHAT A SCARED, UNDERAGE GIRL IS DOING ALONE IN A CASINO? I DON'T THINK SO.
SO, WHAT-- I'M YOUR HOSTAGE OR SOMETHING?
OR OMETHING.
OH, GOD. IS THAT THE GUN YOU USED TO SHOOT--?
NO! I WOULD NEVER HURT GEE. I LOVED HIM. HE SAVED ME, CLEANED ME UP, GAVE ME A LIFE.
CKPOT
NOT THAT THE POLICE BELIEVE ME. ONCE THEY SAW MY RECORD--THE TROUBLE I GOT INTO BEFORE GEE RESCUED ME--I...I...
I'M NOT THAT GUY ANYMORE. JUST TELL ME WHERE YOU'VE BEEN, GREEN JEANS, AND I'LL--

LET. HER. GO.

LOT OF EXCITEMENT FOR A *SCHOOL NIGHT*, WOULDN'T YOU SAY?

SNEAKING INTO CASINOS, REPORTS OF STOLEN AIRBOATS, AND *ANOTHER* CAR WRECK ON THE TRAIL--IN WHICH WE FOUND YOUR *BACKPACK* AND CELL, MISS COOPER.

MR. RITZ--

--I-IS HE OKAY?

HE'S BEEN AIRLIFTED TO BAPTIST HOSPITAL. THEY LISTED HIM AS *CRITICAL* AS OF TEN MINUTES AGO.

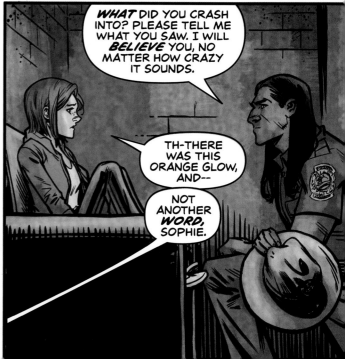

WHAT DID YOU CRASH INTO? PLEASE TELL ME WHAT YOU SAW. I WILL *BELIEVE* YOU, NO MATTER HOW CRAZY IT SOUNDS.

TH-THERE WAS THIS ORANGE GLOW, AND--

NOT ANOTHER *WORD*, SOPHIE.

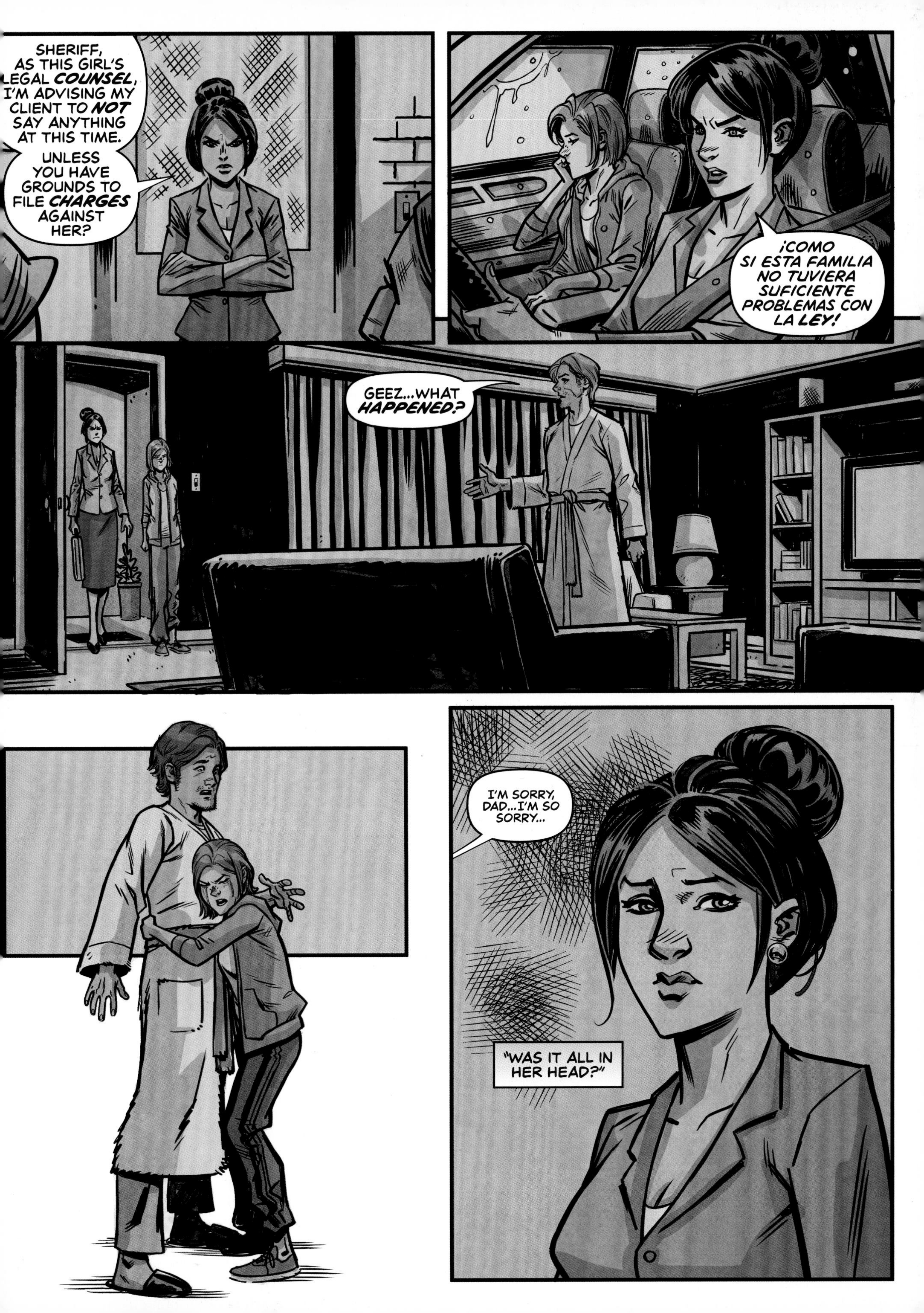
SHERIFF, AS THIS GIRL'S LEGAL COUNSEL, I'M ADVISING MY CLIENT TO NOT SAY ANYTHING AT THIS TIME.
UNLESS YOU HAVE GROUNDS TO FILE CHARGES AGAINST HER?
¡COMO SI ESTA FAMILIA NO TUVIERA SUFICIENTE PROBLEMAS CON LA LEY!
GEEZ...WHAT HAPPENED?
I'M SORRY, DAD...I'M SO SORRY...
"WAS IT ALL IN HER HEAD?"

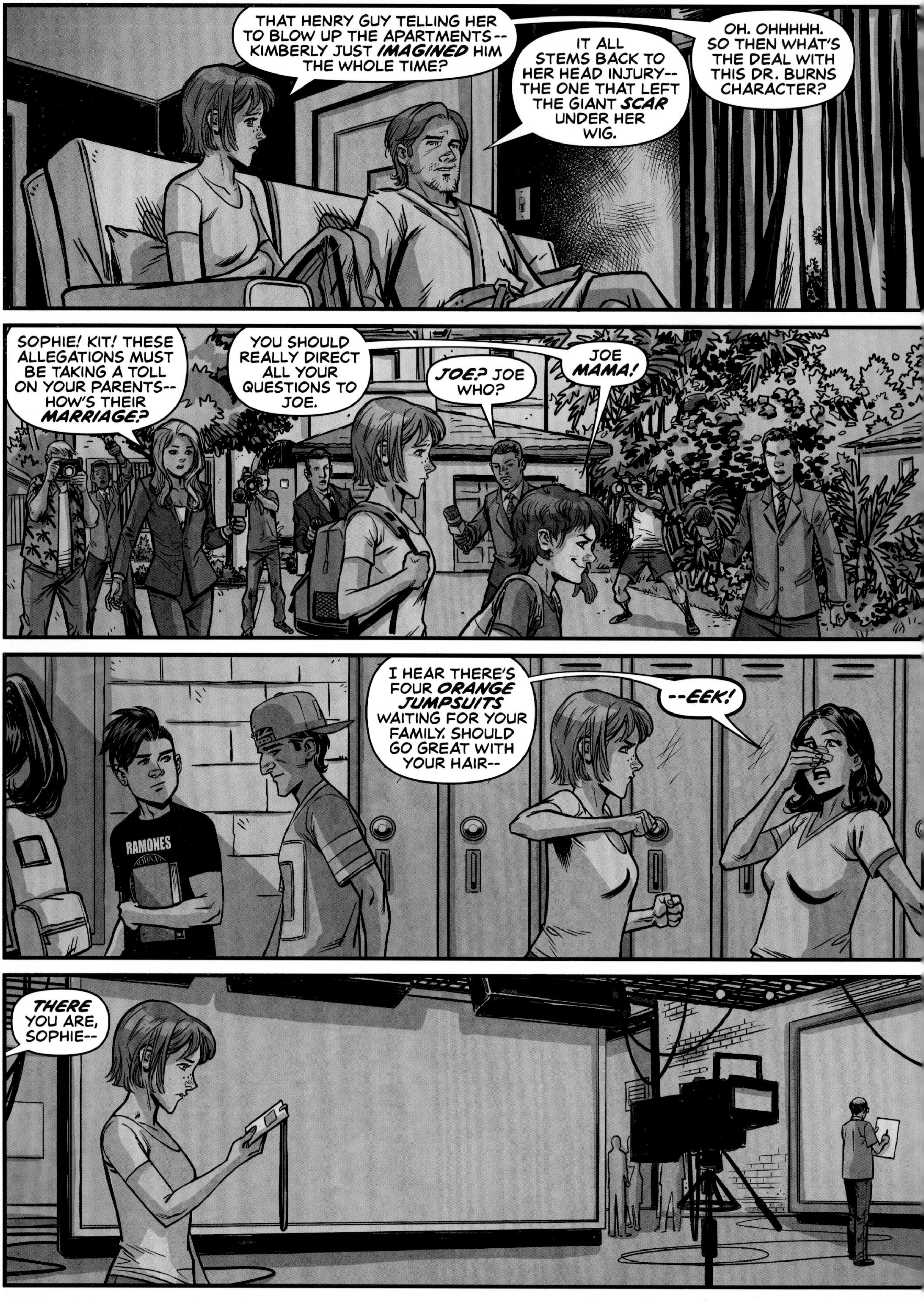
THAT HENRY GUY TELLING HER TO BLOW UP THE APARTMENTS-- KIMBERLY JUST IMAGINED HIM THE WHOLE TIME?
IT ALL STEMS BACK TO HER HEAD INJURY-- THE ONE THAT LEFT THE GIANT SCAR UNDER HER WIG.
OH. OHHHHH. SO THEN WHAT'S THE DEAL WITH THIS DR. BURNS CHARACTER?
SOPHIE! KIT! THESE ALLEGATIONS MUST BE TAKING A TOLL ON YOUR PARENTS-- HOW'S THEIR MARRIAGE?
YOU SHOULD REALLY DIRECT ALL YOUR QUESTIONS TO JOE.
JOE? JOE WHO?
JOE MAMA!
RAMONES
I HEAR THERE'S FOUR ORANGE JUMPSUITS WAITING FOR YOUR FAMILY. SHOULD GO GREAT WITH YOUR HAIR--
--EEK!
THERE YOU ARE, SOPHIE--

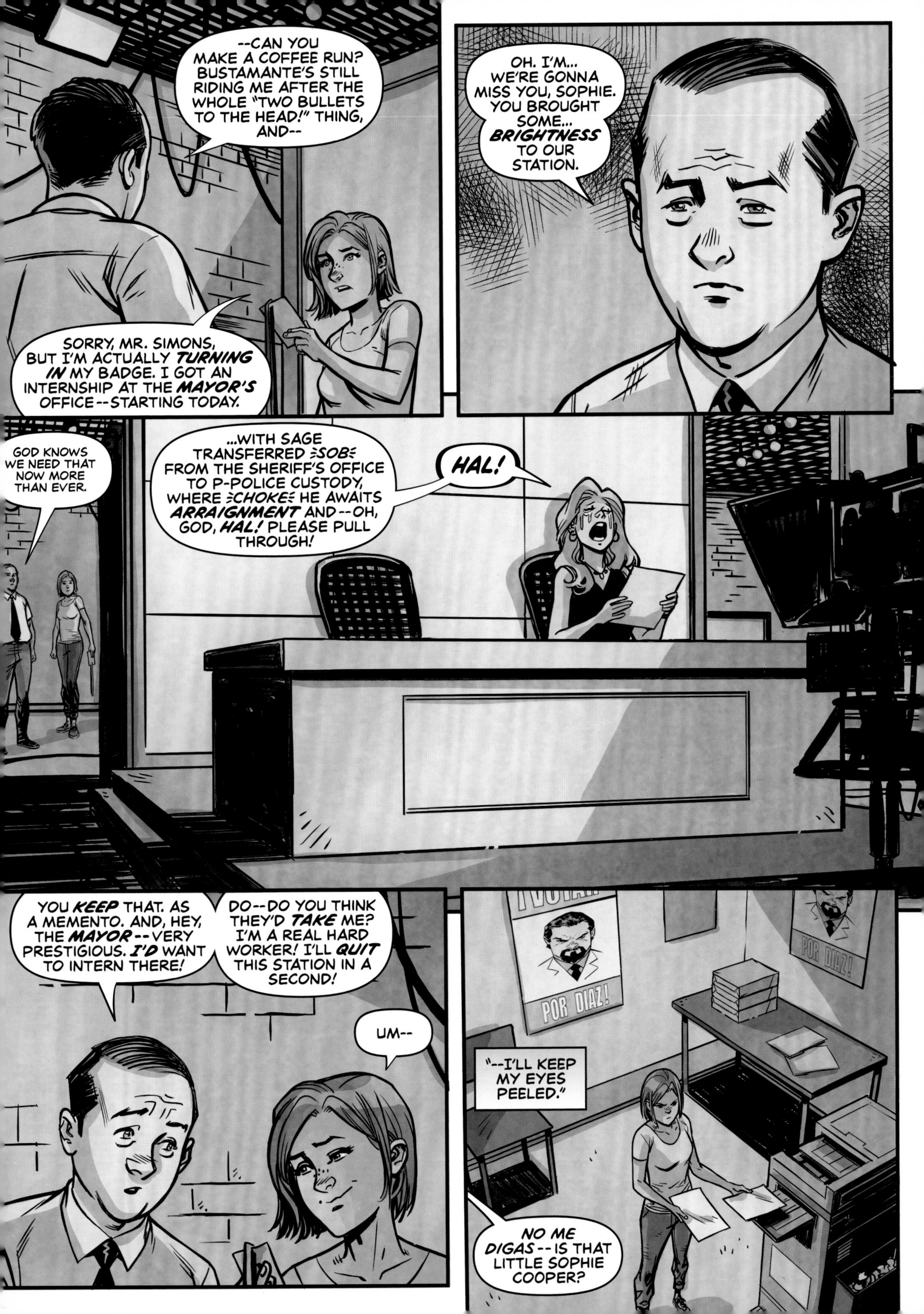
--CAN YOU MAKE A COFFEE RUN? BUSTAMANTE'S STILL RIDING ME AFTER THE WHOLE "TWO BULLETS TO THE HEAD!" THING, AND--
SORRY, MR. SIMONS, BUT I'M ACTUALLY ***TURNING IN*** MY BADGE. I GOT AN INTERNSHIP AT THE ***MAYOR'S*** OFFICE--STARTING TODAY.
OH. I'M... WE'RE GONNA MISS YOU, SOPHIE. YOU BROUGHT SOME... ***BRIGHTNESS*** TO OUR STATION.
GOD KNOWS WE NEED THAT NOW MORE THAN EVER.
...WITH SAGE TRANSFERRED *SOB* FROM THE SHERIFF'S OFFICE TO P-POLICE CUSTODY, WHERE *CHOKE* HE AWAITS ***ARRAIGNMENT*** AND--OH, GOD, ***HAL!*** PLEASE PULL THROUGH!
HAL!
YOU ***KEEP*** THAT. AS A MEMENTO. AND, HEY, THE ***MAYOR***--VERY PRESTIGIOUS. ***I'D*** WANT TO INTERN THERE!
DO--DO YOU THINK THEY'D ***TAKE*** ME? I'M A REAL HARD WORKER! I'LL ***QUIT*** THIS STATION IN A SECOND!
UM--
POR DIAZ!
POR DIAZ!
"--I'LL KEEP MY EYES PEELED."
NO ME DIGAS--IS THAT LITTLE SOPHIE COOPER?

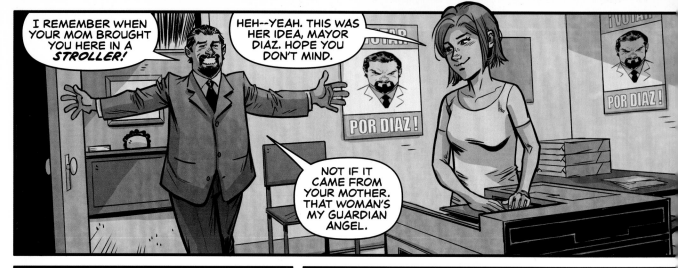

I REMEMBER WHEN YOUR MOM BROUGHT YOU HERE IN A **STROLLER!**

HEH--YEAH. THIS WAS HER IDEA, MAYOR DIAZ. HOPE YOU DON'T MIND.

NOT IF IT CAME FROM YOUR MOTHER. THAT WOMAN'S MY GUARDIAN ANGEL.

AND I'M PRETTY SURE YOU'RE **HERS.** THANKS FOR STICKING BY HER-- BY **US**--WHILE WE DEAL WITH...YOU KNOW...

POR SU PUESTO. HOW'S YOUR DAD? ANYTHING I CAN DO TO HELP?

AS MAYOR, CAN YOU **BAN** ALL TV NEWS IN MIAMI? FOREVER?

HA! YOU HELP ME GET **RE-ELECTED,** AND I'LL SEE WHAT I CAN DO.

FAIR ENOUGH.

PERDONEME, SEÑOR ALCALDE. MIND IF I BORROW YOUR NEWEST EMPLOYEE FOR AN **ERRAND?**

BY ALL MEANS, DULCE. AND SOPHIE, HELP YOURSELF TO AS MANY **POSTERS** AND **BUTTONS** AS YOU WANT.

IN FACT, GIVE SOME TO ALL YOUR **FRIENDS**-- ESPECIALLY IF THEY'RE OLD ENOUGH TO **VOTE!**

YEAH. SURE. **ALL** MY FRIENDS.

OKAY, HERE'S A CHANCE FOR YOU TO EARN BACK SOME OF MY **TRUST**, SOPHIA DEL CARMEN COOPER.

PRINT OUT THE DEPOSIT SLIPS ON THIS JUMP DRIVE AND DELIVER THEM TO THE BANK FOR THE CAMPAIGN'S OPERATING ACCOUNT.

BANK? **WHICH** BANK?

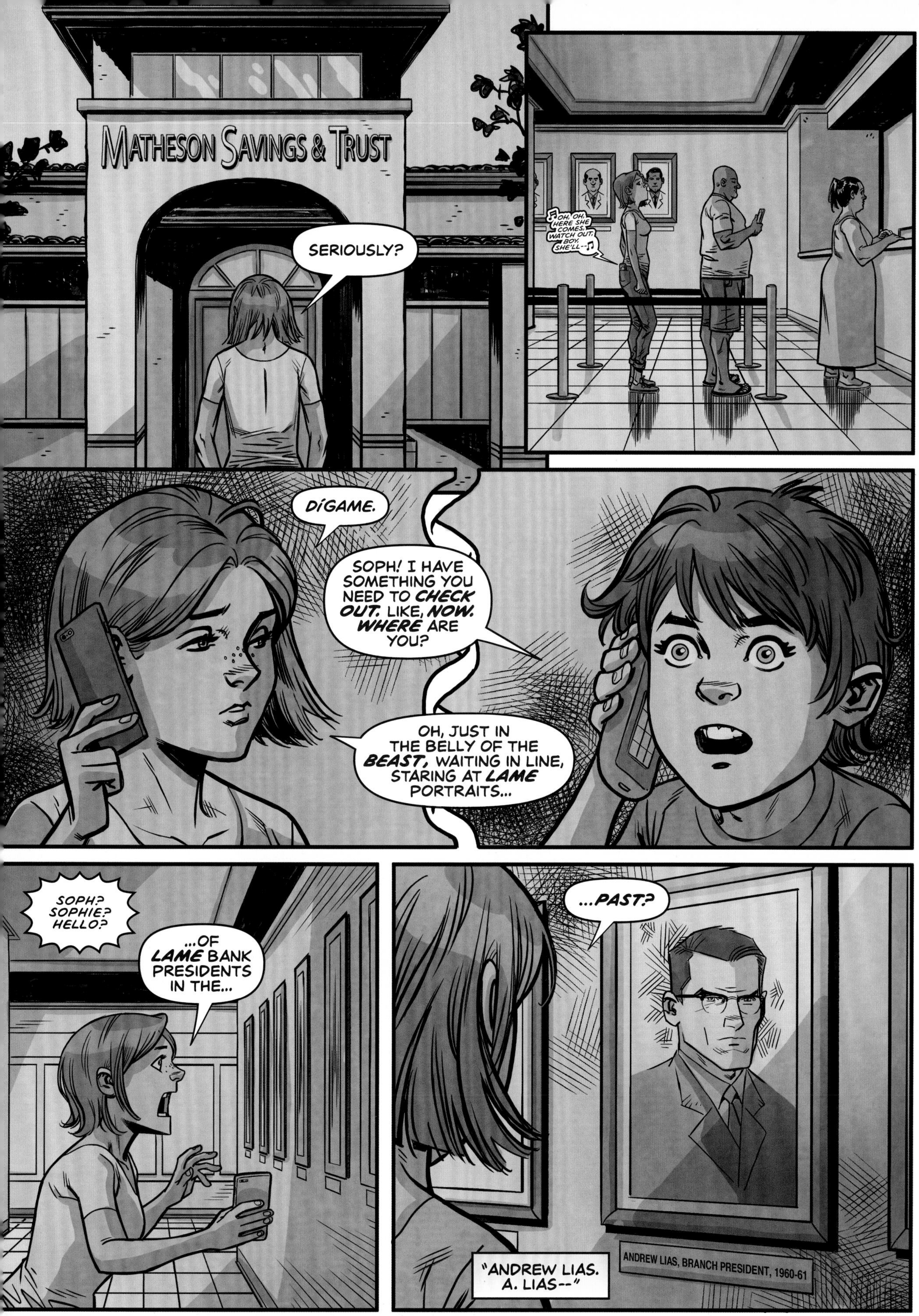
MATHESON SAVINGS & TRUST
SERIOUSLY?
♫ OH, OH, HERE SHE COMES, WATCH OUT, BOY, SHE'LL-- ♫
DíGAME.
SOPH! I HAVE SOMETHING YOU NEED TO CHECK OUT. LIKE, NOW. WHERE ARE YOU?
OH, JUST IN THE BELLY OF THE BEAST, WAITING IN LINE, STARING AT LAME PORTRAITS...
SOPH? SOPHIE? HELLO?
...OF LAME BANK PRESIDENTS IN THE...
...PAST?
ANDREW LIAS, BRANCH PRESIDENT, 1960-61
"ANDREW LIAS. A. LIAS--"

--OR *ALIAS.* CLEVER.

VISIT CUBA

WELL DONE, "ROBIN." WERE YOU ABLE TO TURN UP ANYTHING ELSE ON HIM?

NOTHING. IT'S LIKE HE JUST SHOWED UP IN 1960, VANISHED IN '61--

AND SHOWED UP AGAIN *NOW.* WHY *NOW?*

IF WE CAN PUT A *PIN* IN THAT QUESTION, THIS IS WHAT I WANTED TO SHOW YOU. WELL, *PLAY* FOR YOU.

... *PERFECT* FOR THE NEW LINE? THE, THE--HOW DO YOU SAY?--*JUXTAPOSITION* OF THE NATURE WITH THE SEVERITY OF THE CONCRETE.

CUBA

YES, GEE, IT'S A GREAT BACKDROP, BUT THE DRY CLEANING'S GONNA BE A NIGHTMARE. LOOK AT YOUR JEANS,

THE LASER POINTER-- IT MUST STILL BE AIMED AT THE *WINDOW,* EVEN AFTER I DROPPED IT.

WAIT--IS THAT FROM YOUR *SURVEILLANCE* RIG? IT'S STILL *BROADCASTING?*

YES AND YES. AND THANKS FOR *STEALING* IT, BY THE WAY.

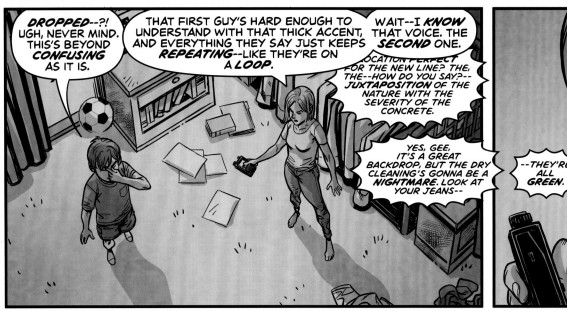

DROPPED--?! UGH, NEVER MIND. THIS'S BEYOND *CONFUSING* AS IT IS.

THAT FIRST GUY'S HARD ENOUGH TO UNDERSTAND WITH THAT THICK ACCENT, AND EVERYTHING THEY SAY JUST KEEPS *REPEATING*--LIKE THEY'RE ON A *LOOP.*

WAIT--I *KNOW* THAT VOICE. THE *SECOND* ONE.

...LOCATION PERFECT FOR THE NEW LINE? THE, THE--HOW DO YOU SAY?-- JUXTAPOSITION OF THE NATURE WITH THE SEVERITY OF THE CONCRETE.

YES, GEE, IT'S A GREAT BACKDROP, BUT THE DRY CLEANING'S GONNA BE A NIGHTMARE. LOOK AT YOUR JEANS--

--THEY'RE ALL *GREEN.*

GREEN JEANS.

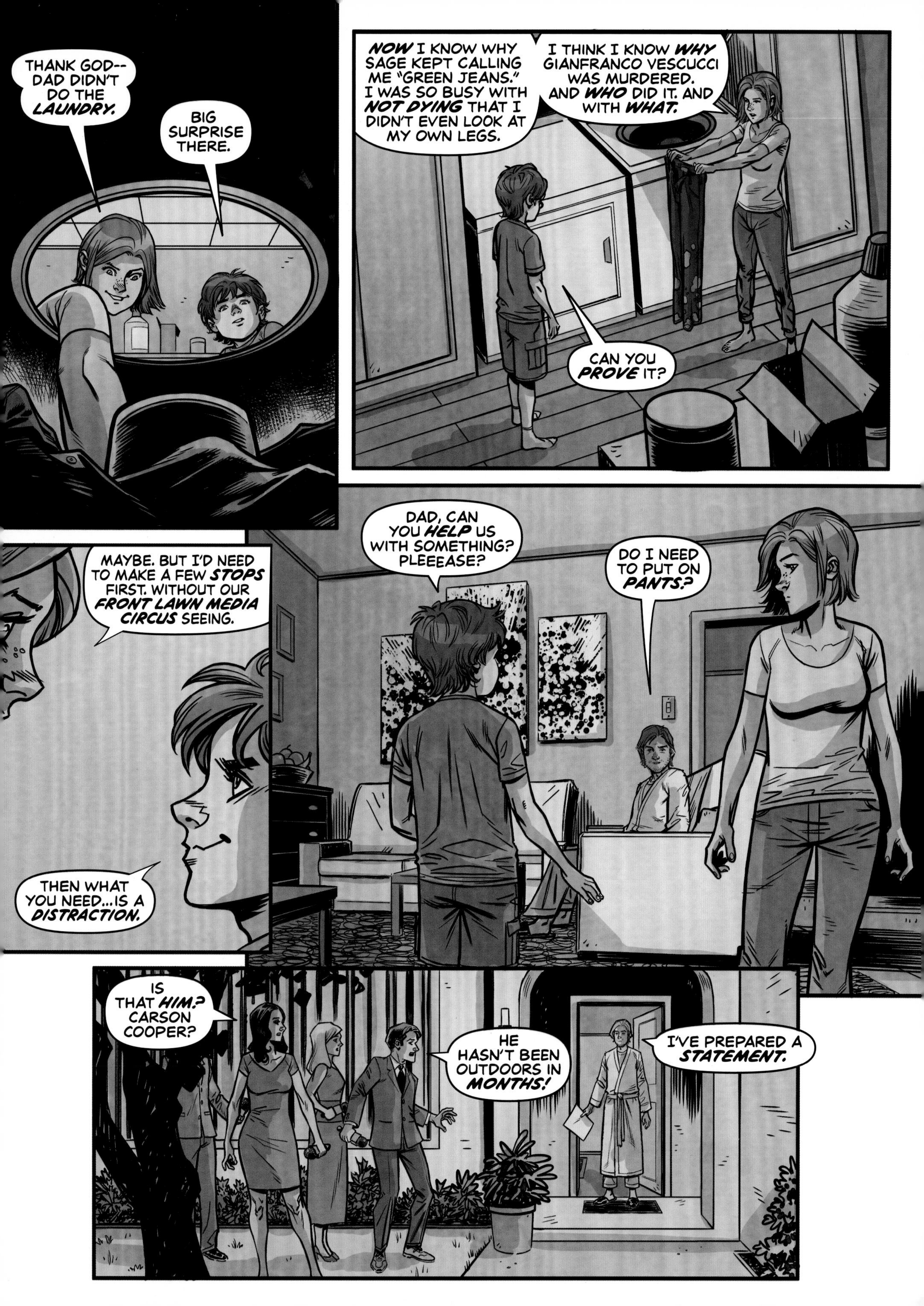
THANK GOD--DAD DIDN'T DO THE LAUNDRY.
BIG SURPRISE THERE.
NOW I KNOW WHY SAGE KEPT CALLING ME "GREEN JEANS." I WAS SO BUSY WITH NOT DYING THAT I DIDN'T EVEN LOOK AT MY OWN LEGS.
I THINK I KNOW WHY GIANFRANCO VESCUCCI WAS MURDERED. AND WHO DID IT. AND WITH WHAT.
CAN YOU PROVE IT?
MAYBE. BUT I'D NEED TO MAKE A FEW STOPS FIRST. WITHOUT OUR FRONT LAWN MEDIA CIRCUS SEEING.
THEN WHAT YOU NEED...IS A DISTRACTION.
DAD, CAN YOU HELP US WITH SOMETHING? PLEEEASE?
DO I NEED TO PUT ON PANTS?
IS THAT HIM? CARSON COOPER?
HE HASN'T BEEN OUTDOORS IN MONTHS!
I'VE PREPARED A STATEMENT.

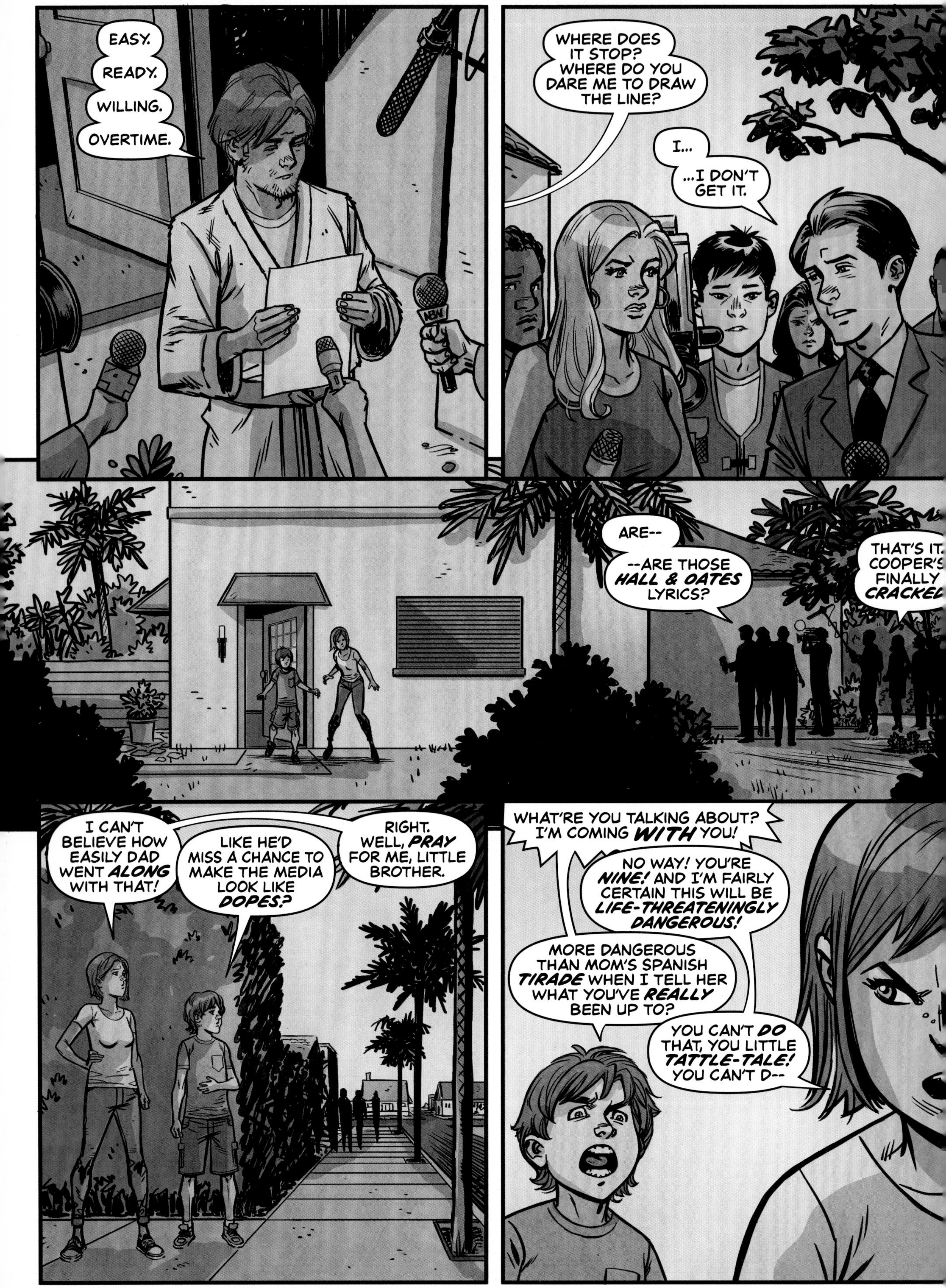
EASY.
READY.
WILLING.
OVERTIME.
WHERE DOES IT STOP? WHERE DO YOU DARE ME TO DRAW THE LINE?
I...
...I DON'T GET IT.
ARE--
--ARE THOSE HALL & OATES LYRICS?
THAT'S IT. COOPER'S FINALLY CRACKED
I CAN'T BELIEVE HOW EASILY DAD WENT ALONG WITH THAT!
LIKE HE'D MISS A CHANCE TO MAKE THE MEDIA LOOK LIKE DOPES?
RIGHT. WELL, PRAY FOR ME, LITTLE BROTHER.
WHAT'RE YOU TALKING ABOUT? I'M COMING WITH YOU!
NO WAY! YOU'RE NINE! AND I'M FAIRLY CERTAIN THIS WILL BE LIFE-THREATENINGLY DANGEROUS!
MORE DANGEROUS THAN MOM'S SPANISH TIRADE WHEN I TELL HER WHAT YOU'VE REALLY BEEN UP TO?
YOU CAN'T DO THAT, YOU LITTLE TATTLE-TALE! YOU CAN'T D--

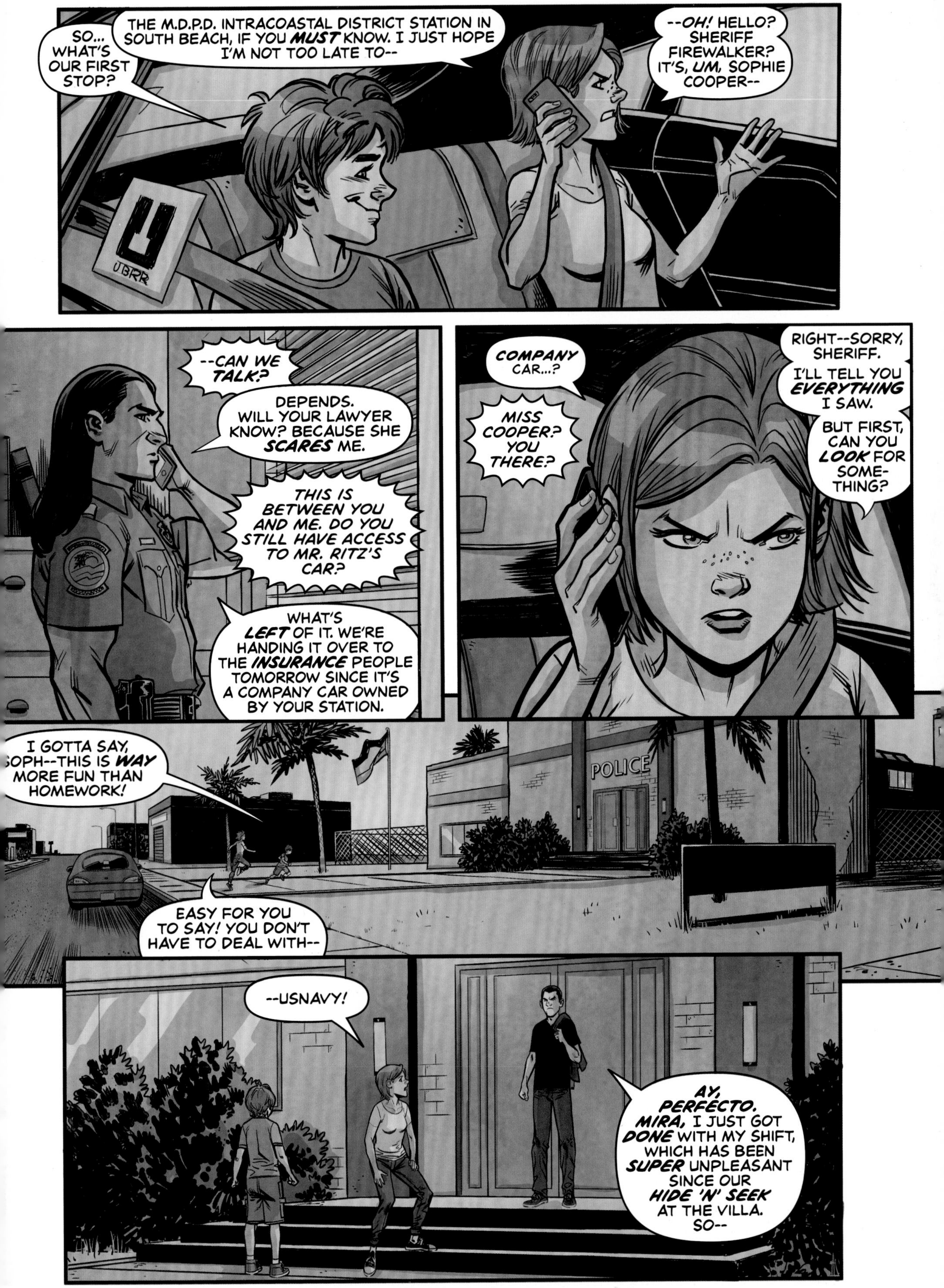
SO... WHAT'S OUR FIRST STOP?
THE M.D.P.D. INTRACOASTAL DISTRICT STATION IN SOUTH BEACH, IF YOU MUST KNOW. I JUST HOPE I'M NOT TOO LATE TO--
--OH! HELLO? SHERIFF FIREWALKER? IT'S, UM, SOPHIE COOPER--
UBRR
--CAN WE TALK?
DEPENDS. WILL YOUR LAWYER KNOW? BECAUSE SHE SCARES ME.
THIS IS BETWEEN YOU AND ME. DO YOU STILL HAVE ACCESS TO MR. RITZ'S CAR?
WHAT'S LEFT OF IT. WE'RE HANDING IT OVER TO THE INSURANCE PEOPLE TOMORROW SINCE IT'S A COMPANY CAR OWNED BY YOUR STATION.
COMPANY CAR...?
MISS COOPER? YOU THERE?
RIGHT--SORRY, SHERIFF.
I'LL TELL YOU EVERYTHING I SAW.
BUT FIRST, CAN YOU LOOK FOR SOME-THING?
I GOTTA SAY, SOPH--THIS IS WAY MORE FUN THAN HOMEWORK!
POLICE
EASY FOR YOU TO SAY! YOU DON'T HAVE TO DEAL WITH--
--USNAVY!
AY, PERFECTO. MIRA, I JUST GOT DONE WITH MY SHIFT, WHICH HAS BEEN SUPER UNPLEASANT SINCE OUR HIDE 'N' SEEK AT THE VILLA. SO--

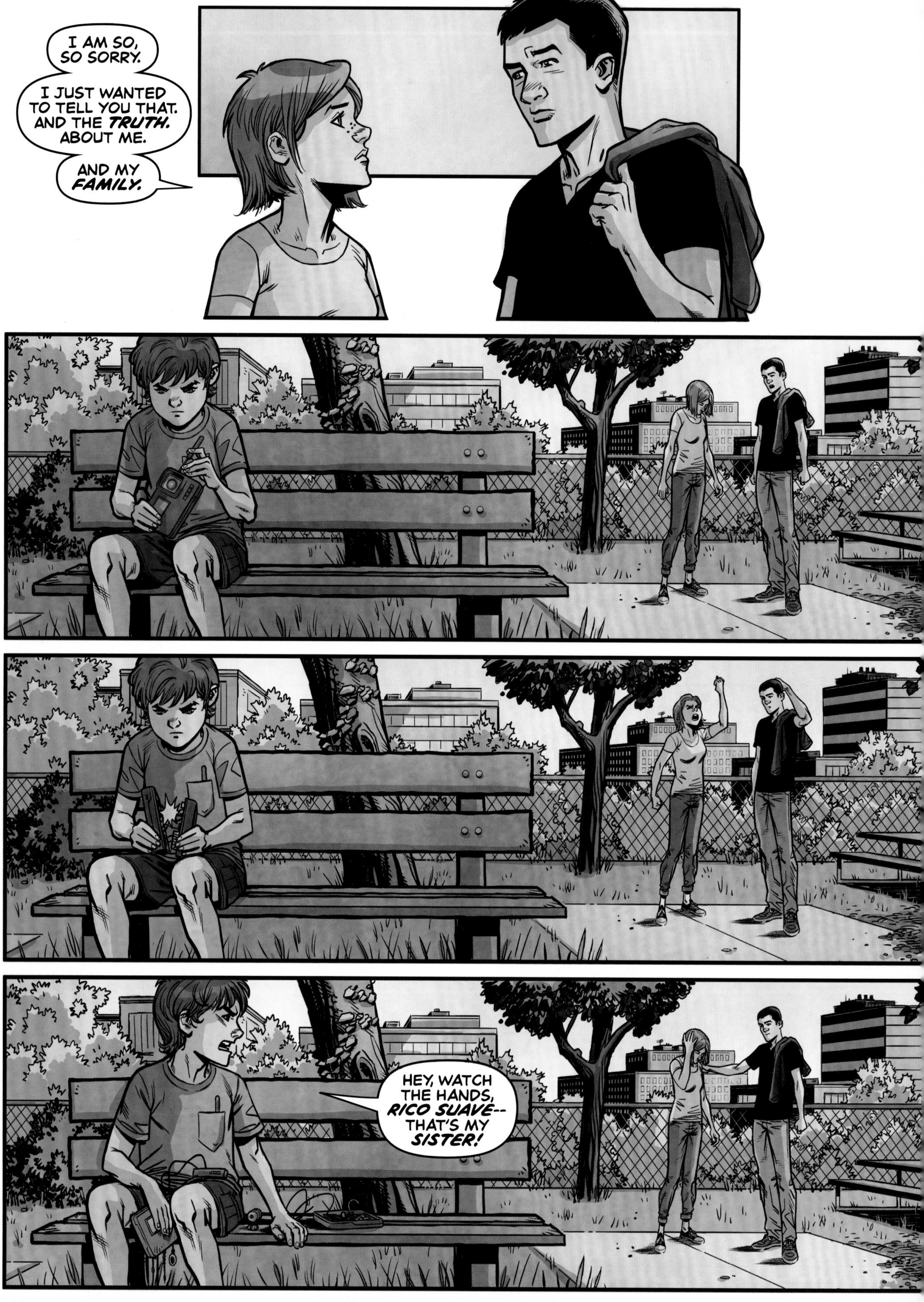
I AM SO, SO SORRY.
I JUST WANTED TO TELL YOU THAT. AND THE *TRUTH.* ABOUT ME.
AND MY *FAMILY.*
HEY, WATCH THE HANDS, *RICO SUAVE*-- THAT'S MY *SISTER!*

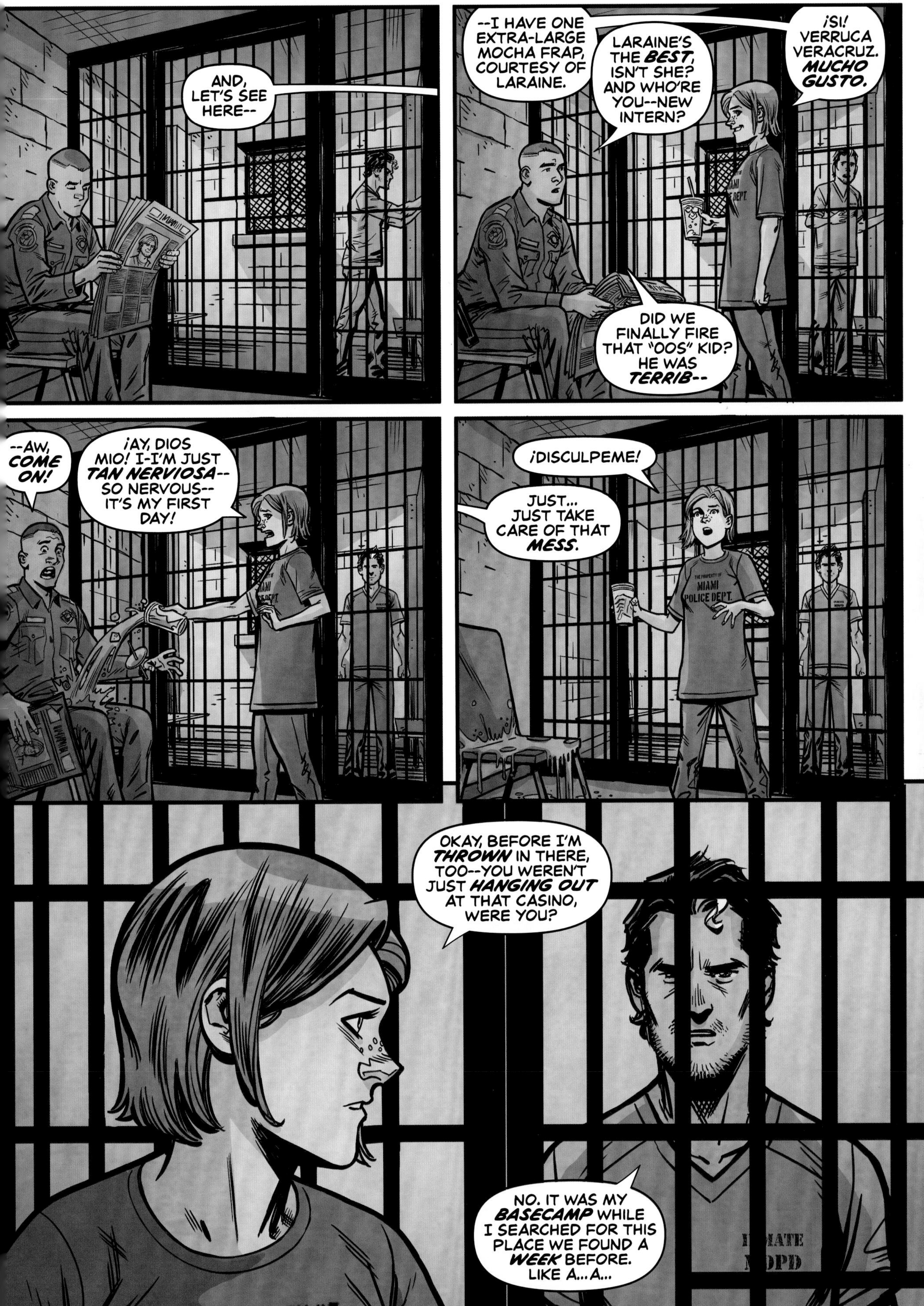

AND, LET'S SEE HERE--
--I HAVE ONE EXTRA-LARGE MOCHA FRAP, COURTESY OF LARAINE.
LARAINE'S THE BEST, ISN'T SHE? AND WHO'RE YOU--NEW INTERN?
¡SI! VERRUCA VERACRUZ. MUCHO GUSTO.
DID WE FINALLY FIRE THAT "OOS" KID? HE WAS TERRIB--
--AW, COME ON!
¡AY, DIOS MIO! I-I'M JUST TAN NERVIOSA--SO NERVOUS--IT'S MY FIRST DAY!
¡DISCULPEME!
JUST... JUST TAKE CARE OF THAT MESS.
THE PROPERTY OF MIAMI POLICE DEPT.
OKAY, BEFORE I'M THROWN IN THERE, TOO--YOU WEREN'T JUST HANGING OUT AT THAT CASINO, WERE YOU?
NO. IT WAS MY BASECAMP WHILE I SEARCHED FOR THIS PLACE WE FOUND A WEEK BEFORE. LIKE A...A...

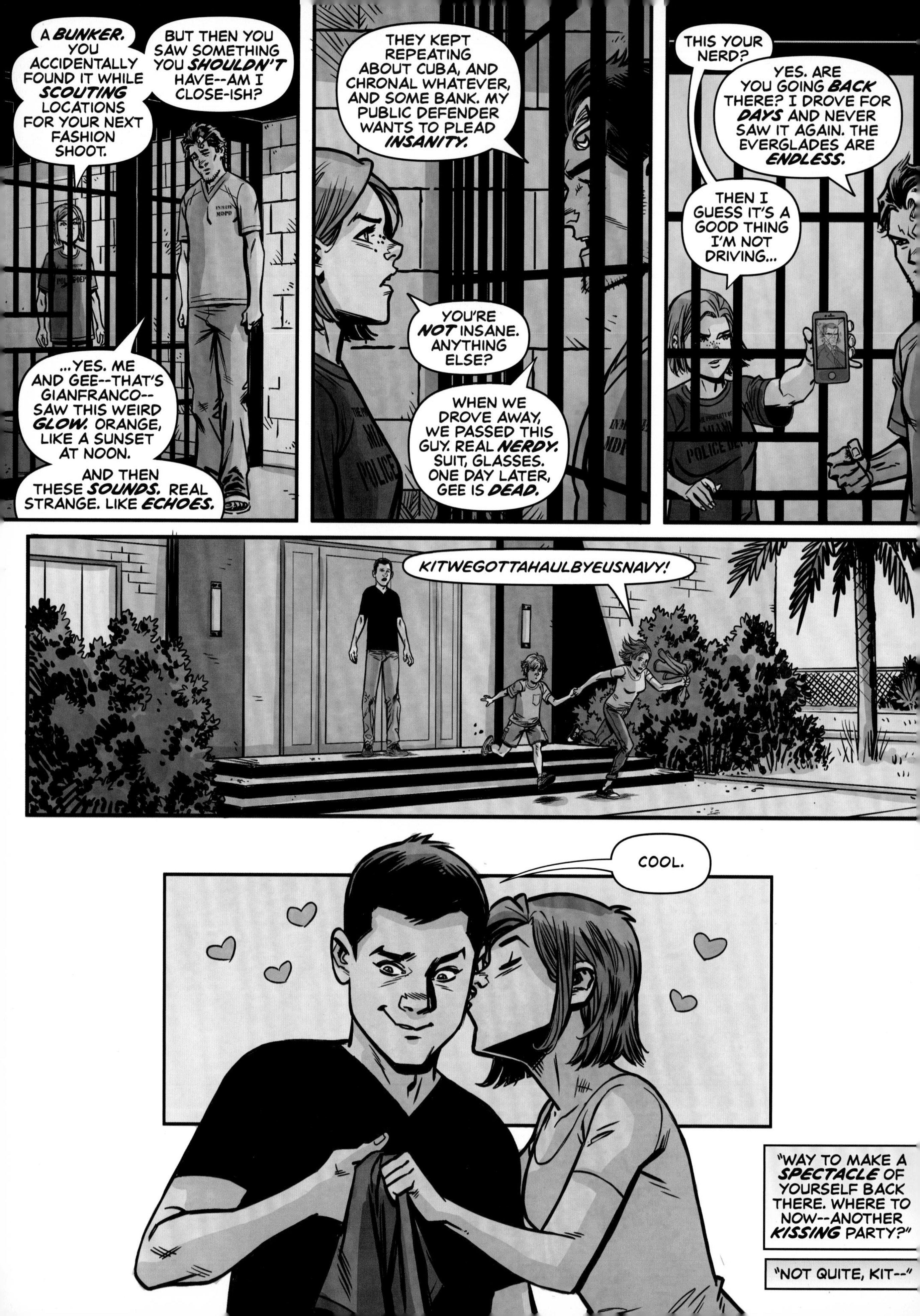
A BUNKER. YOU ACCIDENTALLY FOUND IT WHILE SCOUTING LOCATIONS FOR YOUR NEXT FASHION SHOOT.
BUT THEN YOU SAW SOMETHING YOU SHOULDN'T HAVE--AM I CLOSE-ISH?
...YES. ME AND GEE--THAT'S GIANFRANCO--SAW THIS WEIRD GLOW. ORANGE, LIKE A SUNSET AT NOON.
AND THEN THESE SOUNDS. REAL STRANGE. LIKE ECHOES.
THEY KEPT REPEATING ABOUT CUBA, AND CHRONAL WHATEVER, AND SOME BANK. MY PUBLIC DEFENDER WANTS TO PLEAD INSANITY.
YOU'RE NOT INSANE. ANYTHING ELSE?
WHEN WE DROVE AWAY, WE PASSED THIS GUY. REAL NERDY. SUIT, GLASSES. ONE DAY LATER, GEE IS DEAD.
THIS YOUR NERD?
YES. ARE YOU GOING BACK THERE? I DROVE FOR DAYS AND NEVER SAW IT AGAIN. THE EVERGLADES ARE ENDLESS.
THEN I GUESS IT'S A GOOD THING I'M NOT DRIVING...
KITWEGOTTAHAULBYEUSNAVY!
COOL.
"WAY TO MAKE A SPECTACLE OF YOURSELF BACK THERE. WHERE TO NOW--ANOTHER KISSING PARTY?"
"NOT QUITE, KIT--"

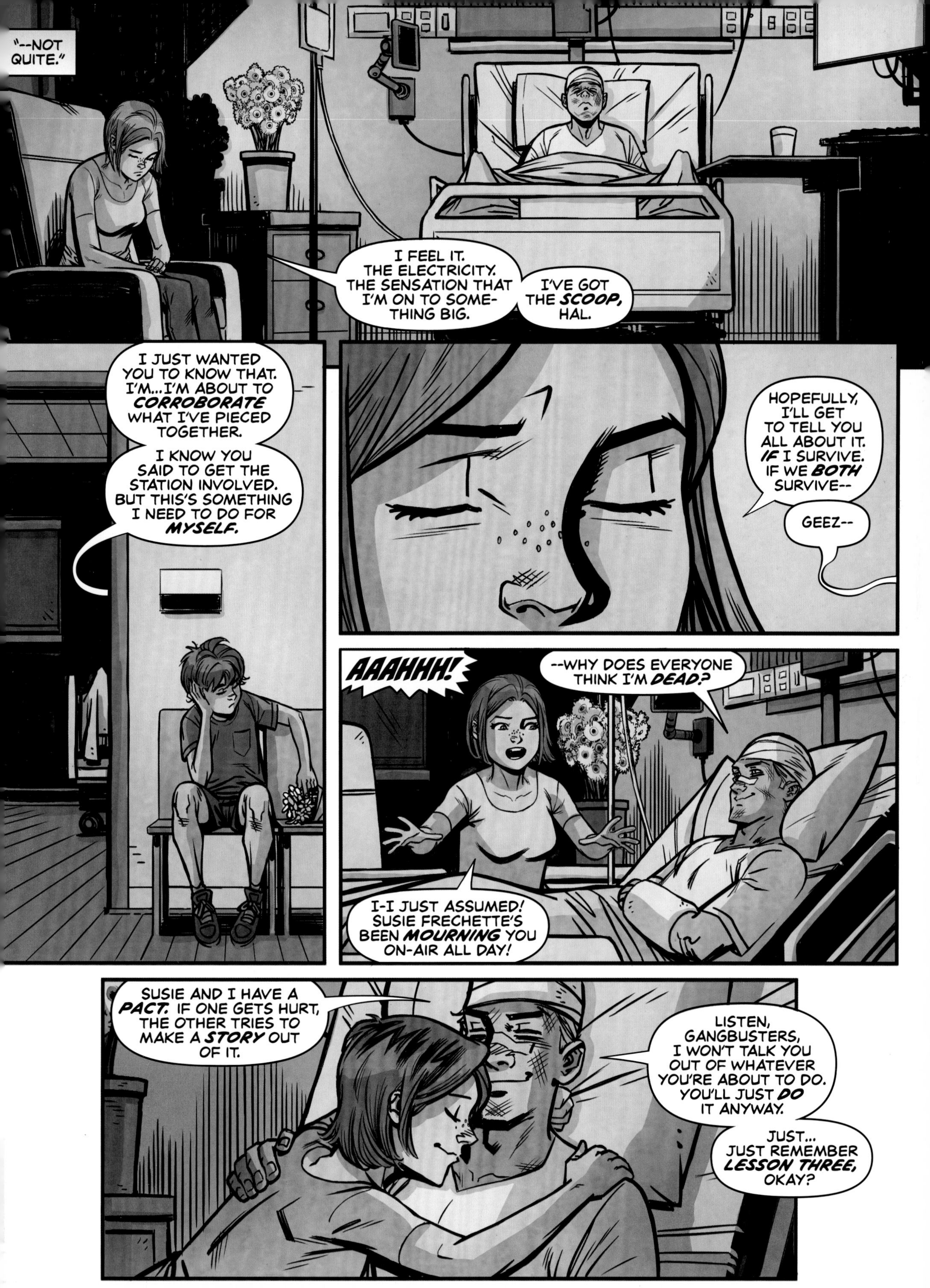
"--NOT QUITE."
I FEEL IT. THE ELECTRICITY. THE SENSATION THAT I'M ON TO SOME-THING BIG.
I'VE GOT THE SCOOP, HAL.
I JUST WANTED YOU TO KNOW THAT. I'M...I'M ABOUT TO CORROBORATE WHAT I'VE PIECED TOGETHER.
I KNOW YOU SAID TO GET THE STATION INVOLVED. BUT THIS'S SOMETHING I NEED TO DO FOR MYSELF.
HOPEFULLY, I'LL GET TO TELL YOU ALL ABOUT IT. IF I SURVIVE. IF WE BOTH SURVIVE--
GEEZ--
AAAHHH!
--WHY DOES EVERYONE THINK I'M DEAD?
I-I JUST ASSUMED! SUSIE FRECHETTE'S BEEN MOURNING YOU ON-AIR ALL DAY!
SUSIE AND I HAVE A PACT. IF ONE GETS HURT, THE OTHER TRIES TO MAKE A STORY OUT OF IT.
LISTEN, GANGBUSTERS, I WON'T TALK YOU OUT OF WHATEVER YOU'RE ABOUT TO DO. YOU'LL JUST DO IT ANYWAY.
JUST... JUST REMEMBER LESSON THREE, OKAY?

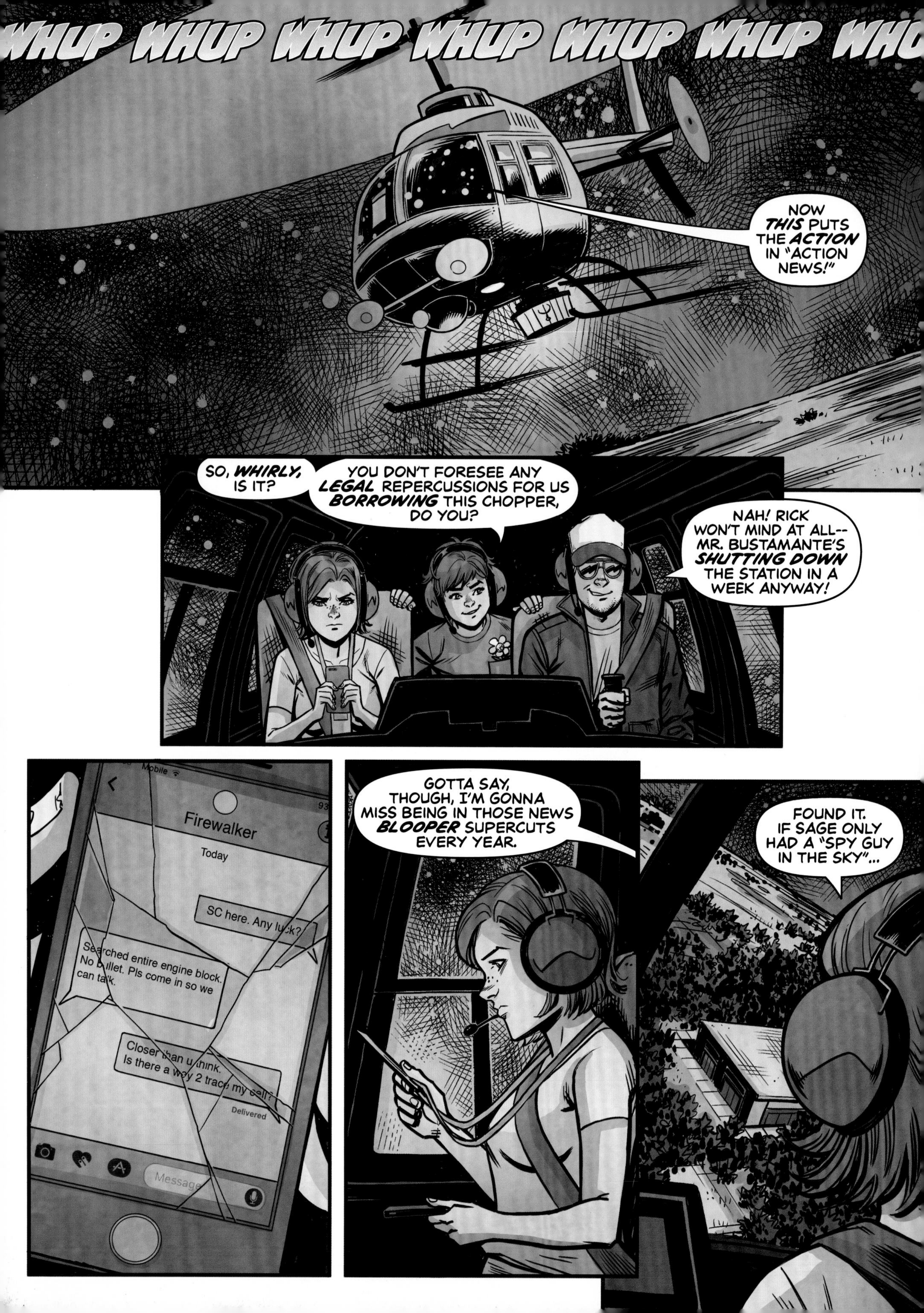
WHUP WHUP WHUP WHUP WHUP WHUP WHU
NOW THIS PUTS THE ACTION IN "ACTION NEWS!"
SO, WHIRLY, IS IT?
YOU DON'T FORESEE ANY LEGAL REPERCUSSIONS FOR US BORROWING THIS CHOPPER, DO YOU?
NAH! RICK WON'T MIND AT ALL-- MR. BUSTAMANTE'S SHUTTING DOWN THE STATION IN A WEEK ANYWAY!
Firewalker
Today
SC here. Any luck?
Searched entire engine block. No bullet. Pls come in so we can talk.
Closer than u think. Is there a way 2 trace my cell?
Delivered
Message
GOTTA SAY, THOUGH, I'M GONNA MISS BEING IN THOSE NEWS BLOOPER SUPERCUTS EVERY YEAR.
FOUND IT. IF SAGE ONLY HAD A "SPY GUY IN THE SKY"...

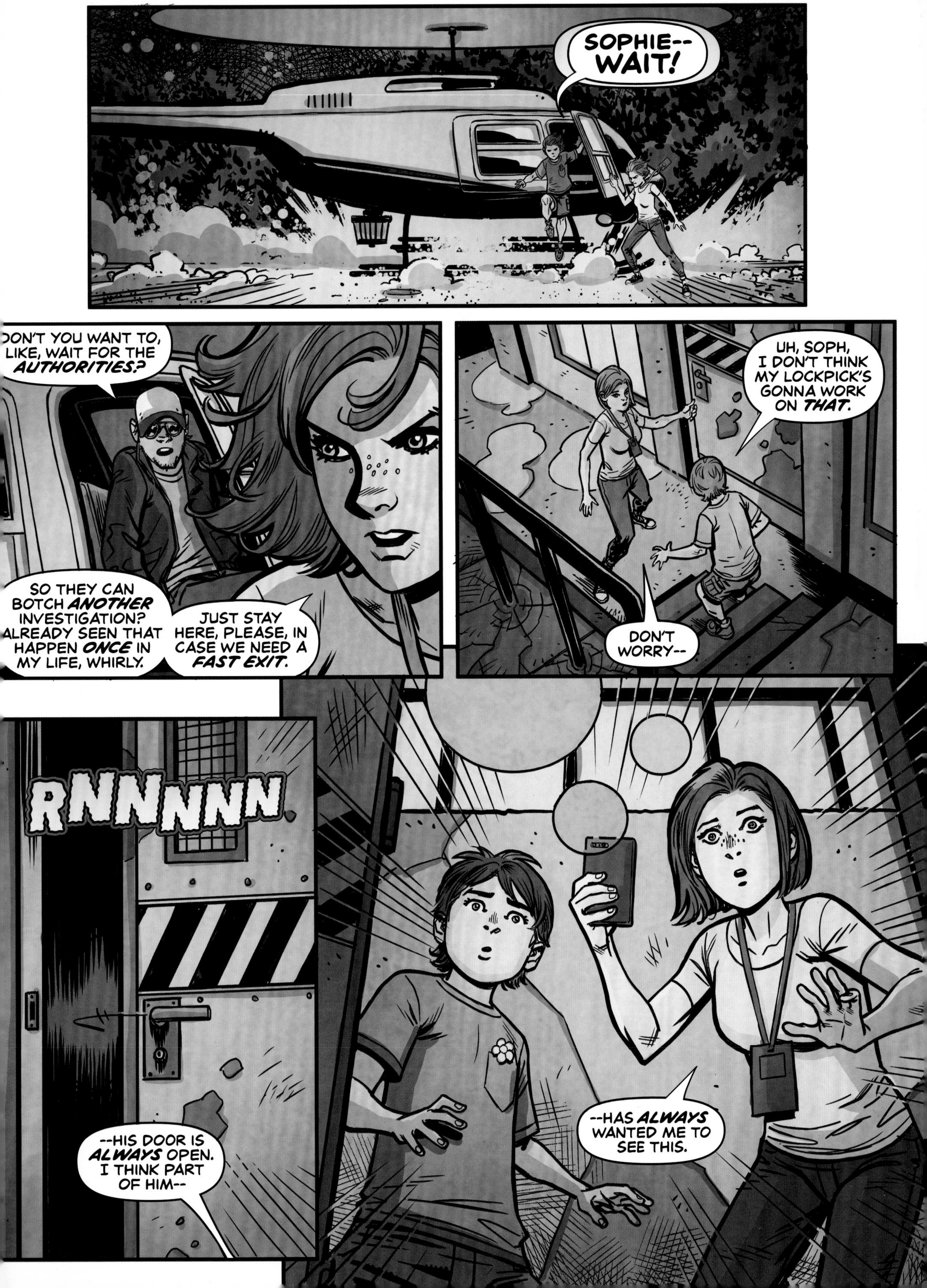
SOPHIE-- WAIT!
DON'T YOU WANT TO, LIKE, WAIT FOR THE AUTHORITIES?
SO THEY CAN BOTCH ANOTHER INVESTIGATION? ALREADY SEEN THAT HAPPEN ONCE IN MY LIFE, WHIRLY.
JUST STAY HERE, PLEASE, IN CASE WE NEED A FAST EXIT.
UH, SOPH, I DON'T THINK MY LOCKPICK'S GONNA WORK ON THAT.
DON'T WORRY--
RNNNNN
--HIS DOOR IS ALWAYS OPEN. I THINK PART OF HIM--
--HAS ALWAYS WANTED ME TO SEE THIS.

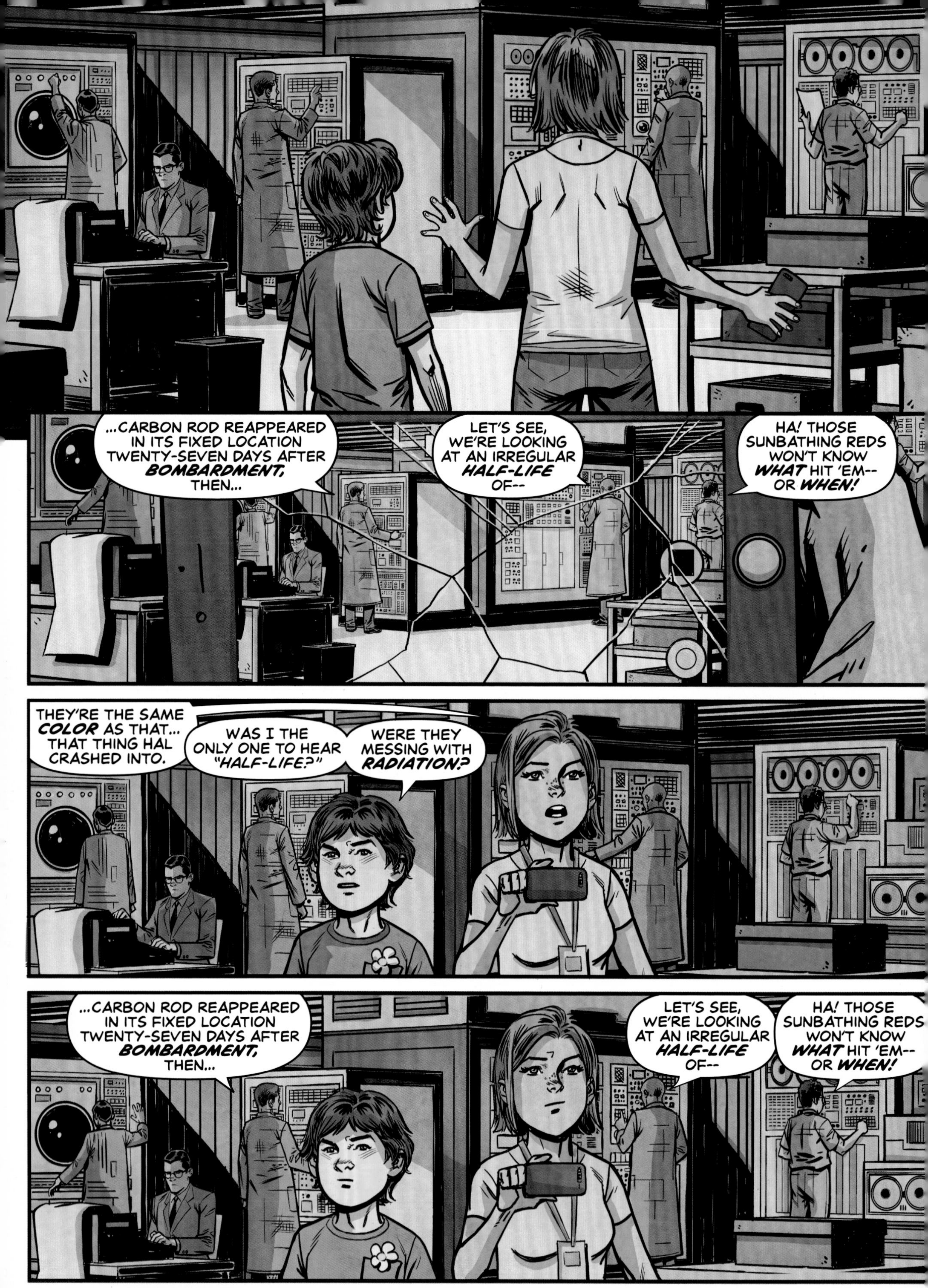
...CARBON ROD REAPPEARED IN ITS FIXED LOCATION TWENTY-SEVEN DAYS AFTER BOMBARDMENT, THEN...
LET'S SEE, WE'RE LOOKING AT AN IRREGULAR HALF-LIFE OF--
HA! THOSE SUNBATHING REDS WON'T KNOW WHAT HIT 'EM-- OR WHEN!
THEY'RE THE SAME COLOR AS THAT... THAT THING HAL CRASHED INTO.
WAS I THE ONLY ONE TO HEAR "HALF-LIFE?"
WERE THEY MESSING WITH RADIATION?
...CARBON ROD REAPPEARED IN ITS FIXED LOCATION TWENTY-SEVEN DAYS AFTER BOMBARDMENT, THEN...
LET'S SEE, WE'RE LOOKING AT AN IRREGULAR HALF-LIFE OF--
HA! THOSE SUNBATHING REDS WON'T KNOW WHAT HIT 'EM-- OR WHEN!

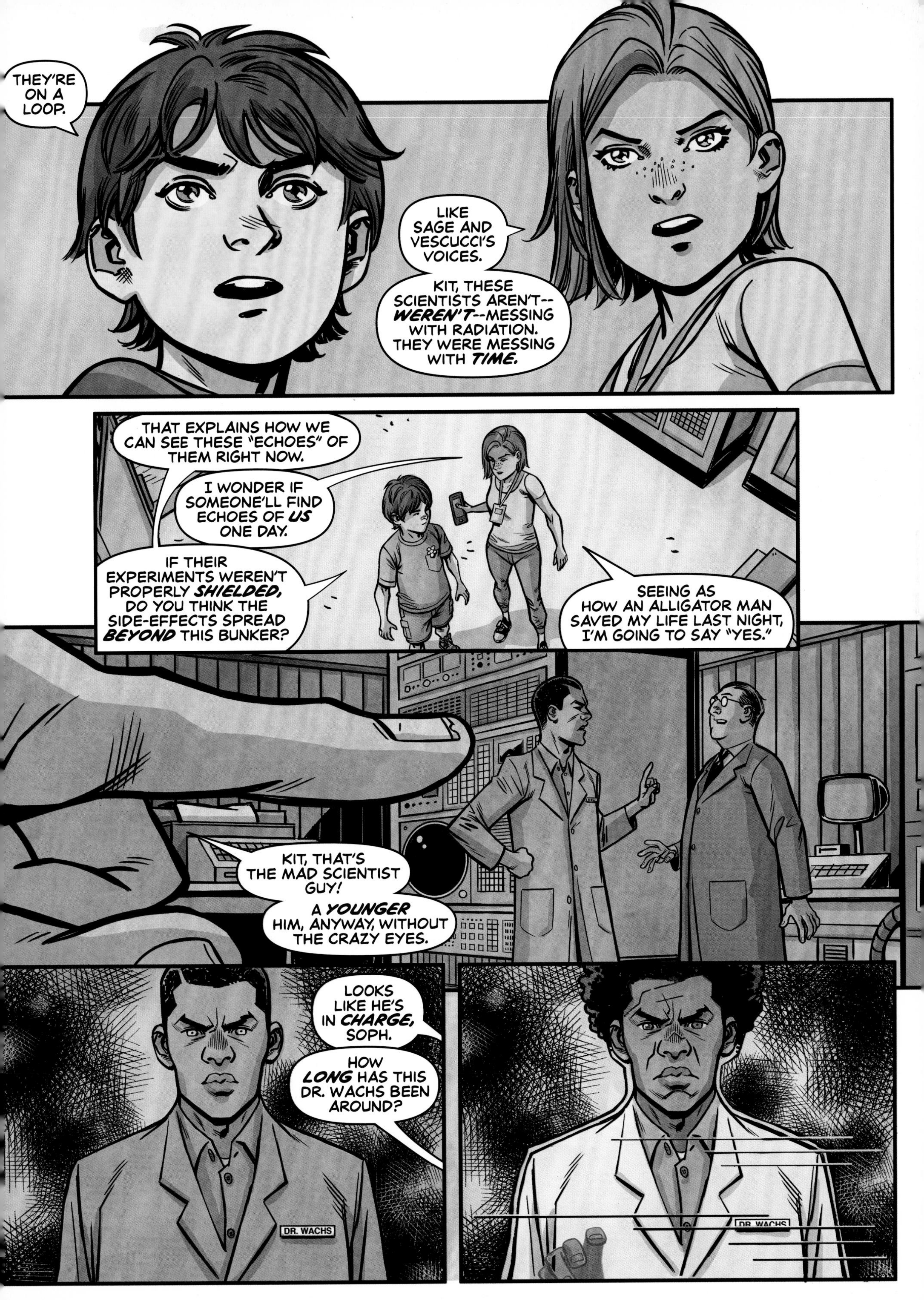
THEY'RE ON A LOOP.
LIKE SAGE AND VESCUCCI'S VOICES.
KIT, THESE SCIENTISTS AREN'T-- WEREN'T--MESSING WITH RADIATION. THEY WERE MESSING WITH TIME.
THAT EXPLAINS HOW WE CAN SEE THESE "ECHOES" OF THEM RIGHT NOW.
I WONDER IF SOMEONE'LL FIND ECHOES OF US ONE DAY.
IF THEIR EXPERIMENTS WEREN'T PROPERLY SHIELDED, DO YOU THINK THE SIDE-EFFECTS SPREAD BEYOND THIS BUNKER?
SEEING AS HOW AN ALLIGATOR MAN SAVED MY LIFE LAST NIGHT, I'M GOING TO SAY "YES."
KIT, THAT'S THE MAD SCIENTIST GUY!
A YOUNGER HIM, ANYWAY, WITHOUT THE CRAZY EYES.
LOOKS LIKE HE'S IN CHARGE, SOPH.
HOW LONG HAS THIS DR. WACHS BEEN AROUND?
DR. WACHS
DR. WACHS

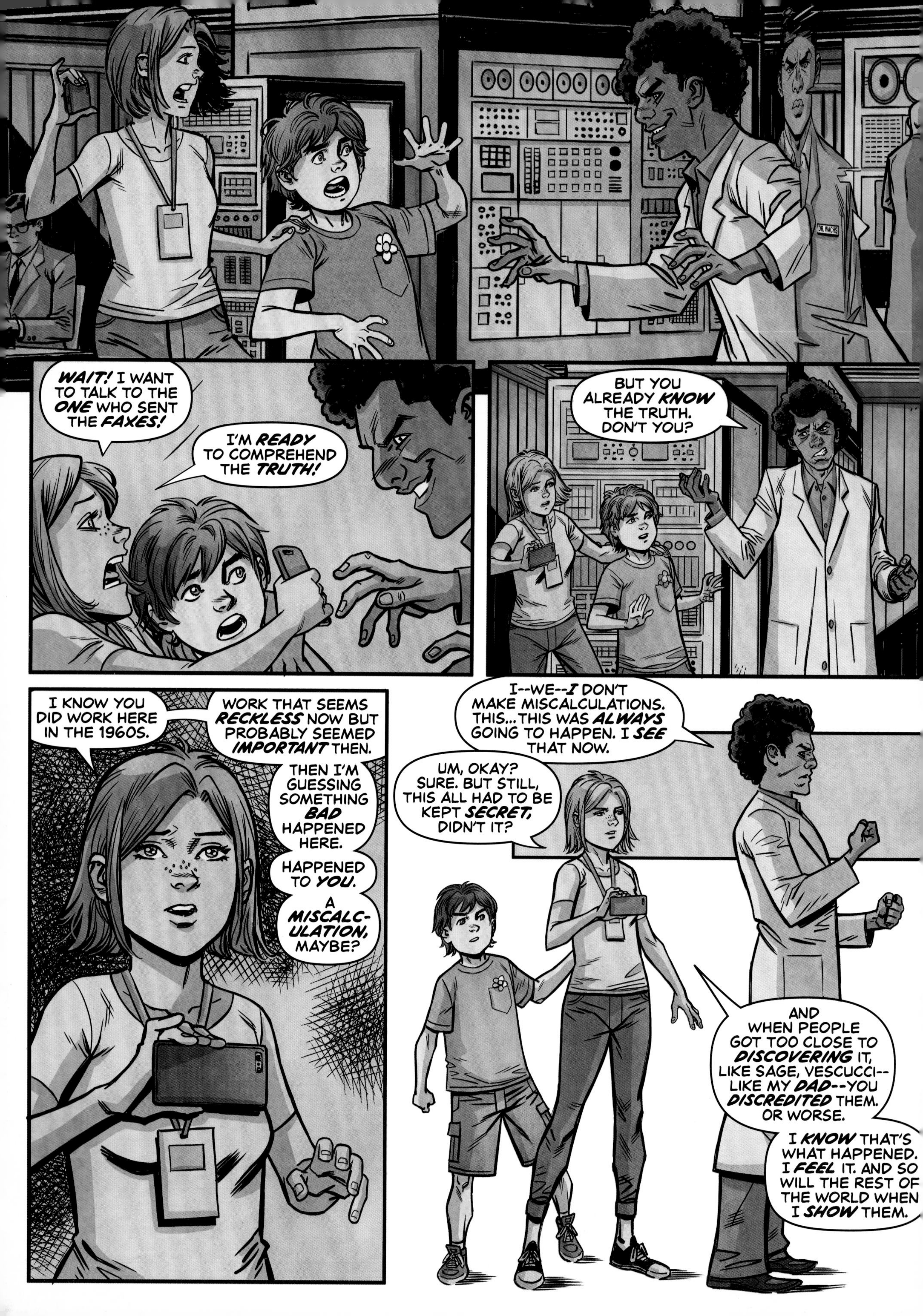

DR. WACHS
WAIT! I WANT TO TALK TO THE ONE WHO SENT THE FAXES!
I'M READY TO COMPREHEND THE TRUTH!
BUT YOU ALREADY KNOW THE TRUTH. DON'T YOU?
I KNOW YOU DID WORK HERE IN THE 1960S.
WORK THAT SEEMS RECKLESS NOW BUT PROBABLY SEEMED IMPORTANT THEN.
THEN I'M GUESSING SOMETHING BAD HAPPENED HERE.
HAPPENED TO YOU.
A MISCALC-ULATION, MAYBE?
I--WE--I DON'T MAKE MISCALCULATIONS. THIS...THIS WAS ALWAYS GOING TO HAPPEN. I SEE THAT NOW.
UM, OKAY? SURE. BUT STILL, THIS ALL HAD TO BE KEPT SECRET, DIDN'T IT?
AND WHEN PEOPLE GOT TOO CLOSE TO DISCOVERING IT, LIKE SAGE, VESCUCCI--LIKE MY DAD--YOU DISCREDITED THEM. OR WORSE.
I KNOW THAT'S WHAT HAPPENED. I FEEL IT. AND SO WILL THE REST OF THE WORLD WHEN I SHOW THEM.

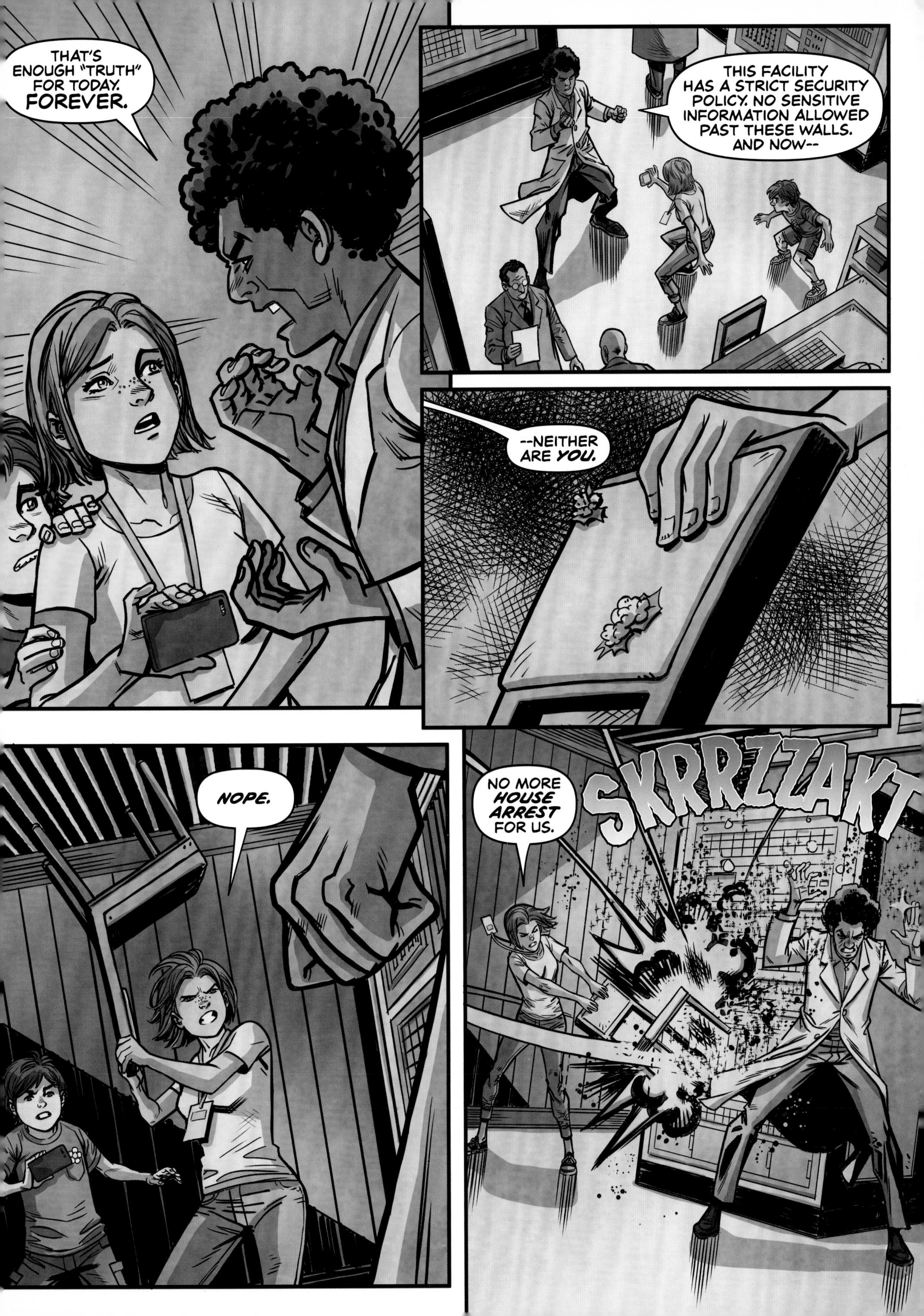
THAT'S ENOUGH "TRUTH" FOR TODAY. FOREVER.
THIS FACILITY HAS A STRICT SECURITY POLICY. NO SENSITIVE INFORMATION ALLOWED PAST THESE WALLS. AND NOW--
--NEITHER ARE YOU.
NOPE.
NO MORE HOUSE ARREST FOR US.
SKRRZZAKT

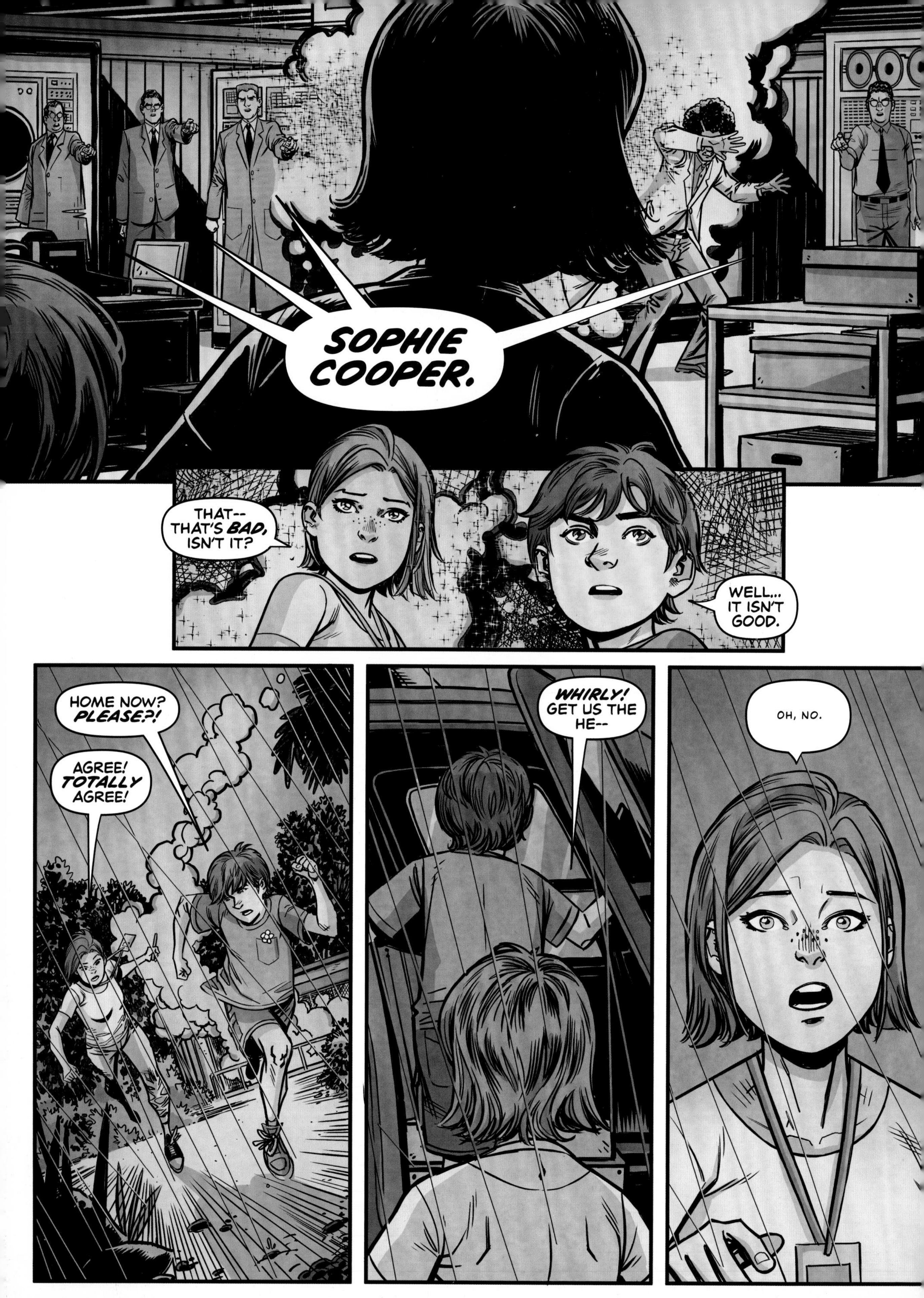
SOPHIE COOPER.
THAT-- THAT'S BAD, ISN'T IT?
WELL... IT ISN'T GOOD.
HOME NOW? PLEASE?!
AGREE! TOTALLY AGREE!
WHIRLY! GET US THE HE--
OH, NO.

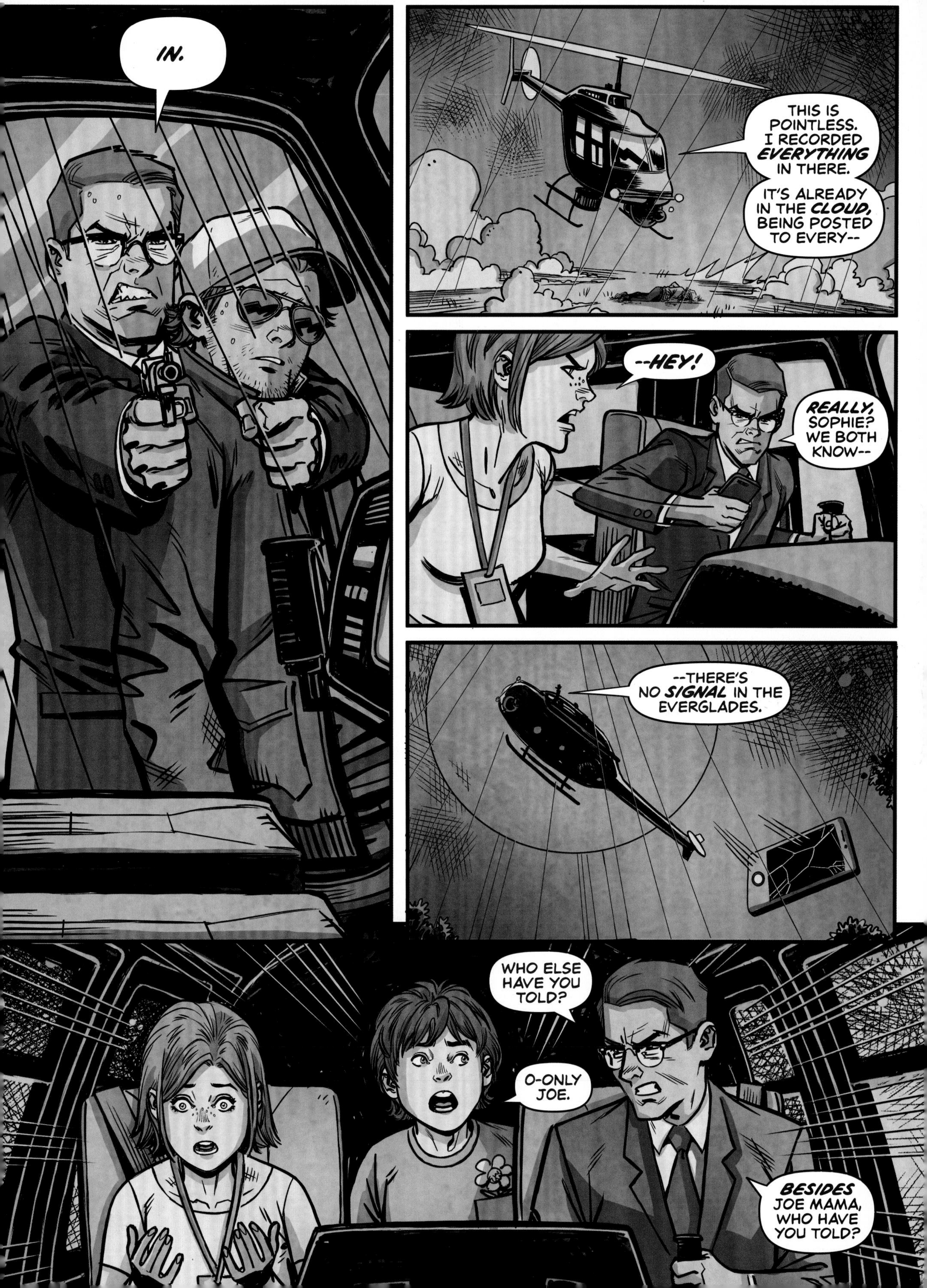
IN.
THIS IS POINTLESS. I RECORDED EVERYTHING IN THERE.
IT'S ALREADY IN THE CLOUD, BEING POSTED TO EVERY--
--HEY!
REALLY, SOPHIE? WE BOTH KNOW--
--THERE'S NO SIGNAL IN THE EVERGLADES.
WHO ELSE HAVE YOU TOLD?
O-ONLY JOE.
BESIDES JOE MAMA, WHO HAVE YOU TOLD?

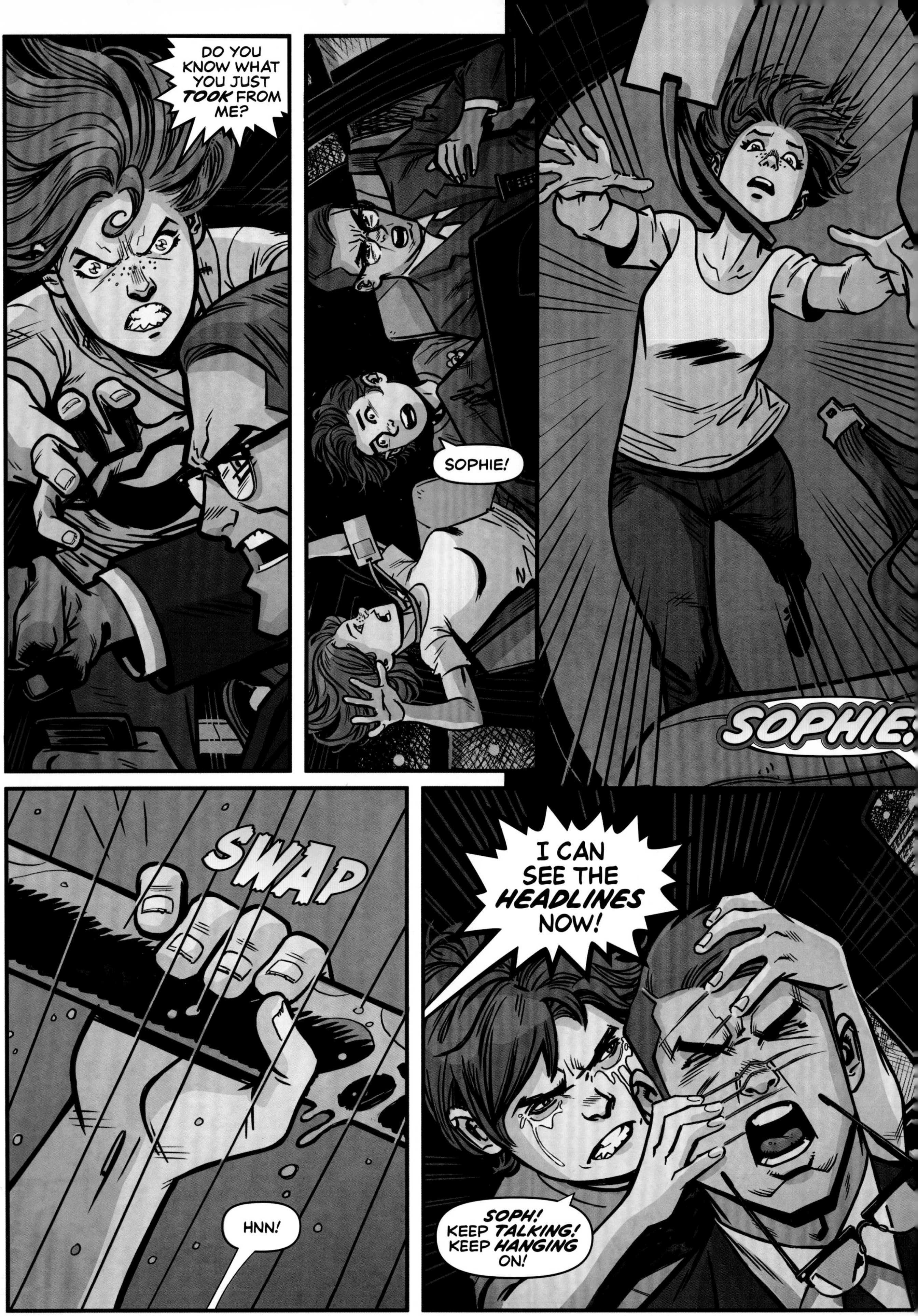
DO YOU KNOW WHAT YOU JUST *TOOK* FROM ME?
SOPHIE!
SOPHIE!
SWAP
HNN!
I CAN SEE THE *HEADLINES* NOW!
SOPH! KEEP *TALKING!* KEEP *HANGING* ON!

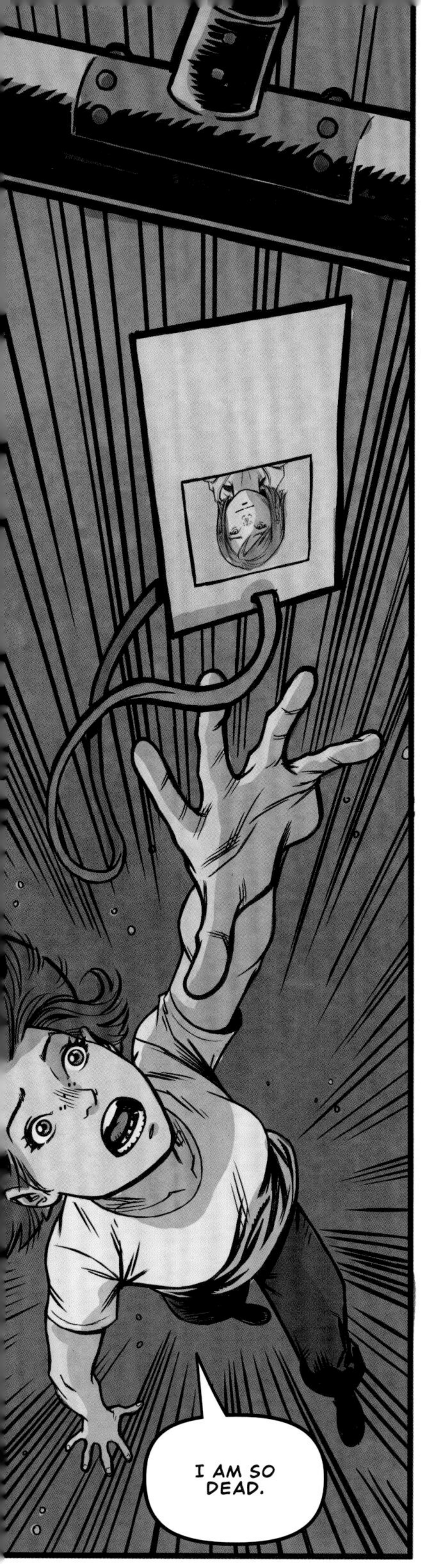
I AM SO
DEAD.

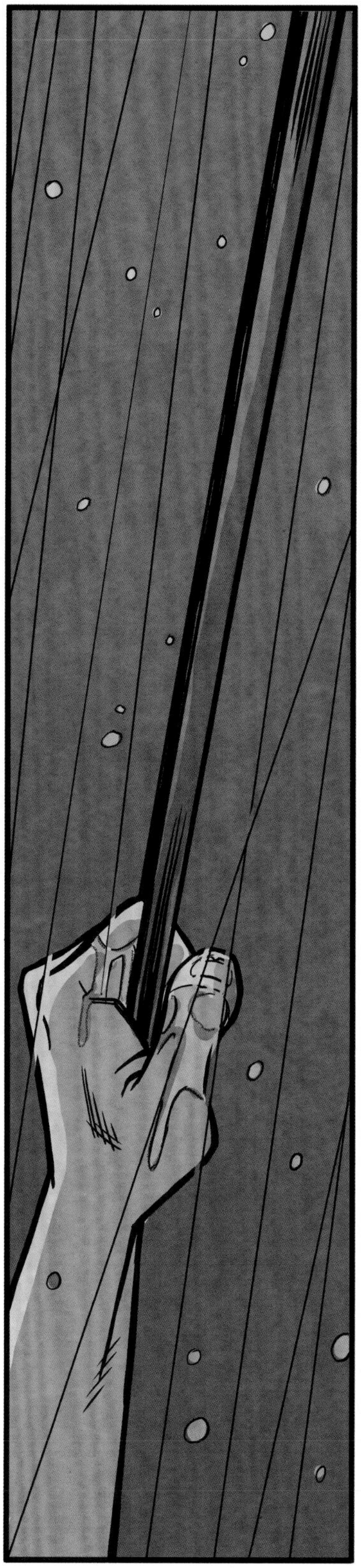

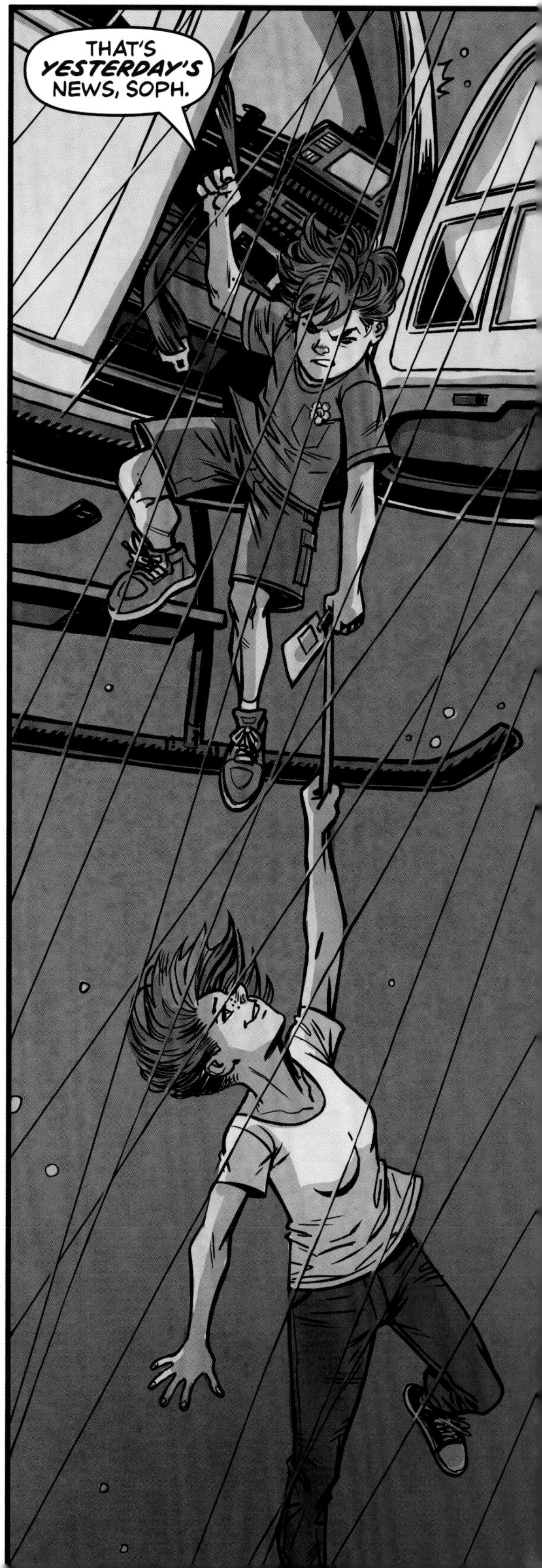
THAT'S
YESTERDAY'S
NEWS, SOPH.

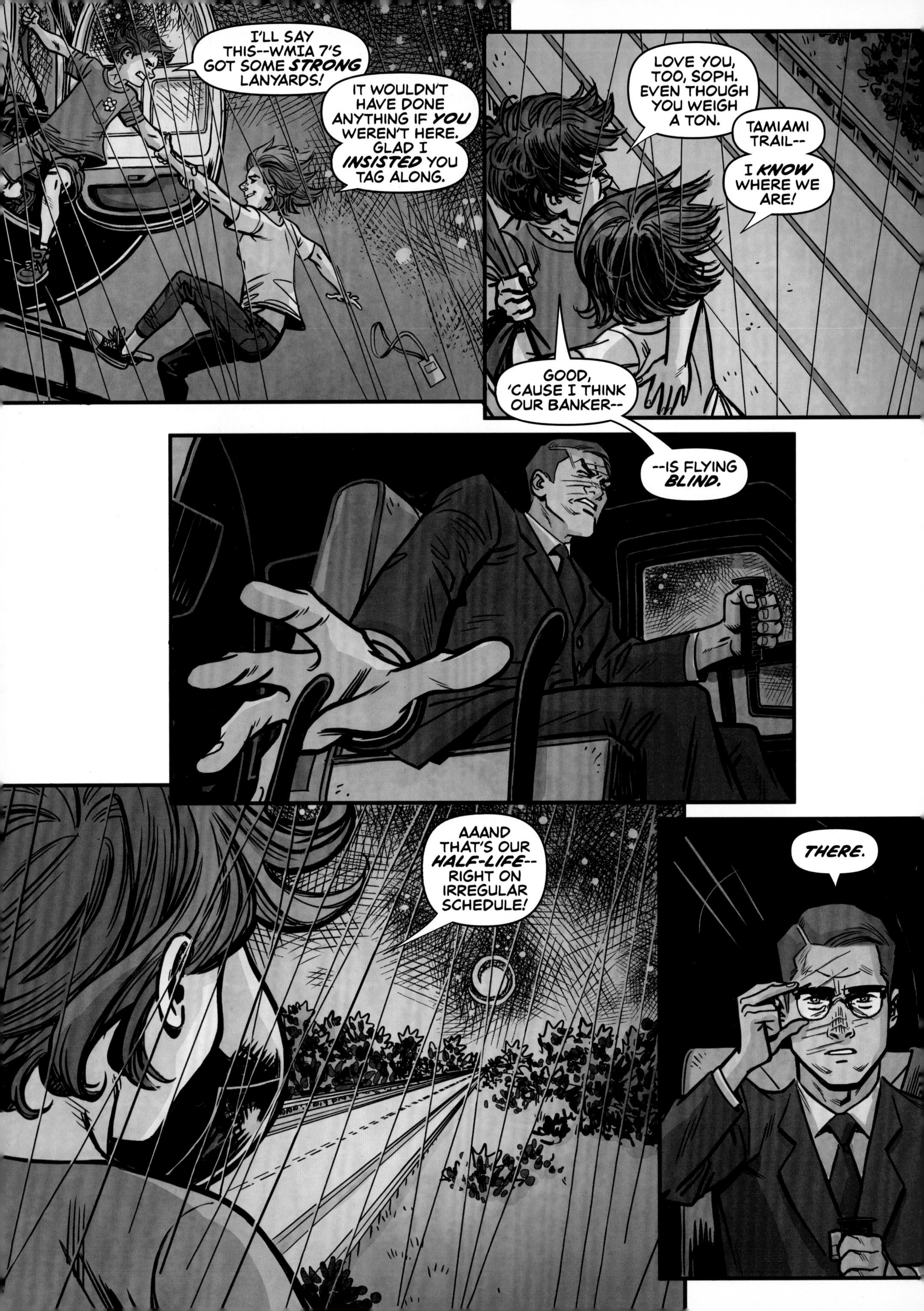
I'LL SAY THIS--WMIA 7'S GOT SOME STRONG LANYARDS!
IT WOULDN'T HAVE DONE ANYTHING IF YOU WEREN'T HERE. GLAD I INSISTED YOU TAG ALONG.
LOVE YOU, TOO, SOPH. EVEN THOUGH YOU WEIGH A TON.
TAMIAMI TRAIL--
I KNOW WHERE WE ARE!
GOOD, 'CAUSE I THINK OUR BANKER--
--IS FLYING BLIND.
AAAND THAT'S OUR HALF-LIFE-- RIGHT ON IRREGULAR SCHEDULE!
THERE.

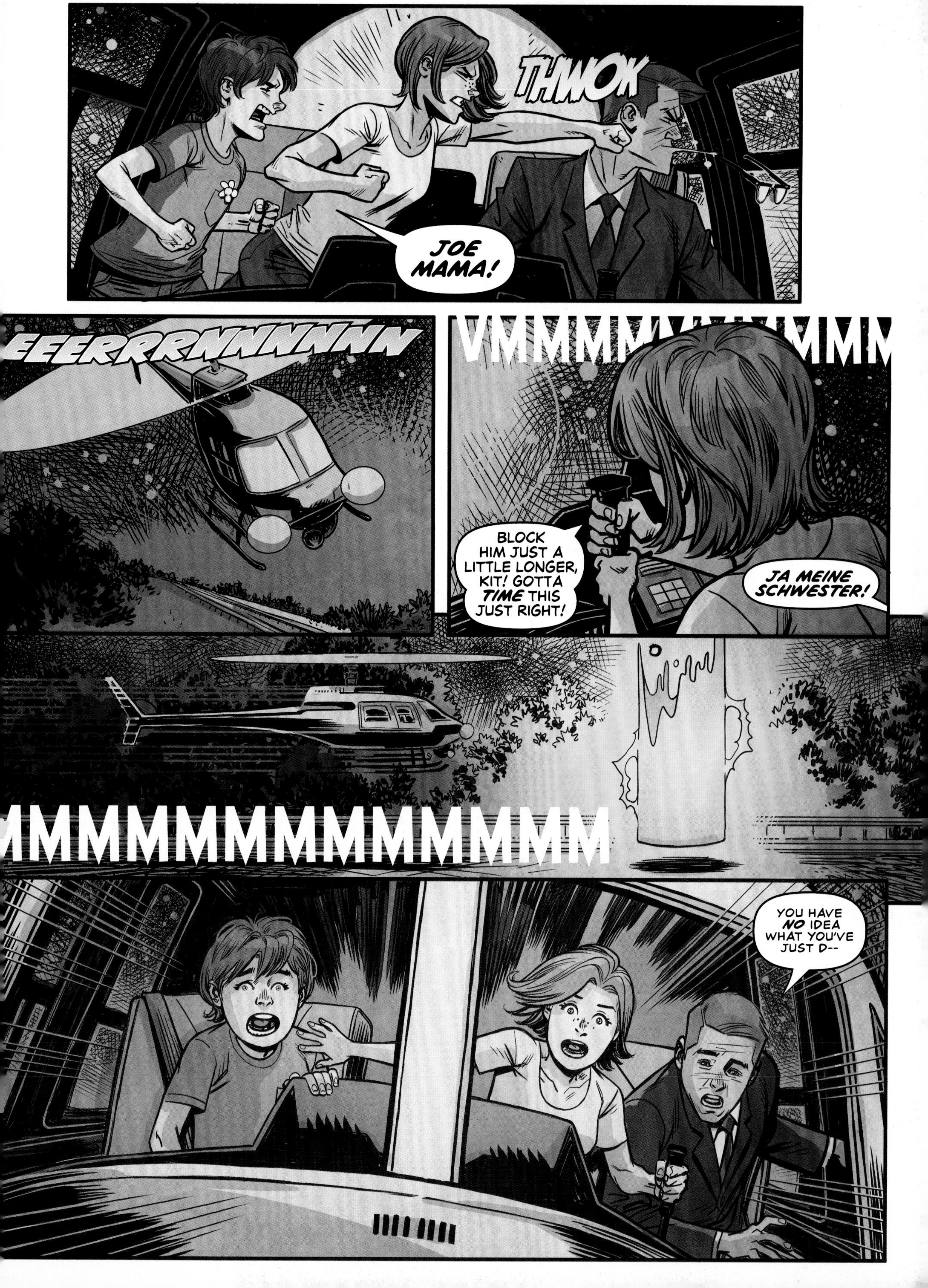
THWOK
JOE MAMA!
EEERRRNNNNNNN
VMMMMMMMMMMMM
BLOCK HIM JUST A LITTLE LONGER, KIT! GOTTA *TIME* THIS JUST RIGHT!
JA MEINE SCHWESTER!
MMMMMMMMMMMMM
YOU HAVE *NO* IDEA WHAT YOU'VE JUST D--

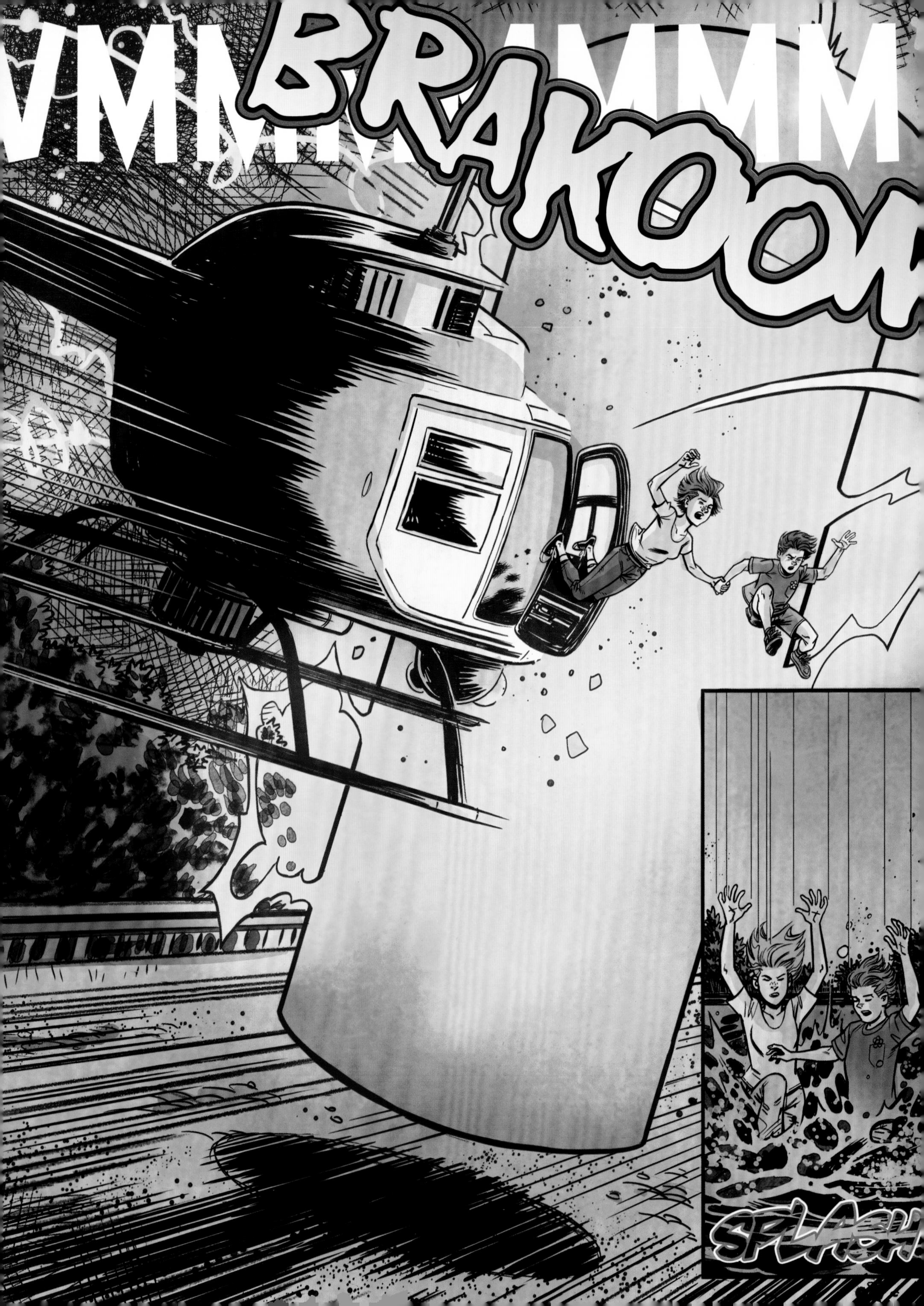
VMMMMMMMMM
BRAKOOM
SPLASH

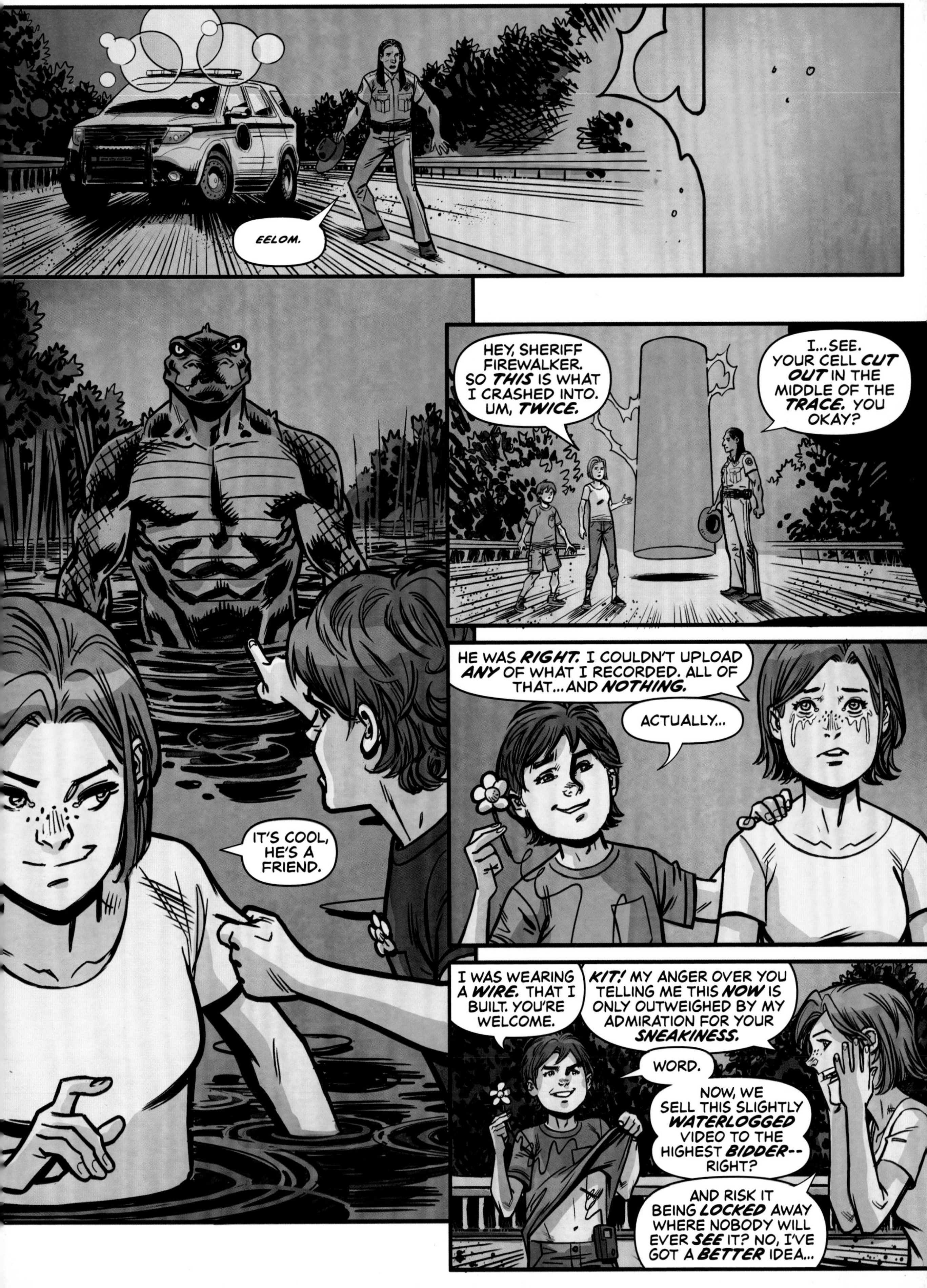
EELOM.
IT'S COOL, HE'S A FRIEND.
HEY, SHERIFF FIREWALKER. SO THIS IS WHAT I CRASHED INTO. UM, TWICE.
I...SEE. YOUR CELL CUT OUT IN THE MIDDLE OF THE TRACE. YOU OKAY?
HE WAS RIGHT. I COULDN'T UPLOAD ANY OF WHAT I RECORDED. ALL OF THAT...AND NOTHING.
ACTUALLY...
I WAS WEARING A WIRE. THAT I BUILT. YOU'RE WELCOME.
KIT! MY ANGER OVER YOU TELLING ME THIS NOW IS ONLY OUTWEIGHED BY MY ADMIRATION FOR YOUR SNEAKINESS.
WORD.
NOW, WE SELL THIS SLIGHTLY WATERLOGGED VIDEO TO THE HIGHEST BIDDER-- RIGHT?
AND RISK IT BEING LOCKED AWAY WHERE NOBODY WILL EVER SEE IT? NO, I'VE GOT A BETTER IDEA...

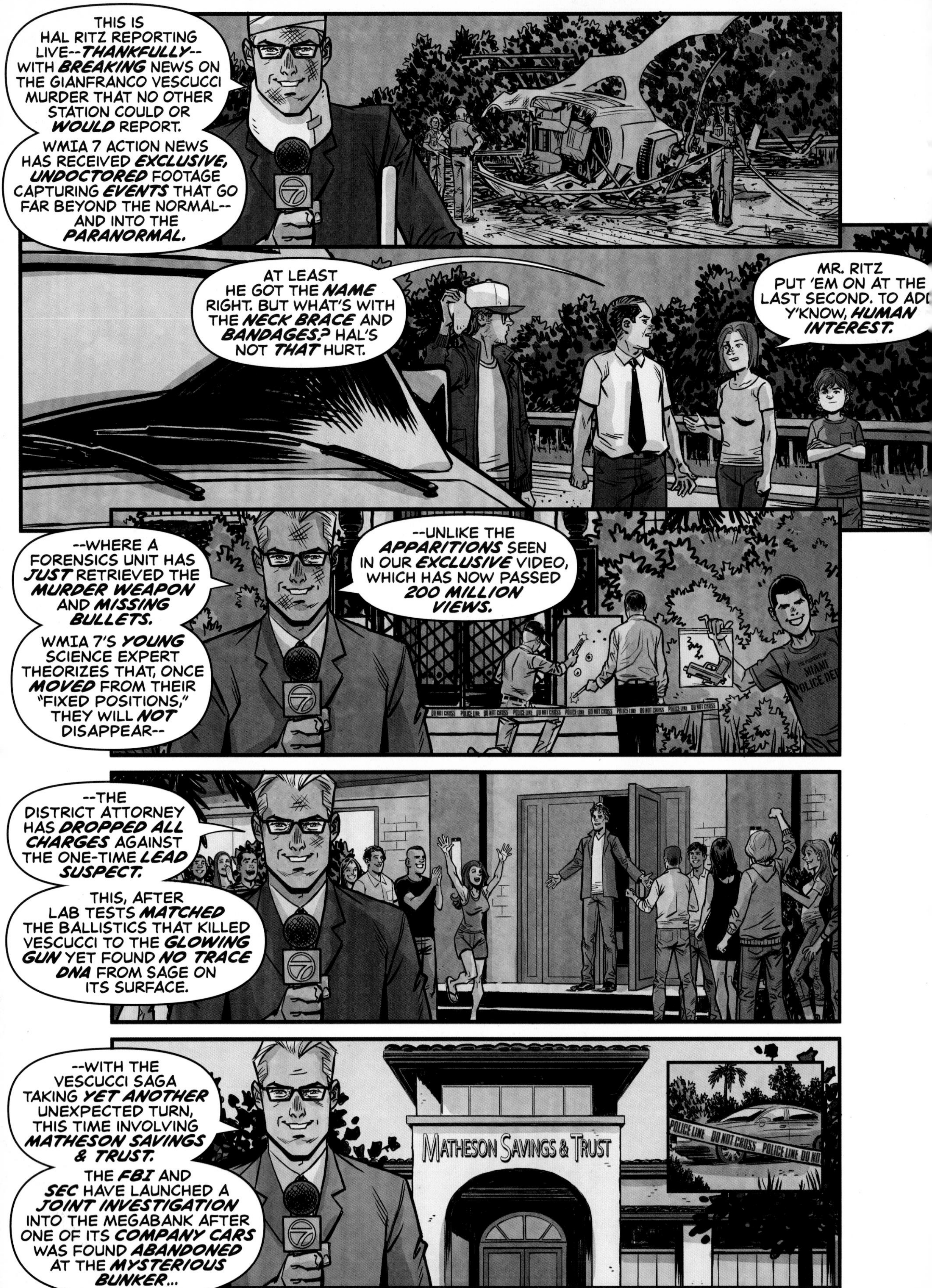
THIS IS HAL RITZ REPORTING LIVE--THANKFULLY--WITH BREAKING NEWS ON THE GIANFRANCO VESCUCCI MURDER THAT NO OTHER STATION COULD OR WOULD REPORT.
WMIA 7 ACTION NEWS HAS RECEIVED EXCLUSIVE, UNDOCTORED FOOTAGE CAPTURING EVENTS THAT GO FAR BEYOND THE NORMAL--AND INTO THE PARANORMAL.
AT LEAST HE GOT THE NAME RIGHT. BUT WHAT'S WITH THE NECK BRACE AND BANDAGES? HAL'S NOT THAT HURT.
MR. RITZ PUT 'EM ON AT THE LAST SECOND. TO ADD Y'KNOW, HUMAN INTEREST.
--WHERE A FORENSICS UNIT HAS JUST RETRIEVED THE MURDER WEAPON AND MISSING BULLETS.
WMIA 7'S YOUNG SCIENCE EXPERT THEORIZES THAT, ONCE MOVED FROM THEIR "FIXED POSITIONS," THEY WILL NOT DISAPPEAR--
--UNLIKE THE APPARITIONS SEEN IN OUR EXCLUSIVE VIDEO, WHICH HAS NOW PASSED 200 MILLION VIEWS.
--THE DISTRICT ATTORNEY HAS DROPPED ALL CHARGES AGAINST THE ONE-TIME LEAD SUSPECT.
THIS, AFTER LAB TESTS MATCHED THE BALLISTICS THAT KILLED VESCUCCI TO THE GLOWING GUN YET FOUND NO TRACE DNA FROM SAGE ON ITS SURFACE.
--WITH THE VESCUCCI SAGA TAKING YET ANOTHER UNEXPECTED TURN, THIS TIME INVOLVING MATHESON SAVINGS & TRUST.
THE FBI AND SEC HAVE LAUNCHED A JOINT INVESTIGATION INTO THE MEGABANK AFTER ONE OF ITS COMPANY CARS WAS FOUND ABANDONED AT THE MYSTERIOUS BUNKER...
MATHESON SAVINGS & TRUST
POLICE LINE DO NOT CROSS POLICE LINE

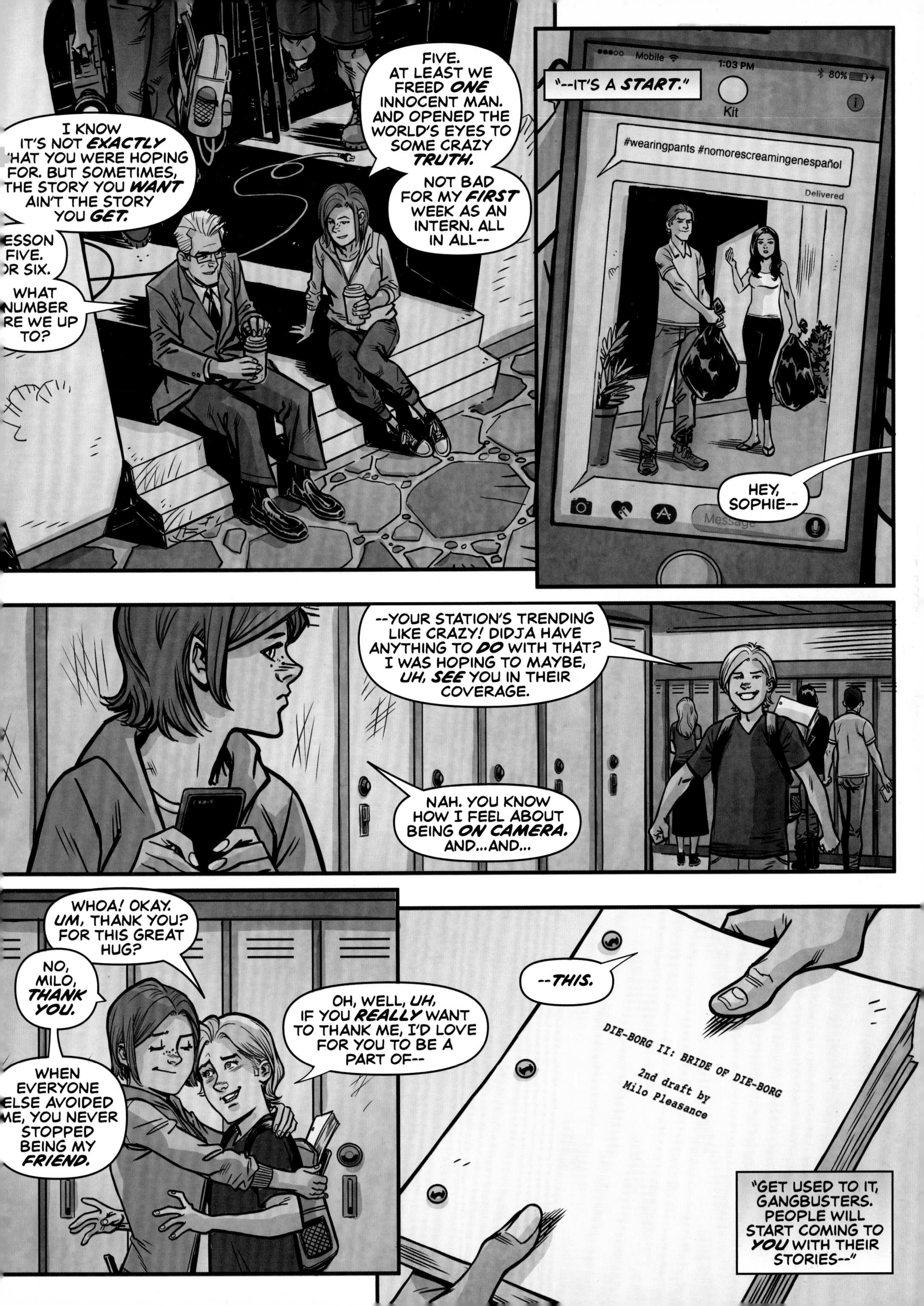
I KNOW IT'S NOT *EXACTLY* 'HAT YOU WERE HOPING FOR. BUT SOMETIMES, THE STORY YOU *WANT* AIN'T THE STORY YOU *GET.*
ESSON FIVE. OR SIX.
WHAT NUMBER RE WE UP TO?
FIVE. AT LEAST WE FREED *ONE* INNOCENT MAN. AND OPENED THE WORLD'S EYES TO SOME CRAZY *TRUTH.*
NOT BAD FOR MY *FIRST* WEEK AS AN INTERN. ALL IN ALL--
"--IT'S A *START.*"
Mobile
1:03 PM
80%
Kit
#wearingpants #nomorescreamingenespañol
Delivered
Message
HEY, SOPHIE--
--YOUR STATION'S TRENDING LIKE CRAZY! DIDJA HAVE ANYTHING TO *DO* WITH THAT? I WAS HOPING TO MAYBE, *UH, SEE* YOU IN THEIR COVERAGE.
NAH. YOU KNOW HOW I FEEL ABOUT BEING *ON CAMERA.* AND...AND...
WHOA! OKAY. *UM,* THANK YOU? FOR THIS GREAT HUG?
NO, MILO, *THANK YOU.*
WHEN EVERYONE ELSE AVOIDED ME, YOU NEVER STOPPED BEING MY *FRIEND.*
OH, WELL, *UH,* IF YOU *REALLY* WANT TO THANK ME, I'D LOVE FOR YOU TO BE A PART OF--
--*THIS.*
DIE-BORG II: BRIDE OF DIE-BORG
2nd draft by
Milo Pleasance
"GET USED TO IT, GANGBUSTERS. PEOPLE WILL START COMING TO *YOU* WITH THEIR STORIES--"

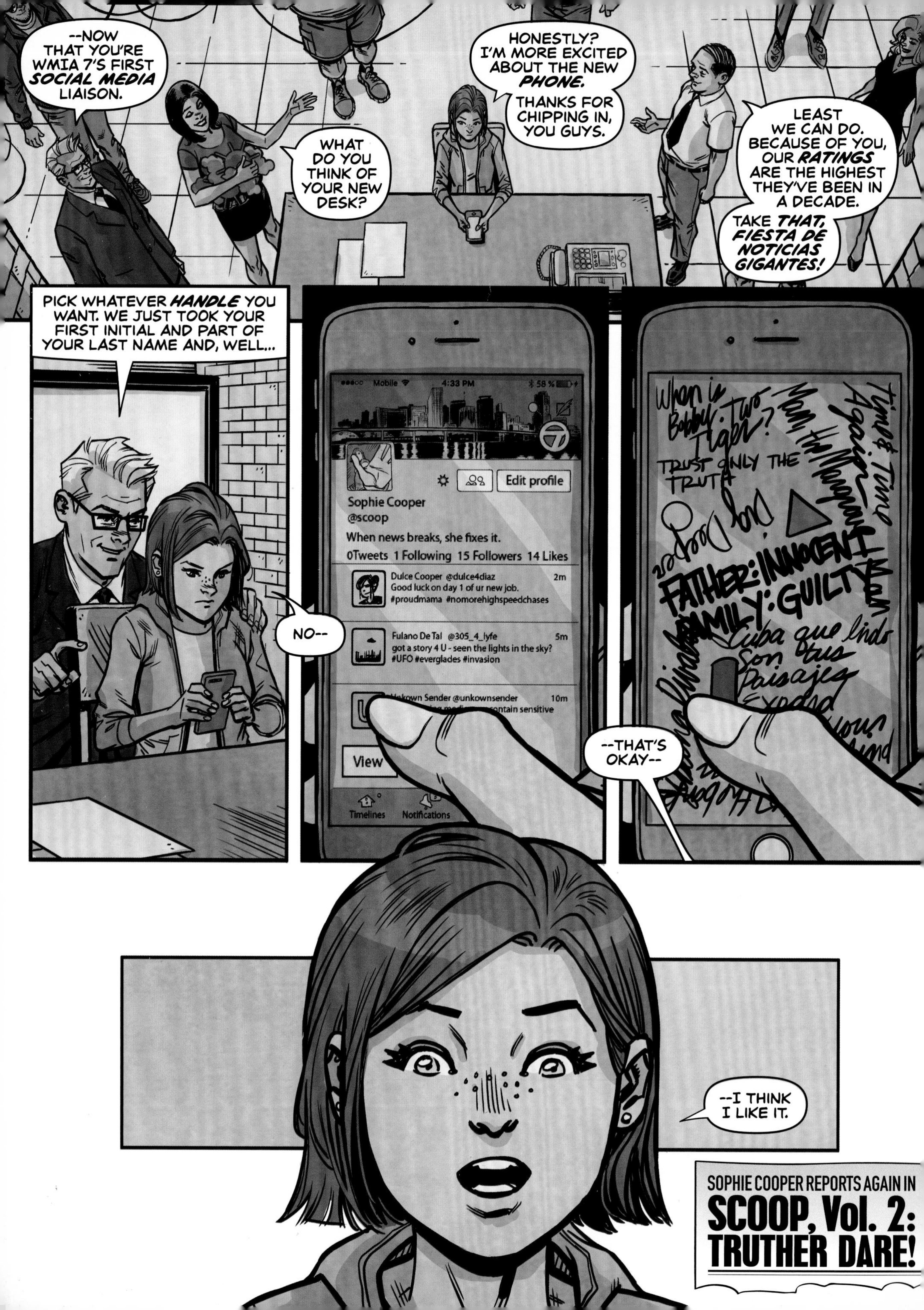

--NOW THAT YOU'RE WMIA 7'S FIRST SOCIAL MEDIA LIAISON.
WHAT DO YOU THINK OF YOUR NEW DESK?
HONESTLY? I'M MORE EXCITED ABOUT THE NEW PHONE.
THANKS FOR CHIPPING IN, YOU GUYS.
LEAST WE CAN DO. BECAUSE OF YOU, OUR RATINGS ARE THE HIGHEST THEY'VE BEEN IN A DECADE.
TAKE THAT, FIESTA DE NOTICIAS GIGANTES!
PICK WHATEVER HANDLE YOU WANT. WE JUST TOOK YOUR FIRST INITIAL AND PART OF YOUR LAST NAME AND, WELL...
NO--
Mobile 4:33 PM 58 %
Edit profile
Sophie Cooper
@scoop
When news breaks, she fixes it.
0Tweets 1 Following 15 Followers 14 Likes
Dulce Cooper @dulce4diaz 2m
Good luck on day 1 of ur new job. #proudmama #nomorehighspeedchases
Fulano De Tal @305_4_lyfe 5m
got a story 4 U - seen the lights in the sky? #UFO #everglades #invasion
Unkown Sender @unkownsender 10m
View
Timelines Notifications
TRUST ONLY THE TRUTH
FATHER: INNOCENT
FAMILY: GUILTY
Cuba que lindo Son tus Paisajes
--THAT'S OKAY--
--I THINK I LIKE IT.
SOPHIE COOPER REPORTS AGAIN IN
SCOOP, Vol. 2: TRUTHER DARE!

BEHIND THE CREATION

SOPHIE

Sophie was always going to be a redhead for two reasons: 1) I wanted to emphasize her status as a social outcast in a visual way, and the red hair definitely stands out in a lineup; and 2) I'm the proud parent of a tall, freckled redhead. A lot of people think redheads have a lower pain threshold than blondes and brunettes (anesthesiologists give redheads different dosages of pain killers before surgeries compared to other people), but I believe redheads are just more sensitive overall than other people—and that isn't a bad thing. Sophie's sensitivity is precisely what makes her such a diligent crusader for justice and perceptive enough to connect the clues in ways that others can't.

Of course, Joe Cooper (no relation) took these ideas and brought Sophie to life on the page. He even added in fun details like Soph's cracked cell phone and chewed fingernails to hint at the financial and emotional stress she and her family have endured under the media's glare. Pete Pantazis and Alba Cardona then took this approach to a whole other level by coming up with the perfect shade of firebrand red for Sophie's hair while making sure her skin tone matched with the rest of the Cuban American Coopers.

KIT

Kit is very much based on my younger brother, Chris. They're both tech savants, total smart alecks, and devoted brothers who always stick by their older siblings. Joe really nailed Kit's impish grin, and he draws Kit to look and act like an actual child (as opposed to a miniature adult). To me, the tight-knit banter between Sophie and Kit is the heart and soul of *Scoop*, and Joe's talent with character acting makes the Cooper kids' moments together seem authentic and emotional.

FIREWALKER

Growing up in Miami, I was lucky enough to be surrounded by a tremendous array of cultures. My elementary school took annual field trips to the Miccosukee reservation, where we would go on airboat rides, watch alligator wrestling, and learn about the incredibly resourceful tribe that adapted to live in South Florida's beautiful—but often dangerous—Everglades.

With the same ease of skill he applied to pretty much everything else in this book, Joe took these early inspirations and made them manifest in Sheriff Firewalker. What started out as kind of an homage to the late, great Sonny Landham (*Predator*, *The Warriors*, and a little Chuck Norris flick called—yep—*Firewalker*) evolved into a pretty cool character that I hope we get to explore in future volumes. After a few initial sketches, Joe added alligator teeth to Firewalker's sheriff hat to differentiate it from the Southwestern-style wardrobe usually seen on Native American characters in film and TV. It's these little details that Joe includes in *Scoop*'s diverse characters and backgrounds—coupled with Alba and Pete's vibrant color palette—that make me feel like I'm back in my hometown.

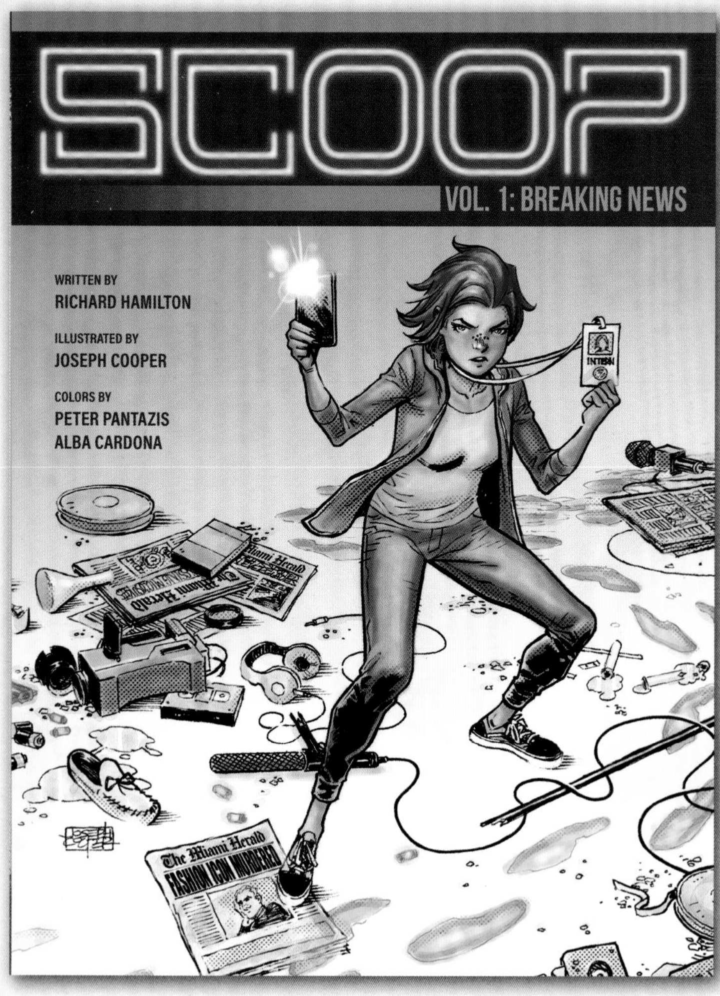
SCOOP
VOL. 1: BREAKING NEWS
WRITTEN BY
RICHARD HAMILTON
ILLUSTRATED BY
JOSEPH COOPER
COLORS BY
PETER PANTAZIS
ALBA CARDONA
The Miami Herald
FASHION ICON MURDERED

COVER

This cover actually came together pretty quickly (well, quickly for me—I didn't have to pencil, ink, and color the darn thing like Joe did). But I still think it's a nice case study for the power of collaboration in which the comics medium excels. My basic idea was to have Sophie holding out her cell phone and intern badge in kind of a *Kolchak: The Night Stalker* pose (I often joke that Soph is our very own "Carla Kolchak"), with broken TV news equipment littered around her. Our editor, Mark, added to the concept by suggesting that we include some sci-fi elements and front-page headlines mixed in with the debris. And Joe added the footprints, bunker equipment, and poor Bobby Two-Tigers' abandoned moccasin—not to mention the awesome half-tone dots. The end result is an image that I feel perfectly captures Sophie's intrepid personality and the overall paranormal mystery vibe that (hopefully) makes *Scoop* so much fun.

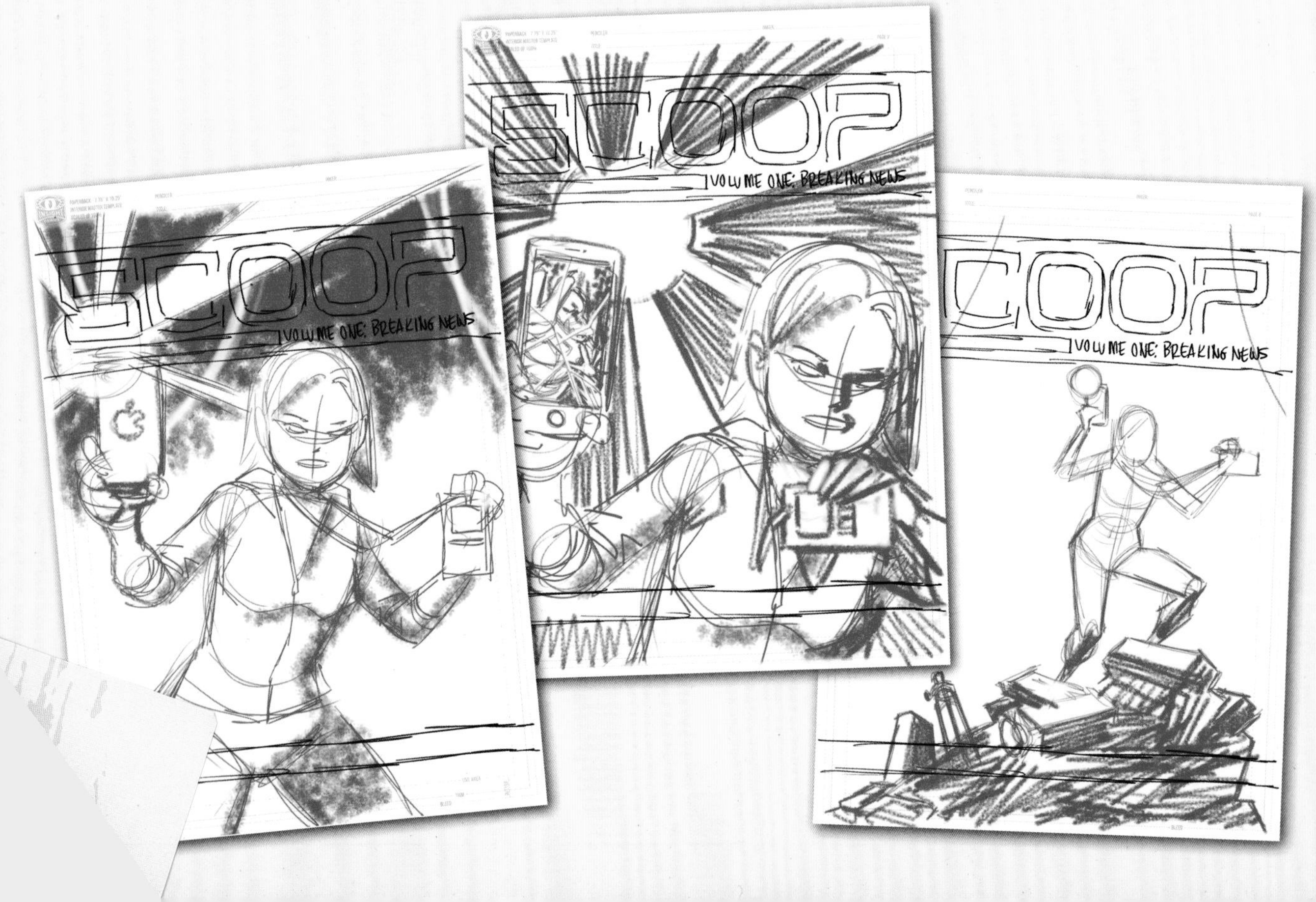
SCOOP
VOLUME ONE: BREAKING NEWS
SCOOP
VOLUME ONE: BREAKING NEWS
SCOOP
VOLUME ONE: BREAKING NEWS

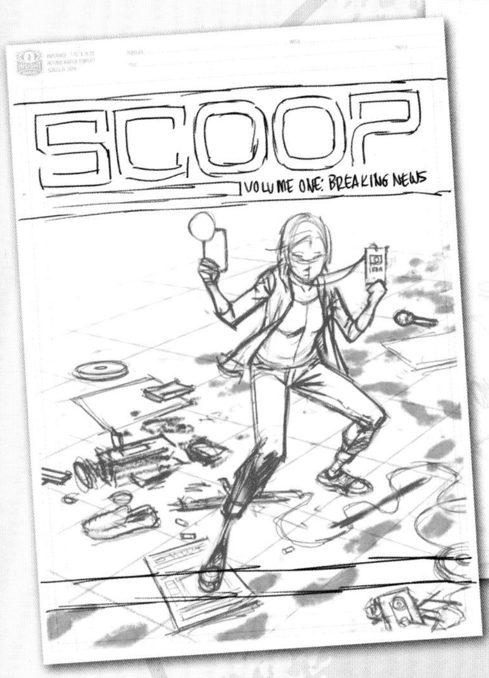
SCOOP
VOLUME ONE: BREAKING NEWS

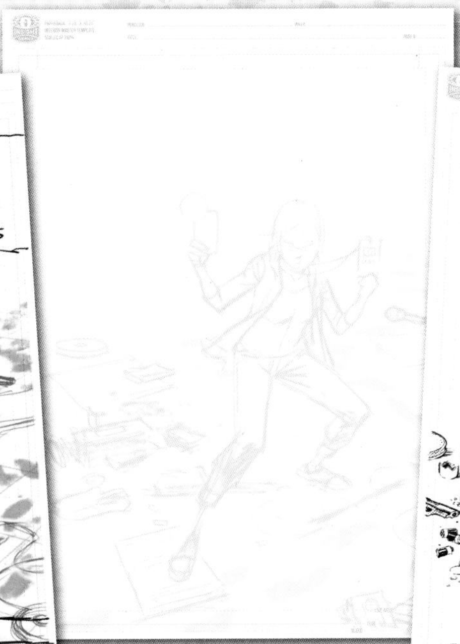

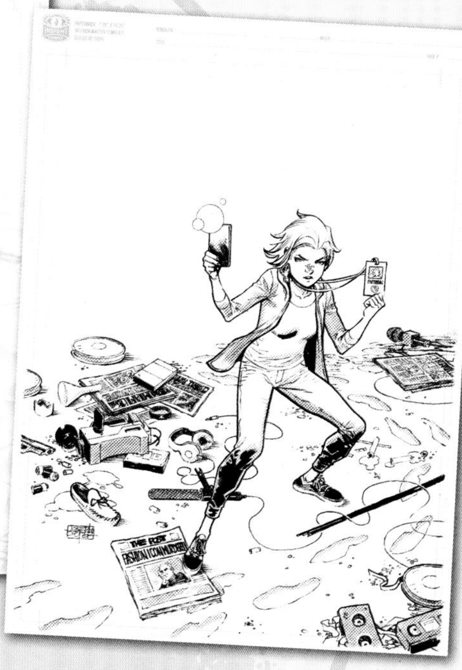

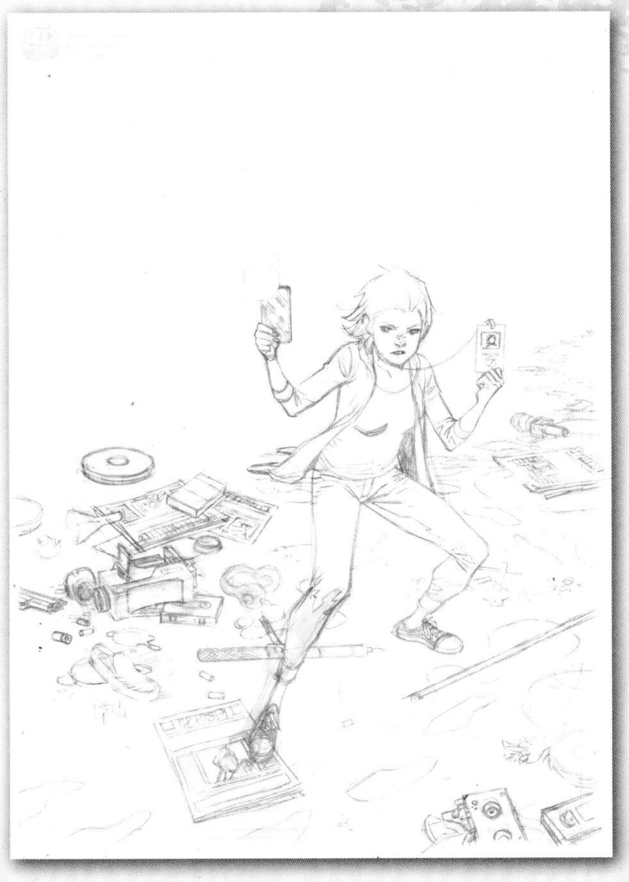

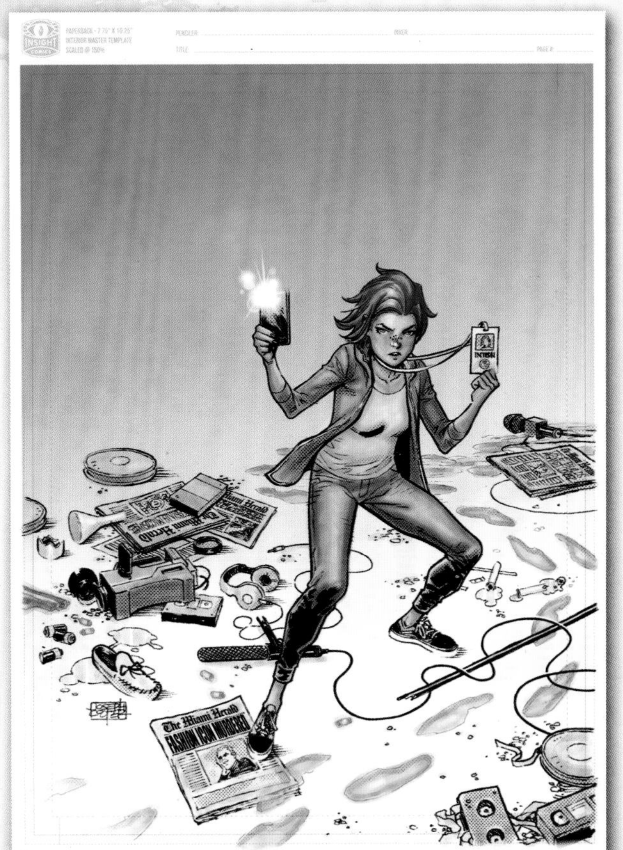
The Miami Herald

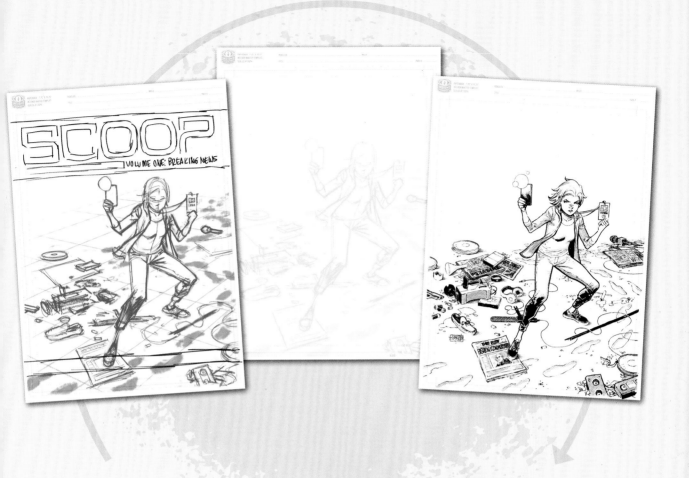

An Imprint of Insight Editions
PO Box 3088
San Rafael, CA 94912
www.insightcomics.com

Find us on Facebook:
www.facebook.com/InsightEditionsComics

Follow us on Twitter:
@InsightComics

Follow us on Instagram:
Insight_Comics

Library of Congress Cataloging-in-Publication Data available.

ISBN: 978-1-68383-084-9

Publisher: Raoul Goff
Associate Publisher: Vanessa Lopez
Executive Editor: Mark Irwin
Editorial Assistant: Holly Fisher
Senior Production Editor: Elaine Ou
Production Manager: Greg Steffen

ROOTS of PEACE   REPLANTED PAPER

Insight Editions, in association with Roots of Peace, will plant two trees for each tree used in the manufacturing of this book.
Roots of Peace is an internationally renowned humanitarian organization dedicated to eradicating land mines worldwide and converting
war-torn lands into productive farms and wildlife habitats. Roots of Peace will plant two million fruit and nut trees in Afghanistan
and provide farmers there with the skills and support necessary for sustainable land use.

Manufactured in China by Insight Editions

10 9 8 7 6 5 4 3 2 1